METAPHYSICS
TO
METAFICTIONS

Dave Carnie, *Hegel's Chairs* (1992), photograph and mixed media, 24" x 30". Collection of the author.

METAPHYSICS TO METAFICTIONS

Hegel, Nietzsche, and the End of Philosophy

PAUL S. MIKLOWITZ

State University
of New York
Press

SUNY Series in Hegelian Studies
William Desmond, Editor

Cover photo used with permission of the photographer, Dave Carnie.
Quotes from *The Hetrodox Hegel* by Cyril O'Regan are reprinted by
permission of the State University of New York Press © 1994.

Published by
State University of New York Press, Albany

Production by Susan Geraghty
Marketing by Anne Valentine

Printed in the United States of America

For information, address State University of New York
Press, State University Plaza, Albany, N.Y., 12246

Library of Congress Cataloging-in-Publication Data

Miklowitz, Paul S.
    Metaphysics to metafictions : Hegel, Nitzsche, and the end of
philosophy / by Paul S. Miklowitz.
        p.   cm. — (SUNY series in Hegelian studies)
    Includes bibliographical references and index.
    ISBN 0-7914-3877-5 (hc : alk. paper). — ISBN 0-7914-3878-3 (pb)
    1. Hegel, Georg Wilhelm Friedrich, 1770–1831. 2. Nietzsche,
Friedrich Wilhelm, 1844–1900. 3. Metaphysics—History. I. Title.
II. Series.
B2948.M48 1998
193–dc21   97-35112
                                                                    CIP

10 9 8 7 6 5 4 3 2 1

CONTENTS

ACKNOWLEDGMENTS

Although it is impossible to name all of the teachers, colleagues, and friends who have contributed to the interpretations developed here, I would like to make special mention of a few. At Santa Cruz, Maurice Natanson's presentation of Husserl and Sartre made a deep impression on me at a formative time. An echo of the opening sentence of *Edmund Husserl*—"Philosophy, these sullen days, is something of a pensioner in the realm of knowledge"—is discernable in the opening paragraph of my own Introduction. Paul Ricoeur's carefully sustained reading of Hegel's *Phenomenology* in seminars at the University of Chicago first opened that book to me, providing both an exemplary model of pedagogy and the foundation for my own interpretation. At Yale, George Schrader was a friendly and helpful *Doktorvater* throughout the writing of the early drafts, while John E. Smith and Karsten Harries also made constructive suggestions and pointed me toward useful texts in the Hegel and Nietzsche literature.

But philosophical scholarship has always seemed to me a means to an end: originating in the broader genus of "literature," philosophy passes beyond itself again into "literature." Accordingly, the direct and indirect influence of the so-called Yale School of literary criticism, especially Jacques Derrida, Paul de Man, and Harold Bloom, contributed perhaps most of all to the interpretive agenda developed here. Derrida's last seminars at Yale before moving to California, de Man's last course before his death, and Bloom's final classroom treatment of Freud, together, constituted the eschatology of "deconstruction" for me; that event remains the horizon beyond which my concluding chapter struggles to see.

Colleagues and friends who have provided critical readings and/or stimulating discussions of the texts and ideas examined here span a great deal of both space and time. A minimal but essential enumeration must include William Earle, R. J. Hollingdale, Thomas Y. Levin, Babette E. Babich, Lewis Klausner, James B. Cushing, and George Cotkin. I would also like to thank the eager students in my Prize Teaching Fellowship seminar at Yale, to whom this project was first presented in lectures, and to a few extraordinary students among the very many I have taught since coming back to California, especially Karl French, John Conte, and

David Horacek. Finally, my wife Marija Bozic has helped me to live with the gathering weight of these sometimes ponderous pages in many far-flung places on three coasts; her good judgment and remarkable objectivity have sustained my faith in this project even when my own arguments have led to incredulity.

This book is dedicated to Julius and Gloria D. Miklowitz.

CITATION CONVENTIONS

Hegel's *Phenomenology* is cited within parentheses in the text. References give the numbered paragraphs in A. V. Miller's translation, followed by the corresponding page numbers in the Hoffmeister edition. Although I have relied heavily on Miller's usually excellent renderings, some emendations have been made, and I have inserted important or problematic terms from the German in square brackets when this seemed advisable. German terms in brackets are italicized only when they are in Hegel's text.

Bibliographical data for the *Phenomenology* is as follows: G. W. F. Hegel, *Phenomenology of Spirit*, trans. by A. V. Miller with Analysis of the text and Foreword by J. N. Findlay (Oxford: The Clarendon Press, 1977); *Phänomenologie des Geistes*, edited by Johannes Hoffmeister (Hamburg: Felix Meiner Verlag, 1952).

Nietzsche's works are also cited within parentheses in the text. References give abbreviations of the English title, followed by section number and/or name where appropriate. Translations are by Walter Kaufmann and/or R. J. Hollingdale unless otherwise indicated, but I have again made occasional emendations and inserted important or problematic terms from the German in square brackets. Abbreviations for Nietzsche's works cited in the text are as follows: *BT, The Birth of Tragedy* (1872); *UT, Untimely Meditations* (1873–76); *HAH, Human, All Too Human* (1878, 1886); *D, Daybreak* (1881); *GS, The Gay Science* (1882, 1887); *TSZ, Thus Spoke Zarathustra* (1883–85); *BGE, Beyond Good and Evil* (1886); *GM, On the Genealogy of Morals* (1887); *TI, Twilight of the Idols* (1888); *CW, The Case of Wagner* (1888); *WP, The Will to Power* (various dates).

Citation of unpublished notes collected by Nietzsche's editors under the title *The Will to Power* cite both that text and *KSA*, the *Studienausgabe* of Nietzsche's *Sämtliche Werke*, edited by Giorgio Colli and Mazzino Montinari, in fifteen volumes (Berlin: Walter de Gruyter, 1980). Other unpublished materials are also cited in *KSA*; translations are my own unless otherwise indicated.

Other works cited in endnotes receive full bibliographical treatment with their first citation, and in the Bibliography.

PREFACE

Metaphysics to Metafictions is about the fate of idealism in philosophy, about the decline in the prestige and authority of ideas as surrogates for a moribund religious faith. Elevated to a grandiose status by Hegel with hubristic, "absolute" presumption that would have made even Faust blush, the bold claims of metaphysics were burst into fragments under blows from Nietzsche's hammer. Hegel and Nietzsche still mark the definitive extremes in the ambitions of metaphysics; their opposition remains decisive even a century after Nietzsche's death.[1]

In working through this story about the apotheosis and apocalypse of metaphysics, an uncanny sense of déjà vu gradually reconciles us to our own time's impatience with the imposing architecture of idealism. At first already in Hegel but then as dramatically as possible in Nietzsche, attention to the linguistic and narrative structures of metaphysics subverts the foundations of belief altogether. Accordingly, it is the task of this book to offer an account of how philosophical thought has led to a place where credulity has come to be regarded as a naive attitude, "faith" just a childlike commitment to one of many possible stories or fictions—but also how, paradoxically, a different kind of belief in these narratives then becomes possible. For repetition—the recognition of which is fatal to belief in theological claims, since these must be unique and "eternal"—repetition nevertheless redeems "mere stories" from the "legitimation crisis" they inherited from culturally central narratives of transcendence. That is, because stories can be repeated, revised, re-inhabited by different characters, they become enduring instances of the structure of human self-understanding. By virtue of their very repeatability, narratives can reflect "truths" legitimated by recognition among readers of diverse times and places. It is the web—or webs—of such truths that provides the reasonable facsimile, the "virtual reality," of that ideal realm lost, after Hegel, to "enlightened" incredulity.

Exposing the Janus face of this intellectual metamorphosis veiled by Hegel's *Phenomenology of Spirit* and Nietzsche's *Thus Spoke Zarathustra*—exemplary texts for reasons that will become clear in the working through—shall concern us presently. First, however, it would seem appropriate to briefly situate this study in the context of cognate historical and contemporary thinking about the importance of language and narrative in the constitution of knowledge and reality, for the "world view" which it is our purpose here to grasp in its foundations is very wide spread.

Beginning with the more obvious contemporary resonances, the debate concerning whether "modernity" has overcome its "legitimation crises" or instead succumbed to them, passing beyond itself into the ambiguous temporality of the "postmodern," shares with this inquiry much of the same textual history and many of the same problems. In particular, juxtaposition of Jürgen Habermas's penetrating defense of Enlightenment reason, worked out in *The Philosophical Discourse of Modernity*[2] and related writings, with the critical analysis of Jean-Francois Lyotard, especially *The Postmodern Condition: A Report on Knowledge*,[3] reinforces the conclusions arrived at here. Reciprocally, *Metaphysics to Metafictions* contributes to this discourse a way of understanding how now to contend with the residual problems of legitimation that remain after the dust settles in the arena of embattled modernity. Thus, whereas Lyotard's notion of "metanarratives" (*métarécits*) resembles in some respects the "metafictions" that this study finds to have displaced metaphysics, Lyotard's conception leaves the central problem of legitimation substantially unresolved. As an "incredulity toward metanarratives,"[4] Lyotard's heralded "postmodernity" literally does not know what to believe. But Nietzsche already saw that nihilism has a double aspect, and that the disillusionment with old values does not imply the abandonment of all values: on the contrary, such aporetic skepticism is merely a "pathological *transitional stage*," a "consequence of decadence."[5] Metafictions are not undone by skeptical doubts because they are not advanced with dogmatic epistemological presumptions; rather, they carefully maintain their plurality and avoid naive presumption with irony.

Correlatively, Habermas's attempt to recover the "unfinished project" of modernity by appropriating nihilism as itself an attitude within, and inseparable from, the discourse of reason, paradoxically amounts to much the same view, in practical terms, as Lyotard defends. Habermas wishes to maintain that the credibility of the universality of reason—which the Enlightenment enthroned in place of the falling deity and "his" scriptural authority—survives even the critical attack reason makes on itself through a parade of post-Kantian thinkers. Habermas maintains that a "performative contradiction" undoes the negative dialectics of Nietzsche and of Horkheimer and Adorno, while Heidegger and Derrida are repudiated for their supposedly disingenuous appeal to a mystification of absence. In a significantly extensive footnote at the very end of the important transitional "Excursus on Leveling the Genre Distinction between Philosophy and Literature," Habermas suggests that Nietzsche, Heidegger, Adorno, and Derrida all still "believe they have to tear philosophy away from the madness of expounding a theory that has the last word"[6]—that is, all supposedly still regard the metaphysical pretensions of philosophy, exemplified by Hegel, as fundamental to truth claims in general. However, Habermas then disingenuously criticizes such views for their naivety: such pretensions are merely "long since *abandoned status claims* that philosophy once alleged its answers to have. . . . The fallibilist consciousness of the sciences caught up with philosophy, too, a long time ago."[7] Rather than "absolute knowledge," "we philosophers" are "aware that there is no zero-context for truth claims. They are raised here and now and are open to criticism."[8]

But if the tradition of philosophy since the Greeks, the "tradition of Western metaphysics," is defined by its search for the True and the Universal, then to the extent that "we philosophers" no longer even attempt to make such a search, affirming instead the pragmatic fallibilism of temporary, in principle revisable truth claims, "we" are no longer "doing philosophy" in the traditional sense, but instead "sociology," "social theory," or something even more interdisciplinary. This would be to say that the status of the discipline of "philosophy" is itself in question: a claim whose institutional and pedagogical consequences are one of the principal themes of inquiry in *The Postmodern Condition*. Indeed, Lyotard closes his Introduction with the wry and pointed observation that the dedicatee of his report, the "Institut Polytechnique de Philosophie" is, "at this very postmodern moment" gradually supplanting the Université de Paris VIII (Vincennes) of which it is nominally a part,[9] and he goes on to examine how "polytechnic" concerns, which value production and efficiency, no longer even aspire to provide the kind of systematic and comprehensive understanding which, according to the nineteenth-century conception of education typified by von Humboldt's principles, was the very purpose of education.[10]

The "fallibilism" and "localism" of postmodern intellectual ambitions as Lyotard describes them bear other points of affinity with Habermas's supposedly antithetical *Weltanschauung* as well. In distinguishing "scientific knowledge" from "another kind of knowledge, which I will call narrative,"[11] Lyotard insists on the richer contexts of "*savoir-faire, savoir-vivre, savoir-écouter*" as providing necessary complements to objective claims uttered in propositions and governed by logic[12]—an enrichment of epistemological and ontological options parallel to Habermas's reasons for claiming the superiority of his theory of communicative practice to the traditional modern claims of a "philosophy of the subject" which finds itself in crisis precisely because of the limits of the subjective paradigm.[13] And Lyotard's final attempt to legitimate the postmodern scientific "quest for paralogy" as implying "a politics that would respect both the desire for justice and the desire for the unknown"[14] must lead us to wonder whether "legitimation" is not either in need of a metanarrative or itself one. Thus, the nihilism of Lyotard's "incredulity toward metanarratives" has its counterpart in Habermas's fallibilism just as the consensus Habermas wants to build out of non-coercive rational communication looks very much like Lyotard's "principle that any consensus on the rules defining a game and the 'moves' playable within it *must* be local, in other words, agreed upon by its present players and subject to eventual cancellation."[15] Massimo Riva seems to have noticed this confluence, too; in a brief speculative essay on late-millenium nihilism and Nietzsche's legacy, he offers the hypothesis that "Nihilism might well be considered the 'grand narrative' in the age of the end of 'grand narratives'—the Modern as an *unaccomplished* project as Jürgen Habermas has put it—and that the category of ambivalence, and the linguistic games of paradox, are themselves fundamental elements of a(ny) definition of (Post)-Modernity and its discourse or style."[16]

Metafictions, then, precisely as distinct from traditional metaphysical "metanarratives," are also neither "local narratives" in Lyotard's sense nor the corresponding structure of consensus that is Habermas's holy grail—although the commonality of concerns and analytical claims among all these cultural reflections is also significant. But maintaining consciousness of the scope and ambition of the Hegelian project while at the same time acknowledging that project's implosion with ontotheology can, as we will see, ironically liberate post-Nietzschean thought from the rhetoric of crisis characteristic of the Habermas-Lyotard debate.

Political crisis is perhaps even further from the proper domain of metafictions (the illocutionary force of which is diluted by irony), although overtly political gestures can just as easily emerge out of post-Hegelian aporias. Guy Debord and the "situationists" exemplify this reaction.

Debord's situationist manifesto, first published in Paris in 1967 and destined to play an important role in the following year's student uprising, opens with a prescient epigraph from Feuerbach: "for the present age, which prefers the sign to the thing signified, the copy to the original, representation to reality, the appearance to the essence . . . *illusion* only is sacred, *truth* profane."[17] But the situationists were not interested merely in "publication"; they even made vigorous efforts to escape notoriety—read: reabsorption into and thus appropriation by the "spectacular culture," which is judged to be oppressive in its ubiquity. So, Debord proceeds to describe, in order to subvert, what he calls the "society of the spectacle," for which "All that once was directly lived has become mere representation."[18] And in fact, Feuerbach's lament serves Debord as a call to arms: society is in thrall to "the system" and its surrogate activities; the spectator is alienated from but submits to the objects his unthinking activity has produced[19] such that "reciprocal alienation is the essence and underpinning of society as it exists."[20] Moreover, Debord characterizes this reciprocal alienation in terms of the failure of the Hegelian *Aufhebung* of religion! "The spectacle," he writes, "is the material reconstruction of the religious illusion"; in place of offering "a fallacious paradise" as the "absolute denial of life," the spectacle accomplishes this absolute denial "within material life itself. The spectacle is hence a technological version of the exiling of human powers in a 'world beyond'—and the perfection of separation *within* human beings."[21]

Redemption from this would-be redemption, the reappropriation of human freedom from its entrapment in the web of mass produced images—of "*capital* accumulated to the point where it becomes image"[22]—is announced in Debord's preface and throughout the text as its real purpose: "This book should be read bearing in mind that it was written with the deliberate intention of doing harm to spectacular society."[23] Marx's famous eleventh thesis on Feuerbach is, of course, another subtext of situationist imperatives (evoked, if not invoked, by the choice of epigraph already noted): hence, the effort to change the world, to subvert the society of the spectacle through an appropriation of the very mass-media images that would otherwise enslave. By means of various public "interventions,"[24] the situationist program called for "a reading of the world of representations in mass culture that recognizes the form of control that resides in the world of images and upon an aesthetic strategy that operates by wresting an image or a form of language from its original context and subverting it by methods of re-presentation in a different context."[25]

To achieve these ends, situationist practice resorted most often to what, for traditional aesthetics, would amount to plagiarism. As Greil Marcus describes it, "*détournement*," a key situationist concept of critique and transformation that signifies a vaguely criminal or delinquent kind of diversion, "meant the theft of aesthetic artifacts from the Old World and their revitalization in contexts of one's own devising."[26] Debord's *Mémoires*, for instance, as the title page itself admits, is "composed entirely of prefabricated elements." These include clippings and second-hand fragments of dizzying variety, paratactically enumerated. As Marcus sums it up, "In the combinations of its found, scavenged, or stolen materials, *Mémoires* affirms that everything needed to say whatever one might want to say is already present, accessible to anyone; the book defines a project, and tells a story."[27]

The sphere of possibilities invoked by this practice is clearly evident also in Zarathustra's metafictional legacy—specifically, in the teaching of "eternal return." And there can be no doubt that the topos of repetition (as pastiche, as citation, as ironic appropriation, as imitation, etc.) is a principal structuring principle in contemporary culture.[28] But viewed through the critical juxtaposition of Hegel and Nietzsche, through the destructive power and creative play of repetition from metaphysics to metafictions, a perspective on the underpinnings of that familiar cultural *milieu* opens up, a perspective that points a way toward reconciliation in a self-confident practice that holds no illusions about the inevitability of illusion. It is a practice that must always be wary of political pretensions, however. As if as a warning, Debord discouragingly argues that the creative "man" is ironically bound even tighter in the web of spectacle to the extent of his creativity, since his materials are all part of the system, and their use, even in art, reinforces the power of the system. "The closer his life comes to being his own creation," Debord laments, "the more drastically is he cut off from that life."[29] But the creative attitude that emerges out of Zarathustra's encounter with eternal return acknowledges, positively celebrates the structuring promises of a system in which everything has always already been tried, in which creation is recreation; the system's power is a boon, not a bane, and it does not occasion the stifling of expression implicit in situationist antipathy. Finally, but no less significantly, metafictions, with their winking disdain for the power of collective belief, are less likely to issue in catastrophic political consequences in which creative possibilities are cut off with the cutting short of life itself.[30]

Yet again, metafictions in the sense arrived at here, through a coherent, synthetic interpretation of the legacies of Hegel and Nietzsche, may be distinguished from "metafictions" as the term is sometimes used to identify the narrative practices of a group of contemporary, predominantly American writers of "literary" texts—although, as with the resonances audible in the debate about modernity and postmodernity, the widespread cultural dissemination of this idea in various guises is also important and significant. Practitioners of literary "metafiction" would include William Gass, John Barth, Donald Barthelme, Robert Coover, perhaps Kurt Vonnegut, perhaps Margaret Drabble's *The Realms of Gold*, some of Borges's tales. Gass uses the term to designate a literary correlate to metatheorems in mathematics or the "linguistic oversoul" of metaethical discourse: "everywhere lingos to converse about lingos are being contrived."[31] In a book on the work of Coover, Barthelme, and Gass entitled *The Metafictional Muse*, Larry McCaffery elaborates that each of these writers "frequently created fictions which either reflexively analyzed their own creative processes or which could be read as allegories about the writing process."[32] Formulated even more succinctly, David Lodge simply states that "Metafiction is fiction about fiction: novels and stories that call attention to their fictional status and their own compositional procedures."[33]

Clearly, then, "metafiction" in this sense is a specifically stylistic gesture that may or may not have philosophical implications. In fact, Gass affects irritation at philosophers for a characteristic failure to give form its due: "Philosophers continue to interpret novels as if they were philosophies themselves . . . they have predictably looked for content, not form; they have regarded fictions as ways of viewing reality and not as additions to it."[34] This is true of a certain familiar way of doing philosophy, the expression of which reaches its apogee in Hegel. But at the same time, two elements in this literary practice suggest a bridging of the genre distinction between literature and philosophy-as-metafiction. On the one hand, the fiction writer's relative unconcern with reality, and the concomitant commitment to truth as correspondence, is consistent with the implications of Nietzsche's perspectivism. But on the other, the writer-as-theorist recognizes the philosophical consequences of his method for the constitution of historical reality—the metaphysical function of metafictions, as it were:

> We may indeed suspect that the real power of historical events lies in their descriptions; only by virtue of their passage into language can they continue to occur, and once recorded (even if no more than as gossip), they become peculiarly atemporal.[35]

The metonymy of linking being with history—and history with fiction ("Historians make more history than the men they write about")[36]—calls to mind another reciprocally illuminating contemporary analytic discourse: the "metahistory" of Hayden White. And auspiciously, White's account of the narrative and fictive elements that structure the historian's discourse is directly informed by readings of Hegel and Nietzsche. In the important book *Metahistory: The Historical Imagination in Nineteenth-Century Europe* and in many essays and addresses, White has sought to identify and classify the various literary devices by means of which historians transform the bland recitation of events and dates into stories. Chronicles are not yet histories, White observes; they begin merely with the first recorded entry, proceed largely by chance, and end just as arbitrarily, lacking the teleology and closure which, as Aristotle noted, is essential to good drama. But the historian makes sense of this random reality, effecting a transformation of chronicle into story "by the characterization of some events in the chronicle in terms of inaugural motifs, of others in terms of terminating motifs, and of yet others in terms of transitional motifs."[37] Thus, the difference between "historian" and "fiction writer" is not reducible to an easy distinction between found fact and invented story; the historian, too, relies on invention. "The historian," White maintains, "arranges the events in the chronicle into a hierarchy of significance by assigning events different functions as story elements in such a way as to disclose the formal coherence of a whole set of events considered as a comprehensible process with a discernable beginning, middle and end."[38]

The publication of *Metahistory* provoked vigorous and continuing debate among academic historians in part because White's argument seemed to threaten the discipline with allegations of some sort of regression to the unscientific and widely discredited practice of the philosophy of history. Hegel was (is) seen to be the most egregious exponent of that irresponsible methodology because his representation of historical reality "consists of nothing but plot; its story elements exist only as manifestations, epiphenomena, of the plot structure."[39] But White's identification of the "embarrassment of plot" within historical narrative suggested that, however much a given historian might disavow tendentious interpretation, not to say "absolute knowledge," writing history is also writing and is inevitably structured by extra-historical, writerly criteria and methods.

This line of analysis is sympathetic to the view developed here with regard to the complex and significantly ambivalent role of idealism in the legitimation of metafictions. On White's account, the desire to understand reality as meaningful—something accomplished, as we will see below, by Judeo-Christian ontotheology and then usurped by Hegel's System—is formally satisfied by narrative as such. After all, it is the world, the Real itself, which threatens to look arbitrary and thus meaningless, not our accounts of the world. On the other hand, these meaningful accounts are admitted to be nothing more than "masks," artfully crafted fictions, "the completedness and fullness of which we can only *imagine*, never experience."[40] Thus, White does not indict idealism for its secret fictive structure without also reversing the polarities and revealing historical reality as similarly the expression of imagination. "Insofar as historical stories can be completed, can be given narrative closure, can be shown to have had a *plot* all along," White concludes, "they give to reality the odor of the *ideal*."[41] This is the thesis of the dialectic of nihilism, succinctly formulated: the "passive nihilism" of the disillusion of the old values, to be followed by the "active nihilism" of recreation.[42] But the re-creation of metafictions takes shape out of a playful practice; it may participate in the passionate conviction of what Nietzsche called "brief habits,"[43] but it is much too self-critical and ironic to make the idealist's usual claims on eternity or universality.

Repetition and consequent reservations about truth both characterize metafictions, then—reservations that stem from the embarrassment of recognition ("We've heard this story before," wink wink), while it is ironically this same capacity to recognize a familiar truth that makes it possible for metafictions to satisfy the demands of credulity. The trick for the writer of metafictions is to find an interesting way to manipulate available elements, to perform variations on themes implied by the forms of speculation themselves. In other words, one must come to terms with one's precursors, whose collective efforts together constitute the body of texts that can serve as models of form. As Harold Bloom memorably put it, distilling his influential theory of the anxiety of influence into an epigram, "the central problem for the latecomer necessarily is *repetition*, for repetition dialectically raised to re-creation is the ephebe's road of excess, leading away from the horror of finding himself to be only a copy or a replica."[44] Having struggled through the legitimation crisis brought on by the Enlightenment's evisceration of religious transcendence as absolute authority, and having striven to somehow universalize the self by means of the philosophy of subjectivity as rational surrogate for that transcendent authority, contemporary sensibilities have become wary of claiming too much about whatever is not the self, just as any unproblematic autonomy has equally come to be regarded with suspicion. Consequently, as David Lodge notes in writing of the literary context, metafiction "is a mode that many contemporary writers find particularly appealing, weighted down, as they are, by their awareness of their literary antecedents, oppressed by the fear that whatever they might have to say has been said before, and condemned to self-consciousness by the climate of modern culture."[45]

But the weight of the past, and the stormy climate of modern culture, are not only obstacles: they are, equally, opportunities. The Bloomian "strong poet," repeating his precursors through his own creative activity, also transforms the past, re-creates it by constituting a self through which others will re-interpret the past.[46] The paradigm of life lived like a dramatic narrative, according to the Nietzschean formula of amor fati, would be manifested, as Richard Rorty explains, by "the genius who can say of the relevant portion of the past, 'Thus I willed it,' because she has found a way to describe that past which the past never knew, and thereby found a self to be which her precursors never knew was possible."[47] It is fitting, then, that we conclude this attempt to sketch a map of the allied territories in which the theoretical construct of metafictions finds its ground and stakes its discursive claims with a backward glance at the precursors who prepared the way.

Contemporary constitutive theories of language and narrative have their origin in the development of consequences that follow from a certain reading of Kant's epistemology, elaborated perhaps most trenchantly by Friedrich Albert Lange and Hans Vaihinger. Leaving aside questions of direct influence with respect to the broad-based dissemination of constructs analogous to metafictions discussed above, a brief examination of Lange's argument in his once popular but now largely neglected masterwork *The History of Materialism and Criticism of its Present Importance* (1873),[48] especially the concluding chapter "The Standpoint of the Ideal," and Vaihinger's belated post-Kantian tract *The Philosophy of 'As if': A System of the Theoretical, Practical and Religious Fictions of Mankind* (1911),[49] can help to establish the patrimony (that is, the legitimacy) of the interpretive framework and its consequent conclusions arrived at here through readings of Hegel and Nietzsche.

Lange's monumental *History of Materialism* is, as its title suggests, concerned principally with descriptive accounts of materialistic doctrines in philosophy from the time of the Greek atomists until the nineteenth century, in order finally to criticize this philosophical attitude and put a kind of equivocal idealism in its place (Lange coins the term *"materiale Idealismus,"* or "materio-idealism," to name his position). "Materialism" is, of course, variously formulated, but all the versions with which Lange takes issue share at least two essential dogmas: belief in the sole reality of matter and in a system of laws to which matter is deterministically bound. Thus, as Bertrand Russell succinctly explains, if "everything that we commonly regard as the motion of matter is subject to laws [of physics] . . . then, although there may be a concurrent world of mind, all its manifestations in human and animal behavior will be such as an ideally skilful physicist could calculate from purely physical data."[50] However, as Lange argues from Kantian principles, the fact that our knowledge of matter is drawn only from its appearances to us, and these appearances are (as materialism itself makes clear) necessarily affected by our physical constitution, it follows that materialism reduces to sensationalism and is accordingly deprived of its proud claims to objective truth. Thus, again in Russell's paraphrase, although "Physics seeks to discover material occurrences not dependent on the physiological and psychical peculiarities of the observer," nevertheless "its facts are only discovered by means of observers."[51]

In Lange's view, the epistemological compromises implied by these observations are problematic only for the doctrine of materialism itself and its advocates; indeed, for the wider view of human knowing Lange recommends, materialist paradoxes point toward the unique potential of speculative idealism in formulating the transcendental hypotheses upon which all distinctly human accomplishment has always been grounded. Accordingly, the two long volumes of Lange's historical criticism lead at last to positive suggestions sketched in the final chapter "The Standpoint of the Ideal," in which an essentially poetic vision of the Real is affirmed to be indispensable to the finding of any value in what, as simply given to sense, is neither harmonious nor even intelligible. Emphasizing the role played by what Kant had called the "transcendental unity of apperception" in the constitution of the phenomenal world—the idealist kernel of the critical philosophy that Hegel was also to seize upon[52]—Lange observes that "the task of producing harmony among phenomena and of linking the manifold that is given to us into unity belongs not merely to the synthetic factors of experience, but also to those of speculation."[53] Both optimism and pessimism, Lange insists, have their source in this capacity for forming pictures of the world "upon the ideal within us,"[54] without which comparison "we should not be able to form a judgment as to the quality of the world."[55] Ethical evaluation thus appears as an aesthetic act that provides a necessary complement to the "certainty" striven for by science. For, although materialism usefully serves to oppose metaphysical "pretensions to penetrate into the essence of nature," nevertheless "the highest functions of the free human spirit" are beyond its reach; in the end, the scientist's devotion to his calling can only pass beyond an "unstimulating" [arm an Anregungen] or "barren" [steril] servitude to unliving matter by "borrowing from Idealism."[56]

"Let us accustom ourselves, then," Lange writes in conclusion, "to attribute a higher worth than hitherto to the principle of the creative idea in itself,"[57] for "One thing is certain, that man needs to supplement reality by an ideal world of his own creation, and that the highest and noblest functions of his mind co-operate in such creations."[58] Let us acknowledge, then, the constitutive contribution we ourselves make to our experience of the world-as-valuable. More, let us not lament the fact that mere facts don't matter, and that what matters can neither be established nor refuted by facts; indeed, "Who will refute a Mass of Palestrina, or who will convict Raphael's Madonna of error?"[59] In a passage of considerable literary power which is lent argumentative weight by the many preceding pages of erudition, Lange declares:

> For the universe, as mere natural science enables us to comprehend it [begreifen], we can as little feel enthusiasm as for an "Iliad" spelt out letter by letter [eine buchstabirte Ilias]. But if we embrace the whole as a unity, then in the act of synthesis we bring our own nature [unser eignes Wesen] into the object, just as we shape the landscape that we gaze at [Anschauung] into harmony, however much disharmony in particulars may be concealed by it. All comprehension [Zusammenfassung] follows aesthetic principles, and every step towards the whole is a step towards the Ideal.[60]

The methodological conception of metafictions, conceived as fictions that serve the purposes of metaphysics, is thus prefigured in the subjective constitution of Kant's transcendental unity of apperception and its consequent regulative epistemological dualism, radicalized as Nietzsche's "perspectivism," informed by Lange's "Standpoint of the Ideal." Indeed, Nietzsche's indebtedness to Lange has often enough been noted but suffers from the comparative disregard currently accorded his precursor. Significantly, Hans Vaihinger examined the dynamics of this influence in some detail, focusing especially on Nietzsche's early essay "On Truth and Lies in a Non-Moral Sense" ("nonmoral lying" is understood to be "the conscious deviation from reality to be found in myth, art, metaphor, etc."[61]) and The Birth of Tragedy ("Art is the conscious creation of an aesthetic illusion").[62] Thus, picking up the thread where Lange leaves it so as to trace still more precisely the intellectual-historical consequences that proceed from Kant's critical idealism to the reductio ad absurdum of Nietzsche's nihilism stands Hans Vaihinger—who acknowledges Kant's antinomies as a "profound influence" on his own thought,[63] describes himself as "a disciple of F. A. Lange,"[64] and displays an abiding fascination for Nietzsche, whom he credits with also having recognized that "life and science are not possible without imaginary, therefore false conceptions."[65]

For Vaihinger, the great lesson of Kant's critical prolegomena to future metaphysics (a lesson learned and further elaborated by Lange) lies in the change of attitude occasioned by a strong-minded repudiation of dogmatism accompanied by an almost ironic profession of the essential importance of precisely that which is thus so decisively compromised. "The principle of fictionalism," Vaihinger writes, "is as follows: 'An idea whose theoretical untruth or incorrectness, and therewith its falsity, is admitted, is not for that reason practically valueless and useless; for such an idea, in spite of its theoretical nullity, may have great practical importance."[66] Distinguishing this stance from "pragmatism" in that, for the latter, the fruitful is therefore also "true," and affirming once again the precedent of Kant, for whom "a large number of ideas, not only in metaphysics but also in mathematics, physics and jurisprudence, were Fictions" and for whom metaphysical ideas "were definitely called 'heuristic Fictions,'"[67] Vaihinger articulates his central notion of "the 'As if' world." Formed by means of "thought-constructs . . . called Scientific Fictions," which are marked as "conscious creations by their 'As if' character," Vaihinger paradoxically insists that "the world of the 'unreal' is just as important as the world of the so-called real or actual (in the ordinary sense of the word); indeed it is far more important for ethics and aesthetics."[68]

The Philosophy of 'As if' thus stakes out a postmetaphysical position which is, with respect to the question of "legitimation," closely analogous to the condition of metafictions. Recognizing metaphysical claims to be, in Lange's words, a "supplement to reality" that the mind itself creates as its "highest and noblest function,"[69] Vaihinger reiterates that "it is just in these ideas and ideals that the highest values of mankind lie," adding provocatively that the "'true value' of these ideas lies in style, the form, as it were, of the conceptual architecture [Vorstellungsarchitektur]."[70] Far from standing in need of transcendent validation, such conceptions cheerfully announce their own lack of any such grounding—or rather, the philosopher who wishes to protect time-honored "ideas and ideals" from corrosive incredulity confesses to this lack in the hope of thereby disarming the inevitable objections.

But here is the rub. Historically, habits of belief have required the validation of authority for all but the very most extraordinary minds; indeed, even extraordinary minds cannot create ex nihilo. It is not "objections" that the "standpoint of the ideal" will face, but something more primitive: pleas, prayers, desperate demands for direction, for dogma; if these demands fail to be satisfied, if reassurance is not forthcoming, such primitive appeals may turn hostile and even violent. The history of philosophy itself teaches this lesson: the enlightened agnosticism of Kant is not, after all, immediately succeeded by Nietzsche's perspectivism—nor is perspectivism yet "eternal return." Intervening between Kant and Nietzsche, between modern optimism and the seeds of postmodern nihilism, lies that great "retrograde step" (in Nietzsche's phrase) taken by Hegel's ironic accomplishment of the modern project.

Lange and Vaihinger both fail to assimilate Hegel's post-critical mysticism and so fail to notice the formal repetition of what could no longer be taken literally with respect to content implicit in the "epilogic" of absolute knowing. Neither adequately contends with the paradox of an eviscerated idealism couched in subjunctive conditionals, which either fails to measure up to its own hard-headed modesty or else simply lacks the didactic force it might have inherited from the disabused dogmas it would supplant. And neither is therefore positioned to appreciate how "eternal return" functions in Nietzsche's thought to provide a mechanism by means of which affirmation and disavowal are simultaneously possible—a mechanism that does not leave a legacy of specific claims, but rather a new attitude toward the expressive potentials of form. Absent the transcendent validation of the dead God, and refusing as unintelligible the dream of absolute creative priority, metafictions answer the demand for legitimation with the ironic credulity of re-creation.

INTRODUCTION

Kant would not see, what Plato before him would not see, that the
"intelligible world" is a world of poetry, and that it is just this
which constitutes its value and dignity.

—F. A. Lange

Few people would deny that we live today in a time of vertiginous change. States rise and fall as they always have, but television and radio have awesomely increased our consciousness of their number while at the same time diminishing their foreignness. The status of knowledge in the sciences is as fickle as are the benefits and risks of what the sciences produce. Art has been liberated from the constraints of convention to the extent that blank canvases hang in museums and musical works are composed entirely of silence. Even advertisers recognize that we have all become weary and wary of truth claims—it is more effective these days to sketch a style with a light and colorful hand than to pontificate on the preeminence of one's product, however persuasively. The nineteenth-century ideal of comprehensive understanding has crumbled under its own weight; ours is a time of fragmentation and dissolution in which probability has supplanted certainty, in which naive totalities have been toppled by revelations of their incompleteness.

But the contemporary attitude of nonchalance toward presumptions of authority by precisely those beliefs and things that have been respected until recently as "authoritative" is not merely a fashion of the moment. Admittedly, nihilism seems to attract paradoxically passionate embraces from time to time in the history of our culture. But what makes the form of the current crisis seem so poised for the hammer, whether it be the iconoclast's or the sculptor's, is its suddenness and definitiveness. Although our own history shows us many anticipations and repetitions of the prophetic stance of "wisdom" that we no longer take seriously (because its very repetition has worn out the credulity of those who would be "enlightened" by it), nevertheless that incredulity marks a rupture of what would be "world historical" proportions if it were audible as a bang and not a whimper.

"What is novel about the position we take toward philosophy," Nietzsche writes in an unpublished note from 1881, "is a conviction that no prior age shared: *that we do not possess the truth*. All earlier men

1

'possessed the truth,' even the skeptics."[1] From at least the time of Plato, Truth about the Real had been affirmed by Western thinkers as a transcendent Ideal, the *telos* of thought and object of the philosopher's proper attention and ambition. But with the Enlightenment, immanent reason began to displace the beyond as sufficient unto itself—at least for the discovery, if not quite the constitution of, truth and reality. Kant's account of the mind's a priori structures, reflexive possession of which grounds the universality and necessity of knowledge claims in mathematics and pure natural science, represents a further step toward recognizing the constituted nature of "truth" and phenomenal "reality." But the most blatant manifestation of that potentially subversive attitude, both in theory and in practice, ironically appears in the *deification* of reason, and thus the complete overcoming of any troublesome "otherness," which is worked out in Hegel's *Phenomenology of Spirit*. As first of all an affirmative gesture, the epistemological consequences of so brazenly usurping the divine come into view only in Hegel's wake; that is, only since "the 'true world' finally became a fable," as Nietzsche was to put it.

In the realm of ideas, then, in "metaphysics"—that most fundamental of inquiries into the nature of being itself—the crucial professors of Truth and "truth" respectively are surely Hegel and Nietzsche.

Hegel's bold project of speculative metaphysics is perhaps the most grandiose testament to intellectual optimism ever attempted in the entire history of philosophy. Believing in the universality of Reason, Hegel never doubts that the course of dialectic is objectively necessary and that it must lead to wisdom. The "love of wisdom" that drove Socrates to practice a tirelessly *critical* dialectic is finally fulfilled twenty-three centuries later in "absolute knowing," a standpoint audacious in its presumption. As Alexandre Kojève matter-of-factly puts it, Hegel "claims to have attained Wisdom (in and by the *Phenomenology*)."[2] This fantastic accomplishment is carried out through a style of writing no less grandiloquent that is affirmed to be simultaneously the medium and the content of the systematic comprehension of reality. With revolutionary fervor, Hegel proclaims "It is surely not difficult to see that our time is a time of birth and transition to a new period. Spirit has broken with what was hitherto the world of its existence and imagination . . . by the break of day that, like lightning, all at once reveals the shape of the new world" (para. 11; p. 15).[3]

In marked contrast to this heroic optimism, Nietzsche—writing toward the end of the very same century inaugurated by Hegel—reveals transcendent Truth beyond the vicissitudes of phenomenal appearances as a *fiction*, fashioned in various forms and employed in the service of "a *drive to appropriate and conquer*" (WP, section 423 [March–June

1888]; *KSA* 13, p. 326).⁴ Far from the brave new world of Spirit's self-consciousness illuminated by the brilliant lightning of reason's *Begriff*, Nietzsche writes "Everything on our way is slippery and dangerous, and the ice that still supports us has become thin: all of us feel the warm uncanny breath of the thawing wind: *where* we walk, soon no one will *be able* to walk" (*WP*, section 57 [1884]; *KSA* 11, p. 12). Crafting fables that compare the philosopher's pretensions to absolute wisdom with those of a gnat, equally justified in believing itself to be the flying center of the universe,⁵ Nietzsche employs extravagant tropes, verse and song, wild polemics and self-indulgent bombast, pointed irony, and generally a host of dramatic rhetorical postures and polymorphous paratactic strategies that are the very opposite of Hegel's systematic exposition: "I mistrust all systematizers and I avoid them. The will to a system is a lack of integrity" (*TI*, "Maxims and Arrows," section 26). When he does mention Hegel explicitly—and such references are neither frequent nor incisive—Nietzsche is caustic and critical.⁶

But in spite of such obvious antipathy, the majority of writing on Hegel and Nietzsche exploits a very different impression of their relationship. In a useful article on "The Hegel-Nietzsche Problem," Daniel Breazeale describes "an international group of investigators intent upon calling attention to the frequently overlooked *similarities* between Hegel and Nietzsche."⁷ The most influential of these is undoubtedly Walter Kaufmann, but the field is large and varied. Arguments for this improbable kinship exploit parallel use of key metaphors, analogous historical "genealogies," even a supposedly common will to abolish epistemology, in order to conclude dramatically that such evidence demonstrates "Nietzsche's profound Hegelianism" (Kremer-Marietti) or, even more bluntly, that "Nietzsche is an Hegelian" (Zimmermann).⁸

Both of these antithetical impressions, however, miss the point; like antinomies, they serve instead to reveal the inadequacy of epistemological assumptions and habits of reading that expect univocal meaning. So significant a conjunction as Hegel and Nietzsche is not a problem in want of a "solution": it is significant because what is at stake in this juxtaposition of impieties is nothing less than the status of "metaphysical" thinking for our own time. As Fredric Jameson has remarked, "the rhetoric of totality and totalization that derived from . . . the Germanic or Hegelian tradition is the object of a kind of instinctive or automatic denunciation by just about everybody."⁹ In spite of a rise in religious fundamentalisms both in the West and in the East, the "common sense" of a highly technological society is ill disposed toward Hegel's method and the audacity of his claims, while "post-historical" events like the Third Reich make common sense suspicious of the German universal for practical reasons. Unanimity of social opinion, for Hegel the hallmark of Spirit and the essence of freedom, smacks for us of tyranny and fascism, of a fanaticism all the more frightening when it bears brawny nuclear arms. And it was Nietzsche, already before the old century expired, who most vividly struggled to describe the void left by the death of belief in the well-rounded spheres of metaphysical totalities.

In order to understand this struggle, to come to terms with the problematic legacy left by metaphysics, the first three chapters of this study examine in detail the quintessential description of the metaphysically sublimated soul: Hegel's account of Spirit's progress through its self-externalization in history toward the self-consciousness of its *telos* in the standpoint of absolute knowing. The *Phenomenology of Spirit* will accordingly rank as our principal text: it is the most influential of Hegel's writings, and it is frankly descriptive of nineteenth-century consciousness, thus laying the metaphysical foundations with which the larger interpretive concerns of this inquiry will be subsequently engaged. Moreover, as J. N. Findlay notes, "there is no notion or principle to be found in the later system which is not sounded in the *Phenomenology*, usually in more penetrating and enlightening fashion."[10]

In Chapter One, we will follow Hegel's opening moves in the analysis of "Sense-Certainty," where the retreat to abstract sensation as the ground and starting point of philosophy is shown to stand in need of the enormous qualification that such a beginning is necessarily mute—more, that when forced to speak, it can utter only universals when the experience meant is the "concrete content" of what is absolutely particular. Hegel rejects appeals to individual embodiment as unintelligible: the immediacy of feeling lacks any determinate content, and its "truth" turns out to be the mediation of universal linguistic expression. Since philosophy must be articulate, the *Phenomenology* begins with a linguistic bias that prefigures its ultimate linguistic redemption in the philosophical *Begriff*—a structural circularity anticipated in the *Vorrede*, which explicitly begins at the end.

Just as the truth of sense-certainty ironically resides in its other, in the negation and sublation of particularity in the universality of language, the truth of self-certainty similarly devolves on the other. In Chapter Two, the skillful manipulation of irony that encouraged Hegel's initial "linguistic turn" is followed further into the domain of historical action, which is generated by the internal metaphysical opposition of a consciousness that thinks itself determinate. When consciousness encounters itself in the form of another embodied individual, it rebels at the deception and implicitly desires a "recognition" from the other that is really a vision of its own reflection. Desire, for Hegel, is bondage, being most profoundly a desire for the other's desire: lord and bondsman need each other in order to be who they are. And in their struggle, they create history—the chronicle of Spirit's immaturity, the long story of deeds done for the sake of a goal that was at the outset already implicitly achieved.

It is in its explicit achievement, however, that the consequences of each of these dialectical moves become clear. The meaning of historical action is bound up with its temporality and teleology: "The interpretation of history thus necessarily becomes prophecy,"[11] and Hegel is able to pronounce the meaning of history because he proclaims its end. In Chapter Three, the "epilogical" perspective of absolute knowing is revealed as the hidden agenda that from the outset had guided a phenomenological vision that pretended to be purely passive. Adding no new content, no new "shape of Spirit," the meaning of Hegel's absolute is pre-constituted by the imaginative representation of what led up to it. Philosophy paints its grey on grey with synoptic repetition: the *Phenomenology* is an exercise in mnemonic hermeneutics, an a priori reconstruction of Spiritual history from the Action that results from the dynamic encounter of mutually desiring Desire.

As such, the revolutionary claims Hegel makes need to be reevaluated in the light of his own methodological presuppositions. Beginning with the denial that the world is intelligible as immediately given, Hegel insists that experience is always already interpreted—in Nietzsche's words, "facts is precisely what there is not, only interpretations" (*WP*, section 481 [1883–1888]; *KSA* 12, p. 315). Moreover, the interpreted world Hegel examines "phenomenologically" is meaningful only in terms of the philosophical eschatology of its *telos* in the absolute.[12]

But as it turns out, for Hegel the *Urtext* of this interpretation is not the Real itself, the immediacy of which can never be present, but rather the canonical mediation of the Word (always already an interpretation of the divine mind) constituitive of Judeo-Christian ontotheology—in both its traditional Lutheran and heterodox Gnostic forms. Chapter Four therefore concludes the treatment of the *Phenomenology* developed here and provides a transition to the reading of Nietzsche that follows by revealing how Hegel's brash realization of the metaphysical ambitions at the center of Western philosophy retrospectively (hermeneutically) makes explicit the repetition that is the undoing of those ambitions. The teleological character of Judeo-Christian eschatology (which is already implicit in Plato, vestiges of cyclic mysticism notwithstanding) is of course incompatible with repetition—yet Hegel repeats those eschatological promises nevertheless, both in his appropriation of Gnostic apocalypse and in the formal structure of his dialectic, for which the end is already in the beginning. Nietzsche is perhaps the first, but certainly the most influential, thinker to understand what had happened: to grasp that the unintelligibility of simply living life can be mediated by meaning only through repetition, that "redemption" is nothing more than a promise of repetition. And so, for Nietzsche "eternal return" becomes the telling locus of an epistemology of irony re-animating repetitions with "spin"—an attitude toward knowing that still defines the (anti)philosophical presuppositions of cultural activity today.

In Chapter Five, then, Nietzsche's uncompromising exploration of the consequences for "philosophy" of such methodological constructivism is followed to the edge of an abyss that is more a test of character than a philosophical conclusion. Man, already for Hegel, had displaced God; subsequently, the ground of values can no longer be sought in some "beyond." From this perspective of radical immanence, Nietzsche pleads "We, however, *want to become those we are*—human beings who are new, unique, incomparable, who give themselves laws, who create themselves" (*GS*, section 335). Hegel's dialectical overcoming of the penultimate shape of revealed religion must be carried one step further—"The will to truth requires a critique" (*GM*, III, section 24). The appropriation of heterodox ontotheology, itself already a repetition within a repetition by the time it re-emerges in Hegel, is repeated yet again, and flamboyantly, in Nietzsche's usurpation of the figure of the Antichrist, while the "epilogical" circularity of Hegelian dialectic circles back in "eternal return." Accordingly, Hegel's conclusion that the real is an historical externalization of the self is reformulated by Nietzsche in the notion of "aesthetical conduct" (*ästhetisches Verhalten*): although the claims to comprehensive, Rational truth are abandoned ("the correct perception—which would mean the adequate expression of an object in the subject—is a contradictory non-entity"), yet the "suggestive carryover" this aesthetical conduct achieves "would still reveal much more with this permutation of spheres, than the empirical world reveals about the essence of things."[13] The "overleaping" of ontological spheres requires the light feet of Zarathustra's dancing metaphors mobilized in a Dionysian affirmation of the ontologically constitutive power of creative imagination; "philosophers . . . must no longer accept concepts as a gift, nor merely purify and polish them, but first *make* and *create* them" (*WP*, section 409 [1885]; *KSA* 11, pp. 486–87).

The abyss toward which this constitutive theory leads leaves the status of metaphysics as doctrine in the void. As Zarathustra finally learns—and, by example, tries to teach—the origin of affirmation in the creative will of the truth sayer ("the laughing soothsayer") compromises the pretensions to universality that traditionally accompany such utterances. Zarathustra's truths are his alone. And so, whereas for Hegel, the real is implicitly an interpretation, which can therefore be retrospectively elucidated—such being the very task of speculative metaphysics—in Nietzsche, the consequences of this circular constitution of meaning for philosophy's didactic intentions become explicit. If the *Phenomenology* is a metaphysical *Bildungsroman*[14] that weaves the tale of Universal History by telling the story of Spirit's heroic development to the standpoint of absolute self-consciousness, then narrative structure is the very structure of Being itself. Metaphysics becomes metafiction—a story told with bold presumptions to universal scope—presumptions unmasked as such by Nietzsche, who offers a "counterdoctrine" that is in the end itself just one more metafiction, one chronicle among many, the braying of another ass (to paraphrase Zarathustra). For Nietzsche realized not only that belief in the universality of metaphysical presumptions was bankrupt, that the meaning of the world derives from active creation and not passive reception—in the end, Nietzsche knew that creative originality is nevertheless impossible! One is always and inevitably a motley montage "of all that men have ever believed" (*TSZ*, Part II, "On the Land of Education") for "the development of language and the development of consciousness . . . go hand in hand" (*GS*, section 354). Even the self is a metafiction, a synthetic construction of available possibilities; all expression is always already repetition. "What is disagreeable and offends my modesty," Nietzsche wrote to Jacob Burkhardt after the onset of his madness, "is that at bottom I am every name in history."[15]

The concluding chapter of the present inquiry attempts to interpret this great aporia—this vertiginous historical-conceptual limbo separating Hegel's belated optimistic finality from the liberating "active nihilism" of Nietzsche's nascent transvaluation—insofar as it remains definitive of Western intellectual culture approaching the millennium. "Form within yourself an image to which the future shall correspond," Nietzsche counseled the youth of his own already post-modern time, "and forget the superstition that you are epigones."[16] But we are still struggling to form that image in the wake of the death of God—or rather, to formulate criteria by means of which our choices might be legitimated, for there has been no paucity of suggestions. We are still striving to become those we are, but only very gradually is the circular structure of that project of self-creation beginning to be visible through the occluding mists of pride and hope. Both an offense to our modesty and a release from an infinite, impossible burden, the familiar shape of the new can just be made out in the penumbra of the effects of Nietzsche's agon as it returns among us.

CHAPTER ONE

Language and Truth:
The Aufhebung *of Immediacy*

The *Phenomenology of Spirit* begins the arduous process of appropriating human history for philosophical "speculation" with the common-sense hypothesis that there exists a world of which we are conscious. In some fundamental way, we all believe that we exist in a time and place populated by similarly existing objects and other people. Of this "fact" we believe ourselves to be completely certain: only madmen and philosophers are seriously disturbed by doubts. Nevertheless, close scrutiny fortifies these doubts and stands common sense on its head, for the effort to articulate and justify our certainty is fraught with problems.

In this chapter, we will look closely at Hegel's dialectical interrogation of the certainty claimed by sense experience. In Part I, Hegel's moves themselves are followed to an aporetic conclusion: although it is impossible to affirm the immediacy claimed by sense-certainty in the *medium* of affirmation—language—it is equally impossible to deny it altogether. The empiricist claims for the epistemological adequacy of sense data are revealed as naive, even contradictory; still, "being *is*." Hegel's philosophy proceeds from the tragic realization that knowing and being are primordially alienated toward a recovered unity in the conceptual recognition of intersubjective Spirit. But, as will only gradually become clear, the consequences of denying intelligibility to the given world in order to dialectically reconstruct it so that it may finally be appropriated by philosophical understanding are far from indifferent.

Part II of this chapter further examines Hegel's initial "linguistic turn" from naive immediacy to articulate mediation through a reading of readings of "Sense-Certainty." The primacy of expression in Hegel's dialectic is regarded by some commentators as illegitimate, while more contemporary readings turn away from a mute loyalty to "raw feels" to focus instead on the narrative and rhetorical or tropological strategies of the medium itself. The stakes of this ontological commitment to language, so central to current debates, will become progressively clearer as we traverse the course of Hegel's dialectic, arriving at last at the mediated immediacy of philosophical wisdom. But the circularity of this eternal return, and its significance for metaphysical thinking, will remain obscured by Hegel's idealist pretensions; not until Zarathustra struggles with this heaviest of burdens will Hegel's legacy to a post-historical world be assumed and passed on to the philosophers of the future.

PART I. SENSE-CERTAINTY AND EXPRESSION

1. *Deferral of the* Vorrede *and the "immediate" beginning*

It is significant that the *Phenomenology* begins, as it were, at the end. The substantial *Vorrede*, which itself opens with a denial of the very possibility of writing a preface to a project that can only be realized in the praxis of carrying it out, nevertheless advances formulations which are proper to the fully developed philosophical cognition finally reached in Chapter VIII, *Das absolute Wissen*. Even before the claims of a hypothetical naive consciousness can be described, examined, and revised in the first chapter, diligent readers have thus already been prepared for the conclusions ultimately to be reached. "The *fundamental principle* [der *Grundsatz*] of a system of philosophy is its *result*," Hegel writes in a colorful aphorism composed during the period when the *Phenomenology* was gestating in his mind: "Just as we read the last scene of a play, the last page of a novel, or as Sancho considered it better to reveal beforehand the solution to a riddle, so the beginning of a philosophy is indeed also its point of return."[1] Throughout the *Phenomenology*, Hegel will dialectically reevaluate common sense and traditional views again and again from "our" perspective as speculative philosophers in possession of the *Begriff*, a perspective that is both pro- and retro-spective: guiding the analyses from the very outset, the absolute is already implicit in the interpretive impetus of dialectic. The Preface is accordingly a somewhat anomalous text; its special status is evident even in the way it is catalogued in the table of contents, and its extreme difficulty results from the attempt it makes to do the impossible. But because its anticipatory role can be fully understood only in conjunction with its mirror image in the recapitulative structure of absolute knowing, we will return to the Preface in order to evaluate that final apotheosis in Chapter Three. The hermeneutic circularity of Hegel's dialectical method is of central importance to this interpretation, as it provides the key to resolving hotly contested questions about the ontological potency and relevance of the absolute even as it leads philosophical method beyond dialectic toward Nietzsche's metafictional self-consciousness. But this recursive strategy called "dialectic" emerges only in practice; to appreciate its manner of operation it is necessary to play along with Hegel's game and observe closely as "naive" assumptions are systematically enlightened and revealed in their "truth."

With Chapter I of the *Phenomenology*, then—"Sense-Certainty: Or the 'This' and 'Meaning'"—we begin at the beginning. From a certain point of view it may seem that the most primitive form of knowledge, philosophical or otherwise, is that which is derived from the immediate presence of the world to the experience of simple consciousness. Although Hegel does not explicitly associate this attitude with some particular tradition, both the empiricist reduction to the epistemological primacy of what has recently been called "sense data" or "raw feels," as well as the Cartesian antithesis of this view which insists that *self*-certainty must ground all inquiry, are criticized as one-sided and inadequate.[2] It is, in fact, versions of these two alternatives that constitute the opposed moments in Hegel's first phenomenological dialectic.

The chapter opens with a declaration of this hypothetical starting point in a primitive, pre-philosophical knowing; emphatic repetition of the root word *unmittelbar* (immediate) serves to rhetorically underline the methodological determination that cognition remain passive, allowing the thing to show itself:

> The knowledge or knowing which is at the start or is immediately our object cannot be anything else but immediate knowledge itself, a *knowledge* of the *immediate* or of what simply is. Our approach to the object must also be *immediate* or *receptive*. (para. 90; p. 79)

The presumption of this proposal, which Hegel will presently challenge, is quite clear: "immediate knowledge" is possible if, in regarding the object of such knowing, in "apprehending it," we "refrain from trying to comprehend it" (ibid.).[3]

Furthermore, since the passivity of this cognitive attitude is supposed neither to augment nor reduce the "concrete content" of what thus presents *itself*, this primitive sense-certainty "immediately appears as the richest kind of knowledge, indeed a knowledge of infinite wealth" even as it "appears to be the *truest* knowledge" (para. 91; p. 79). Unmediated by understanding, language, or judgment, sense-certainty is a pure knowing *that*, not yet even a knowledge *of*; as such, its object would seem to embody a plenitude of being unreduced by the essentialism of categories nor enlarged by rational schemas. It is not pen and paper that are present to sense-certainty, but merely 'This'. And 'This' is present to a completely unspecific and undetermined consciousness, the pure correlate of this simple knowing.

In fact, however, this is not "knowledge" at all, and "this very *certainty* proves itself to be the most abstract and poorest *truth*" (ibid.). Although sensuous presence as such is indubitable, still the *certainty* (*Gewissheit*) claimed by this hypothetical starting point is too abstract to have a proper content: "its truth contains nothing but the sheer *being* of the thing [Sache]" (ibid.). This is not negligible, as we shall see; "mediation" is itself unintelligible unless there is something that is mediated. And this pure existence cannot be "false": it simply is, and that is its "truth." But negatively, a pure 'This', devoid of properties and qualities, is as cognitively empty as is a pure 'I', devoid of the existential characteristics of consciousness ("a manifold imagining and thinking").

Nevertheless, Hegel will not abandon the "concrete content," which here tempts sense-certainty into asserting that its knowledge is both rich and true. This *assertion* is already being called into question, since claims about the quality and extent of sense-certainty's knowledge imply the mediation of comparative judgments and cannot be "immediate." But although the truth-claims of sense-certainty cannot be maintained, it remains the case that the uttered "meaning" is identified with the particularity which expressions like 'This', 'Here', and 'Now' betray to universality. Hegel's subtitle for this chapter alerts us to the importance of this dialectic: *das Meinen*, the *meaning* (or opinion) which is uniquely *mine*, is dynamically but problematically related to the *saying* which must lose the particularity of individuals in the universality of expression. Hegel's examination of sense-certainty thus must turn from its essential but mute "concrete content" to these very claims about this content, which are from the outset regarded as dubious. With the bias for expression inevitable in any intelligible inquiry, sense-certainty must be forced to speak, even though its speech introduces reflection and mediation where there was supposed to be only immediate content. Immediacy thereby gets reinterpreted as a rhetorical posture of mediation, the construct of a certain narrative about knowledge and its origins. Pure sensual experience does not by itself assert anything at all; for it, "the thing *is*, and it is, merely because it *is*" (para. 91; p. 79). As soon as we ask questions about *what* the thing is we create a rift in the simple unity of immediate certainty.

With this realization, then, Hegel makes his first properly "philosophical" move: we are henceforth not concerned with an innocent self-revelation by sense-certainty of its own immediate content, but rather with a phenomenological examination of the relation between certainty and its object. The double vision of dialectic, which interrogates naive consciousness from the as yet distantly anticipated but already functional perspective of synthetic understanding, deprives sense-certainty of its independence: like self-consciousness in Chapter IV, distinct dialectical moments merge in a process that gives precedence to relation over determination. But the synthetic resolution of mediation presupposes an initial opposition which is not admitted by the simple unity of naive sense-certainty. Therefore, "we" philosophers must begin the process of reconstructing the synthetic unity of absolute knowing by first demonstrating the naivety of the unity claimed by this original presumed immediacy. Faced with complacent sense-certainty, with the smug simplicity of pure presence, "we take a bit of this wealth [ein Stück aus dieses Fülle] and by division *enter into it*: Consciousness, for its part, is in this certainty only as a pure *I*, or *I* am in it only as a pure *This* and the object similarly as a pure *This*" (para. 91; p. 79).

The artificiality of any division between 'This I' and 'This object' must be emphasized here. Although Hegel claims that it is intrinsic to the experience—"It is not just we who make this distinction . . . on the contrary, we find it within sense-certainty itself" (para. 93; p. 80)—it must be admitted that a purely naive certainty does no "finding" at all. Rather, "we" identify these constituent moments upon reflection, thereby introducing a dynamic multiplicity of perspectives into what was originally supposed to be a static unity. Hegel will proceed to overcome immediacy, then, through dialectical analysis initiated by the observation that the two 'Thises' which structure any actual instance of immediacy themselves provide a primitive mediation. Insisting on the actuality of an instance over the abstraction of mere essence, Hegel notes that we know 'This I' because it is not 'This object', and conversely; thus, "each is at the same time *mediated*: I have this certainty *through* something else, viz. the thing; and it, similarly, is in sense-certainty *through* something else, viz. through the 'I'" (para. 92; p. 80).

2. Critiques of object- and subject-centered philosophical starting points

Having made this new distinction between essence and instance, and temporarily privileging the latter, Hegel proceeds to explore the first moment of the historical dialectic proper to this chapter, in which versions of empirical materialism and Cartesian rationalism are opposed and finally overcome.[4] In any given instance of sense-certainty, Hegel reasons, it is first of all the object that is posited as primary and essential: the 'I' that knows it may either be or not be, but the object is "regardless of whether it is known or not; and it remains, even if it is not known, whereas there is no knowledge if the object is not there" (para. 93; pp. 80–81). What, then, is the nature of this obstinate object?

Maintaining an attitude of interrogation that would force sense-certainty to speak for itself,[5] Hegel presumes to answer that 'This' is at least constituted by temporal and spatial aspects. Whatever the object of sense-certainty may be, the immediate particularity claimed by this experience demands that the 'This' is 'Here' 'Now'. Calling these determinations "the twofold shape of its being," Hegel adds that this dialectic is contained in the object of sense-certainty just as the distinct moments 'I' and 'This' were shown to be. Then, to evaluate the truth of empirical materialism and the primacy of the object it claims, Hegel proposes a simple test: specifying some arbitrary content for 'Here' and 'Now', we "write down this truth; a truth cannot lose anything by being written down" (para. 95; p. 81). But specifying any object whatsoever in terms of the primitive coordinates of an immediate 'This' 'Here' 'Now' proves indeed to lose something by being written down: although 'This' may be a tree at midnight for the immediate consciousness that utters 'Here' 'Now', the truth of this statement is contradicted at noon and by the house that stands over 'Here'. Hence, the object of sense-certainty is constantly changing, and the immediate particularity of what is meant eludes utterance. The articulation of spatial and temporal particularity is incompatible with the naive immediacy claimed by sense-certainty.

Before moving on to consider the Cartesian alternative of privileging the subject as the essence of sense-certainty, Hegel draws a lesson of great importance from this attempt to speak for the object. The 'Now' that is preserved in the written testament 'Now is Night' proves to be the opposite of what it initially appears to claim for itself: at noon, the 'Now' of Night is not. And, of course, "[t]he same will be the case with the other form of the 'This,' with 'Here'" (para. 98; p. 82). Assuming the object to be the essence of sense-certainty cannot be sustained if we are to suppose the expressions 'This', 'Here', and 'Now' indeed voice the claims of immediacy, for these expressions prove to be essentially mediated by negation. 'Now' preserves itself from night to day "as a *negative* in general" and is, therefore, "not immediate but mediated; for it is determined as a permanent and self-preserving Now *through* the fact that something else, viz. Day and Night, is not" (para. 96; p. 81). Furthermore, the radical particularity of the immediate presence meant by sense-certainty proves, when that experience is forced to speak, to be expressed in *universals*: although they are supposed to name an experience absolutely unique to the consciousness that has it, an experience so primitive and direct that any further specification would falsify it, 'This', 'Here', and 'Now' are in fact terms that are true for any experience at any time and in any place. The linguistic expression appropriate to the immediacy claimed by sense-certainty is in fact mediated by negation, and the radical particularity that is meant proves when spoken to have the character of a universal:

> A simple thing of this kind which *is* through negation, which is neither This nor That, a *not-This*, and is with equal indifference This as well as That—such a thing we call a *universal*. So it is in fact the universal that is the true [content] of sense-certainty. (para. 96; p. 82)

The "concrete content" and the "true content" of sense-certainty are thus rigidly distinguished by what Derrida will call a "trick of writing": the former remains mute in the fullness of being—a plenitude that, in its self-sufficient immediacy, is indifferent to truth-claims—while the latter introduces the possibilities of articulation and discrimination at the cost of "directly reversing the meaning of what is said, of making it into something else, and thus not letting what is meant *get into words* at all" (para. 110; p. 89). Although we utter mediated universals in the attempt to make sense-certainty speak about immediate particulars, nevertheless "language, as we see, is the more truthful; in it, we ourselves directly refute what we *mean* to say, and since the universal is the true [content] alone, it is just not possible for us to say, or to express in words, a sensuous being that we *mean*" (para. 97; p. 82).

This is a startling claim with far-reaching consequences. It is impossible to abandon immediate sense-experience altogether—even in terms of "truth," pure being cannot be said to be "false" since it makes no assertion at all ("it *is*, merely because it *is*"), as we have seen. Yet every utterance about what is, precisely because it *is* an utterance and not the thing itself, sets an unbridgeable gulf between two domains of being that we naively suppose to be intimately connected. "The sensuous being that is meant," Hegel writes, "*cannot be reached by language*, which belongs to consciousness, i.e., to that which is inherently universal" (para. 110; p. 88). Nietzsche's ontology will also insist on this point: he speaks of independent "spheres" of being, of nerve stimuli transferred to images and again into sounds, such that "we possess nothing but metaphors for things—metaphors which correspond in no way to the original entities."[6] But whereas Nietzsche remains true to this view, and so develops his ideas without "forgetting that he himself is an *artistically creating subject*,"[7] Hegel will attempt to overcome the ontological impasse of indirect expression through the formal innovation of the philosophical *Begriff*. In absolute knowing, the immediate content of what we mean is not alienated by the mediation of images and metaphors, by *Vorstellungen*, but rather assimilated in the synthesis of Substance and Subject.[8]

The success or failure of this project is, of course, subject to evaluation only after we have worked through the analysis which leads Hegel to make such claims. In the meantime, however, having shown that the object of sense-certainty cannot consistently be held to be primary, Hegel next turns to consciousness itself, the "inherently universal" reflective structure to which language is proper. No longer immediate, "pure being" as the "truth" of sense-certainty retains its essential status as an abstract concept mediated by negation and expressed in language (para. 99; p. 82). The material object of naive empiricism, which on inspection proved to be a mediated universal instead of an immediate particular, is cast in a dependent role by the advance of dialectic. Accordingly, the second moment of this dialectic proposes the knowing subject as the essence of sense-certainty: "Its truth is in the object as *my* object, or in its being *mine* [*Meinen*]; it is, because *I* know it" (para. 100; p. 83).

The strategy of this move, as well as its dialectical *Aufhebung*, is straightforward and, by now, familiar. Since the object of sense-certainty is immediately present to experiencing consciousness even though the expressions that name it dissolve it in universality as soon as they are uttered, a new tack is demanded, and it lies close at hand: "the vanishing of the single Now and Here that we mean is prevented by the fact that I hold them fast" (para. 101; p. 83). This new attitude proclaims that it is *my* knowledge which is certain, which is true or false; even if there still remains a "concrete content" of sense-certainty whose status eludes articulation, it is now asserted that the *subject* defines the essence of the meaning-relation for phenomenology. The 'I' is the new locus of truth.

However, Hegel overcomes this posture as soon as it is proposed with the same observation that was employed against the meant particularity of 'Here' and 'Now'. The 'I' is also a universal expression; reference to the uniqueness of my meaning-intention, to the "authentication" of my immediate seeing, does not solve the problem since everyone is 'I' and any other 'I' may intend different 'Heres' and 'Nows'. We see again that absolute existential particularity is unspeakable, but this time the lesson is learned by the self. This is the germ of Hegel's ultimate identification of finite man with infinite absolute Spirit.

Once more, then, we have to modify our position regarding the essence of sense-certainty; but this time, having exhausted the traditional alternatives of both object and subject by dialectizing them as "moments," a third, "synthetic" alternative emerges. Hegel neatly summarizes this first phenomenological dialectic:

> Sense-certainty thus comes to know by experience that its essence is neither in the object nor in the 'I', and that its immediacy is neither an immediacy of the one nor of the other; for in both what I mean is rather something unessential, and the object and the 'I' are universals in which that 'Now' and 'Here' and 'I' which I *mean* do not have a continuing being, or *are* not. Thus we reach the stage where we have to posit the *whole* of sense-certainty as its essence, and no longer any one of its moments. (para. 104; p. 84)

Emphasizing totality and relation, the Hegelian dialectic now locates the meant particularity of immediate sense-certainty in "a pure [act of] intuiting [ein reines Anschauung]" (para. 104; p. 84):[9] when *I mean This*, the universality of the expressions 'I' and 'This' is overcome in the act of their relation. Of course, the immediacy that is essential to this relation remains fundamentally existential; Hegel says that it would "lose its significance entirely" if we retrospectively analyze it or stand at a distance from it; in philosophical analysis we can "point to it," but expression encounters the same paradox of particularity and universality we are already familiar with (para. 105; p. 85). In fact, even "pointing out" is problematic since 'This Now' "has already ceased to be in the act of pointing to it" (para. 106; p. 85); the immediacy of pure intuition is lost in any attempt to name it, even in the most primitive of mere gestures.

Instead, the Now that results from its own dialectic, which is the "true" Now, is no longer a pure or simple immediacy: it has returned to the sense of immediacy through the negation of what it is not. In the first and one of the most lucid illustrations he offers of the dialectical principle called "negation of the negation," Hegel explains how we reach this result in paragraph 107 (pp. 85–86). First, naive sense-certainty asserts the simple immediacy of this 'Now', only to discover (in the second moment of the dialectic) that what was asserted or pointed out is not; rather, it 'has been'. But then, asserting what has been is itself negated by the same inexorable dialectic: "what has been, *is not*; I set aside the second truth, its *having been*, its supersession, and thereby negate the negation of the 'Now', and thus return to the first assertion, that the 'Now' *is*" (para. 107; p. 85); emphasis added). Once again, the universal character of sense-certainty's truth is demonstrated; the return to *this* Now through a plurality of Nows is a *result*, not a beginning, a mediated and not a simple immediacy. Similarly with 'This' and 'Here', the meant particular vanishes in the multiple reference of the universal, which in turn vanishes in multiplicity itself (which logically requires individual parts). Universality is the whole, which is necessarily a sum of its parts, and each part is a whole made up of parts—and thus, in the passing from this 'Here' to that, "what abides is a simple complex of many Heres" (para. 108; p. 86).

3. The "divine nature of language": Mystery and equivocation

We can see, then, that the dialectic of sense-certainty is the history of this attempt to know a particular, frustrated by the logic of knowledge, which yields only universals: the very most primitive dialectic, beginning with nothing more than what is presumed given to consciousness, already involves the dynamism of historical relations. One such is mentioned briefly in paragraph 109 (pp. 86–87). At first, the necessary historicism of consciousness itself is affirmed as a dialectical result; Hegel even makes the apparently contradictory claim that immediate sense-certainty is already historical. This purely theoretical finding is augmented, however, by an example or illustration pertaining to "the practical sphere," taken from Greek antiquity:

we can tell those who assert the truth and certainty of sense-objects that they should go back to the most elementary form of wisdom, viz. the ancient Eleusinian Mysteries of Ceres and Bacchus, and that they have still to learn the secret meaning of the eating of bread and the drinking of wine. . . . Even the animals are not shut out from this wisdom but, on the contrary, show themselves to be most profoundly initiated into it; for they do not just stand idly in front of sensuous things as if these possessed being in-itself [an sich seienden] but, despairing of their reality, and completely assured of their nothingness, they fall to without ceremony and eat them up. (para. 109; p. 87)

Ceres was an Italian deity associated with Demeter, especially ritualistically; Bacchus is, of course, Dionysus. Both Dionysus and Demeter were central to the Eleusinian Mysteries where, in fact, the rites associated with Ceres were also thought to have been performed. So Hegel's reference, although slightly evasive, is nevertheless concrete: the simple material immediacy claimed by sense-certainty reveals not even as much knowledge as beasts possess, who are not deterred by the otherness of what may be so easily mediated by crude physiology. Eating, in fact, will remain an important instance of "mediation" for Hegel, from the lord's immediate satisfaction of his (gastronomic) desires at feasts provided by the mediation of the bondsman's labor, to metaphors of ingestion and digestion in the *Logic*.[10]

But on closer inspection, this first explicit historical illustration in the *Phenomenology*, however incomplete, is complicated and problematic; no event is ever transparently clear to the retrospective gaze that historicizes it, but the "Mysteries" at Eleusis are not even as hermeneutically accessible as, for example, Stoicism and Skepticism are. We know that these rites were open to anyone, including women and slaves (only barbarians and violent criminals were excluded), that they are mentioned by Aristotle and were supported by both Peisistratus and Pericles—but exactly how they transformed the lives of the very many pilgrims who yearly became initiates remains a mystery. Furthermore, Aristotle suggests that what was learned at Eleusis could not be called knowledge in the usual sense at all; rather, the *mystae* underwent "an experience and an influence" (frag. 45). Summarizing the scholarly consensus on this judgment, Lewis Richard Farnell and Herbert Jennings Rose write:

In seeking to guess what the secret of the mysteries was we must first rid ourselves of the notion that it was any esoteric philosophy, or elaborate theology kept hidden from the world at large. Negatively, we have no jot of evidence that the initiates were more intelligent than the rest of Greece. . . . Positively, we have the repeated insistence, from the Homeric Hymn [to Demeter] down, that the initiates saw something which greatly comforted their souls, not that they learned anything of great importance.[11]

To account for such "visions," it has even been provocatively argued that, whatever allegorical drama may have been staged at Eleusis, it was greatly enhanced by a ceremonial wine the initiates were given to drink that contained an hallucinogenic substance derived from ergot of barley[12]—a suggestion that resonates with Hegel's incantation, in his poem "Eleusis" of 1796, "O Ceres, you who are enthroned in Eleusis! / I feel now drunk with enthusiasm."[13] If such was in fact the case, Hegel's reference to ingestion in the *Phenomenology* would seem to be still more significant: not just a ritualistic act with symbolic import, nor merely a rhetorical way of emphasizing simple sensuousness, the assimilated other would be the very vehicle of mystical vision. Further, this experience would be akin to the immediacy here at stake for Hegel, as its content was evidently not mediated by a teaching of any philosophic sort.

However these obscure puzzles might be solved, it is hard not to notice a suggestive affinity between the ambiguities essential to the Eleusinian Mysteries and the occult aura of Hegel's final apotheosis. At the very end of the *Phenomenology*, after the inferior mediation of religious *Vorstellungen* has been superseded by the philosophical *Begriff*, Hegel abruptly invokes a host of Christian images: revelation, Calvary, and, in the concluding verses adapted from Schiller, the personal-divine "Him." If we go on to notice the structural parallels between Hegel's metaphysical historicism and that of the proto-heretical twelfth-century monk Joachim of Fiore,[14] the "divine nature of language"—first so-called in this first chapter on sense-certainty—begins to look like an important early clue. Insofar as it has the power of "directly reversing the meaning of what is said, of making it into something else, and thus not letting what is meant *get into words at all*" (para. 110; p. 89), the divine nature of language is mystery, equivocation, ambiguity. And indeed, when moving beyond sense-certainty to a perceiving that admits mediation and begins distinguishing properties and qualities, Hegel exploits the lexical composition of *Wahrnehmen* (perception) to emphasize the partial and problematic appropriation of the immediately real by a cognition that wishes to speak: "instead of knowing something immediate, I take the truth of it [nehme ich wahr]" (para. 110; p. 89). As we will ultimately see, the sublime irony of Hegel's metaphysical accomplishment is the very abolition of philosophy from the impossible burden of its own questions: a partial "taking for true" leaves the "wealth" of being as both the ground of meaning and as that which exceeds the attempts of language to subsume and supplant it.[15]

Thus, the systematic and comprehensive clarity of philosophical Notions would appear to be incompatible with "language" and expression. But is such incompatibility even intelligible? From the outset, Hegel seems to have set himself the task of transcending language itself in aspiring for the absolute. What can he hope to put in its place? And what will be its status with regard to the tangible and undeniable,[16] even if inexpressible, reality of sensuous experience?

PART II. ON READING SENSE-CERTAINTY

In overcoming the claims made by sense-certainty, it remains unclear whether or not Hegel has also decisively overcome the *Sinnliche* or *gemeinte Einzelne* of actual experience. Is the immediacy of meaning satisfactorily accounted for in the dialectical move Hegel's linguistic bias encourages him to make—or is the *Aufhebung* of immediacy dialectically presupposed and predetermined? Although the universality of sense-certainty's expression is admittedly incompatible with the particularity of the experience that is meant, belief in the reality of that experience survives the dialectical assault on its truth.

Two things are at stake in this somewhat aporetic "result": the status of the overcome but not obliterated *gemeinte Einzelne*, and the medium of mediation itself. Even if sense-certainty speaks falsely, it does and must try to speak. Thus, language is set out from the beginning as the realm, won by a compromise, in which an urgent certainty is mediated—that means alienated, transformed or translated, even negated. And since the elaborate articulations of Science and System, even of history itself, grasp toward the reconciliation of the Absolute,[17] Hegel first tells the "fall story" of a retreat into truth from simpler certainty.

In looking now at some of the readings this puzzling text has provoked, Hegel's own analyses and amplifications may usefully be considered first. The immediacy whose simple presence to consciousness in sense experience proves too mute to base a philosophical understanding of the development of culture on, is in fact the very subject of the *Logic*: "*Being* is the indeterminate *immediate*."[18] When we have seen how Hegel has not abandoned immediacy in overcoming sense-certainty, we will examine a selection from among the remarks other philosophers have made about Hegel's move to mediation. In particular, the critics cluster around questions concerning the legitimacy of this linguistic turn: has Hegel killed sense-consciousness, or at least robbed it of its integrity by forcing it to speak "through an alien medium"?[19]

1. The Immediacy demanded by the Logic

Both of Hegel's Logics, in working toward an elaboration of a Science of Being, carve out a place for immediacy: the certainty of Faith, an intuition necessarily not alienated and falsified, demands it.

Without exploring the suggestion, Charles Taylor notes that "The references to 'pure Being' [in the *Phenomenology*] evoke parallel arguments in the Logic."[20] These "parallel arguments," it turns out, are less equivocal about the status of what we might call "dogmatic immediacy" than their phenomenological counterparts. In spite of the dialectics from 1807, which so rigorously interrogate naive certainty, Hegel writes twenty-three years later that "immediate knowledge is to be accepted as a *fact* [*Tatsache*]."[21]

This passage concludes a dialectical argument which is exercised on behalf of God in Chapter V of the *Encyclopedia Logic*. The chapter, entitled "Third Attitude of Thought to Objectivity: Immediate or Intuitive Knowledge," follows chapters that critically examine the "attitudes of thought to objectivity" in Hegel's precursors: Kant, the empiricist tradition, and the unquestioning belief in reflection and its adequacy to truth of "common sense." Thus, the discussion of immediacy as a dogmatic imperative is placed at the pre-logical level of an as yet unclarified "attitude of thought" (*Stellung des Gedankens*), albeit the third and last of these historically expressed attitudes. Just as Revealed Religion holds the penultimate place in the phenomenological pageant of Spirit's developing self-consciousness, the immediacy claimed by Faith makes a last stand at the threshold of the logical "Doctrine of Being."

The argument Hegel offers, which concludes so dogmatically, is easily rehearsed. Employing a strategy not unlike that of the "ontological argument" as found in Anselm and Descartes, Hegel insists that knowledge of God *must* be immediate because mediation implies negation and error: "insofar as the object in question be the True, the Infinite, the Unconditioned, and we change it into the mediated and conditioned, far from apprehending the truth by thought we have rather inverted it into untruth [in Unwahres verkehren]" (section 62).

Knowledge of God, the certainty of which Hegel questions as little as does Hume's "Philo" in the *Dialogues Concerning Natural Religion*, must nevertheless not be threatened by the perpetual permutations of an empiricist dialectic. Thus, again like Hume's "Philo," Hegel sketches out a subtle theism for which the stripping away of "anthropomorphic conceptions" does not merely reduce God to a "substantially empty essence [erklecklich leeren Wesen]." Rather, the "taking for true" of experience and perception (*Wahrnehmung*) is grounded in the certainty of self that is also the foundation of Faith:

> The principle of *Experience* entails the infinitely important stipulation that, in order to accept and take as true any subject matter, one must *be in contact* [*dabei sein*] with it, or more precisely, one must find this subject matter united with *one's own self-certainty* [*der Gewissheit*

seiner selbst]. . . . This principle is the same as that which in the present day has been termed Faith [Glauben], immediate knowledge [unmittelbares Wissen]. (section 7)

Since the "highest aim" of philosophic science is to bring about a "harmony" (*Übereinstimmung*) of actuality and experience through a "reconciliation of self-conscious reason [selbstbewussten Vernunft] with the reason of existing *things* [*seienden* Vernunft]" (section 6), we may anticipate here that the *Logic* must crucially inform any reading of Hegel's final phenomenological move to Absolute Knowing.[22] In fact, the status of immediacy, the nature of the medium of mediation, and the constitutive role of expression (*Entäußerung*) can finally be made intelligible only from that fully developed dialectical perspective. However, the end is "in" the beginning, and first steps importantly establish direction. Hyppolite does not exaggerate when he says "we can consider the sensuous certainty with which consciousness starts as at once its highest truth and its greatest error."[23]

The relation between the immediate and the Absolute thus deferred until the historical possibilities and actualities of mediation can be fully explored, we return with Hegel to the opening moves of the *Logic*. These pages labor to expose the philosophical instability of unexamined, taken-for-granted ontological presuppositions. Hegel notes that the "other sciences" enjoy the luxury and security of being able simply to assume the existence of a certain class of phenomena; unlike them, philosophy "cannot . . . rest with the existence of its objects as immediately given representations" (section 1). Repeating the dialectical interrogation employed in the overcoming of sense-certainty,[24] Hegel attempts to purge the starting point of presuppositions. This is a preeminently "phenomenological" move, a Cartesian or Husserlian drive toward foundational certainty. What does Hegel's inquiry reveal about these ambitions?

Granting first of all that "some *acquaintance* [*Bekanntschaft*] with its objects . . . philosophy may and even must presume" (section 1), Hegel turns immediately upon this assumption to see what it entails. Such primitive "acquaintance," even though we reach its positing through reflection and thought, seems to make an appeal to intuition through "feelings" that reflection recognizes as resistant to conceptual thematization. These "contents of consciousness," although already "human" and "thought grounded" (*menschliche, Denken begründete*), "do not originally *appear in the form of thought*, but rather as feeling, intuition, representation [Gefühl, Anschauung, Vorstellung]" (section 2).

Hegel is trying to make an important distinction here between supposedly primitive *Gefühle* and *Anschauungen*—which, insofar as they are human, are already determined by thought—and some other kind of experience that is more explicitly and self-consciously reflective. That we have experience of the latter sort is clear and needs no demonstration; but how can the more primitive encounter with Being be accounted for in the very medium of reflective thought which is supposed to be essentially inadequate to it?

Hegel's way of answering this question casts the net of concepts over all experience while at the same time distinguishing the receptive passivity of mere consciousness from the reflective activity of an emerging self-consciousness. "But it is different," he writes, "to have feelings and representations *determined* and *inspired* [*bestimmte* und *durchdrungene*] by thought—than to have *thoughts about them*" (section 2). In a passage which recalls the amusing demonstration offered in the *Phenomenology* that even animals recognize objects as *Denken begründete*—and so, without ceremony, fall to and eat them up (para. 109; p. 87)—Hegel reiterates his wit as well as his argument at this same stage of the dialectic in the *Logic*. To suppose that reflective, self-conscious knowledge exhausts all that is determined by thought, he writes, "would find its parallel if we said that eating was impossible before we have acquired a knowledge of the chemical, botanical, and zoological characters of our food; and that we must delay digestion until we had finished the study of anatomy and physiology" (section 2).

The articulation of the forms of thought that "determine and inspire" even the most primitive of supposed immediacies emerges out of these logical reflections as the imperative of philosophy. Although the "difficulty of making a beginning lies in that a beginning, as *immediate*, makes—or better, itself is—an assumption" (section 1), philosophy steps in swiftly and "puts *thoughts, categories*, or better, *notions* [*Begriffe*][25] in place of representations [Vorstellungen]" (section 3). These "representations"—along with "feelings" and "images," as we have already seen—are thus netted out of the dark sea of unself-conscious immediacy by Hegel's linguistic turn to narration and expression. Accordingly, uninterpreted moments of pure presence "may be regarded as *metaphors* [*Metaphern*] of thoughts and notions" (section 3); a dialectical slight-of-hand redescribes immediacy as precisely that ambiguity the meaning of which it is the hermeneutical project of philosophy to clarify. "To have representations," Hegel scolds, "does not yet imply that we know their meaning" (section 3).

And of course, their meaning is—ambiguous. Rehearsing the entire sense-certainty dialectic in a dense but lucid passage of section 20 in the *Encyclopedia Logic*, Hegel explains how the meant individuality (*Einzelnheit*) that is basic to the distinction between sense and thought cannot itself be captured in the medium of language: language utters universals when what is meant is absolutely particular. Before turning at last to Hegel's commentators in order to examine more closely the consequences of these important early dialectical commitments, it may be useful to quote this passage at length, allowing Hegel to summarize his conclusions for himself:

> Moreover, if the sensible has been determined by *individuality and mutual exclusion* [*Einzelnheit und des Außereinander*], it is well to add that [attributes of sense] are also thoughts and universals; in Logic it will become clear that thought, and the universal, is at once itself and its other, that it overreaches [übergreift] both and lets nothing escape. As *language* is the work of thought, nothing can be said in it which is not universal. What I merely *mean* is *mine* [Was ich nur *meine*, ist *mein*], it belongs to me as this particular individual [Individuum]; but if language expresses only the universal, then I cannot say what I merely mean. And the *unsayable*—feeling, sensation—is not the most excellent and truest, but the most meaningless and untrue. When I say 'the *individual*' ['das *Einzelne*'], 'this individual', 'Here', 'Now', all these are universal terms; *everything* and *anything* is an individual, a This and, if it be sensible, a Here and a Now. Similarly, when I say 'I', I *mean* just myself to the exclusion of all others; but what I say, 'I', is just every I, which [likewise] excludes all others from itself. (section 20)[26]

2. "Sensualism" versus the always already linguistic

We turn now to the critical debate over the legitimacy of Hegel's opening moves. The battle is waged along partisan lines: whereas Feuerbach, Löwith, and Loewenberg defend the integrity of the object of sense-certainty (which, they hold, Hegel has unfairly "impersonated" and abolished), Solomon, Taylor, and Derrida turn their attention away from mute immediacy toward the involved and dynamic mediation of language.

The "loyalist sensualism" of Feuerbach and Löwith, as it might be called, has become an almost canonical target for contemporary commentators more familiar with the language obsession of current philosophical debate. "Hegel's analysis in no sense does away with the singularity of the sense object" insists Martin J. De Nys, but "it does argue that the concrete singular object is internally complex or mediated, and is not a bare, immediate particularity."[27] Robert Solomon agrees, crediting De Nys with "an excellent discussion and refutation of the Feuerbach and Löwith arguments."[28] Although a closer look at these arguments must reach the same conclusion, the consequences of Hegel's analysis can be exposed to scrutiny in the process. Finally, Loewenberg's appeal on behalf of "silent sensualism"—a term he coins himself—formulates this same view in a rather more dramatic way. In so doing,

Loewenberg very clearly illuminates the ontological status of Hegel's linguistic turn: "the beginning of speech is the end of immediacy."[29]

The crux of loyalist sensualism is outrage at Hegel's conceptual bullying. "What an immense difference there is," Feuerbach writes, "between the 'this' as an object of abstract thought and the 'this' as an object of reality! This wife, for example, is my wife, and this house is my house, although everyone speaks, as I do, of his house and his wife as 'this house' and 'this wife'. The indifference and uniformity of the logical 'this' is here interrupted and destroyed by the legal meaning of the word."[30] For Hegel, Feuerbach complains, particularity and universality "flow together, indistinguishable for thought" (p. 43).

We may or may not wish to dispute Feuerbach's "legal" rights of possession over his wife, but his claims to having understood Hegel seem even less certain. His account would attribute to Hegel the foolish view that the "indifference and uniformity" of universals threatens the hearth and home of humble particulars with a kind of ontological terrorism. Rushing to protect his wife from the negating onslaught of the Hegelian *Begriff*, Feuerbach battles the Word bravely on behalf of his favorite objects:

> We have before us in the beginning of the *Phenomenology* nothing other than the contradiction between the word, which is general, and the object, which is always a particular. And the idea that relies only on the word will not overcome this contradiction. Just as the word is not the object, so is the being that is spoken or ideated not real being. (p. 43)

But this quixotic, if rather gallant, skirmish completely misses the point. Hegel's strategy is really quite benign. On the one hand, insisting on mediation denies the absolute otherness of the "objective" and opens the door to the possibility of reconciliation; on the other, Hegel opposes the Romanticism of Fichte, Schelling, Jacobi, and so many others who claimed immediate access to the Absolute through occult intuition. In effect, the famous Preface already makes this point, and in a pithy way: it ironically proclaims its own impossibility in face of the philosophical imperative of phenomenology. The labor of the negative, the parade of historical forms mastered dialectically by Spirit advancing toward self-consciousness, cannot be bypassed so easily. Thus, the "idea" does not merely "rely" on the word—this would indeed lead to an unresolvable contradiction, as Feuerbach notes, between word and object. Rather, the idea becomes word, it externalizes itself (*ent-äußerung*) in expression (*Entäußerung*), it in-forms the *Gestalten* of historical Spirit. And among these manifest shapes or forms, both Feuerbach's wife and house must be included.

Karl Löwith's version of loyalist sensualism is only slightly complicated by his closer attention to language. Just as Feuerbach had characterized the meant sensible particular as the "boundary of thought" (p. 40), Löwith complains that Hegel's starting point "begins with thought rather than with that which is the precondition of all reflection which thought itself cannot anticipate."[31] Refusing to abandon prelinguistic experience to the necessity and ubiquity of mediation, Löwith evokes a "realm of images" (*einem Reich der Bilder*) in which "there are meanings that are not mediated by language [nicht sprachlich vermittelt], for example the meaning of music and painting."[32] But what such meaning may be is hard to say—in fact, it is impossible to say, which is the basis of Löwith's error. "Music and painting" are supposed, on this theory, to be as it were pre-linguistic languages, manipulating pure sense by evading conceptual mediation, but nevertheless conveying some profound meaning. Unfortunately, the metaphor with the arts only points up the naivety of Löwith's sensualism: the linguistic elements—grammar, vocabulary, syntax—of music and painting are too easily specified. Without an exquisite metaphysics like Schopenhauer's to give some content to such aesthetic mysticism, the view seems merely parochial.

Establishing a dualism of word and thing in order to eviscerate the former in contrast to the fullness and plenitude of the latter, Löwith thus separates what Hegel unites. Recalling almost exactly Feuerbach's battle with the windmills of Hegelian mediation, Löwith insists that "actual being is definite existence, here and now, thought and word are abstractly universal."[33] Mistakenly supposing that Hegel means to argue with the claims of immediacy, Löwith petulantly concludes "sense-certainty will never be talked into believing that its object is a universal 'this' mediated by negation."[34]

Jacob Loewenberg's "silent sensualism" comes just as vigorously to the defense of pre-linguistic immediacy as do Feuerbach's and Löwith's loyalisms. According to Loewenberg, in Hegel's chapter on sense-certainty "the task is one of impersonation, involving the subtle art of assuming the attitude of another mind."[35] It is this impersonation that forces sense-certainty "into a false position": "the incongruity of immediacy results from feigning it" (p. 25). Loewenberg distinguishes "simulated" from "real" immediacy in order to argue that "real sensuousness cannot be convicted out of its own mouth because it does not speak at all" (ibid.). Accordingly, when Hegel forces it to speak, thus revealing the supposed truth about universality, he should not be surprised to find that sense-certainty perjures itself: "Immediacy raised to the level of discourse is indeed absurd, but the absurdity inheres in the attempt to formulate a type of experience whose nature beggars all description" (ibid.). The mistake has been to hold sense-certainty "responsible for the implications of our language, a language to which it is manifestly not committed. . . . Cozened into concepts, it inevitably reveals itself as suffused with mediation" (pp. 25–26).

Loewenberg's commentary constantly attends to the meaning-saying dialectic, and so to the problem of saying what we mean. Since sense-certainty has here spoken only under duress, a "real adherent of immediacy might decline to answer altogether and his silence would be an eloquent tribute to the strength of his position" (p. 28). A defender of the speechless certainty of "silent sensualism" thus points out that sense-certainty is asked to describe what it experiences "through an alien medium" (ibid.). Loewenberg repeatedly indicates that "the method of interrogation" specifically causes "the defect of immediacy," the violation of the meant. Meaning is always destroyed by saying because "the beginning of speech is the end of immediacy" (p. 31). Although immediacy will persist throughout the *Phenomenology* as the dialectical moment which opposes mediation, at this early stage the claims of immediacy to truth are shown to be wanting.

Like Feuerbach and Löwith, Loewenberg's position is "dualistic" because it describes immediacy or sensuousness as independent from and incommensurable with all discourse. Moreover, Loewenberg insists that Hegel's *Aufhebung* proceeds illegitimately from correct dualistic premises to reach the

> astonishing conclusion that in the absence of words capable of saying what we mean we must end by meaning what we say. The immediate and its expression being at loggerheads, we are called upon to sacrifice the authenticity of intuition to the ambages of locution. Because the immediate, admittedly inexpressible, turns into its opposite as soon as we open our mouths, we are required to hold that it is other than itself on its own plane of being. The *non sequitur* of this is evident. The contradiction is not in sense-certainty but only *between* it and discourse. (p. 36)

On Loewenberg's account, Hegel succeeds in overcoming sense-certainty only by forcing it to speak and then pointing out that it has done so falsely according to its own lights. This leaves the status of the original, "immediate" intuition very much in limbo, since the account it leaves of itself is importantly ambiguous.

Of course, this criticism presupposes something highly peculiar: that inarticulate immediacy can "claim" to be real, even though it can advance this claim in no language. Since, however, Hegel's explicit concern is with "certainty" (*Gewissheit*), Loewenberg's criticism would seem to expect too much of simple "sensuousness"; he doubts the autonomy of all *Meinung* "in the absence of words capable of saying what we mean." But this is an instructive exaggeration since it tends to reveal the narrative strategy implicit in Hegel's move to mediation; dialectically appropriating what expresses itself only negatively, Hegel is able to comprehend this indeterminacy by casting it in an intelligible role—a role which will later be re-interpreted so as to recover the immediacy here imbedded in the *Aufhebung*, which moves beyond it.

Solomon, recognizing the dialectical synthesis Hegel works on the sensualist dualism, agrees with this interpretation:[36]

> the "truth of sense certainty" is "the universal" (paras. 107, 109, 110, 111). But this does not mean that from here on we will dispense with sense and cease to consider particulars as objects of knowledge. It means only that neither sense nor individual objects (including sensations) are to be considered as *given* prior to the attempt of consciousness to understand them.

This emphasis on engagement and involvement—an account of knowing which takes seriously the synthetic dynamic that essentially distinguishes dialectic from static dualism—is of extreme importance. It at once marks the distinctive feature of contemporary readings of Hegel, in which the Absolute becomes ever more the property of the aphoristic, just as it provides the key for moving on in the *Phenomenology* to the animated encounters of interpreted history that are initiated by the primal conflict between master and slave. As De Nys points out, the dualistic arguments of Feuerbach and Löwith erect an obstacle to dialectic that would invalidate the entire project of the *Phenomenology*. "The dubious character of idealism," Löwith writes, "is bound up with its attitude toward nature. The primary model for theoretical mediation is not the primary world of nature, which produces and reproduces itself without human mediation, but rather the secondary world of human spirit."[37] Refusing the dialectical turn nips Hegel—and all subsequent philosophy!—in the bud.

Thus, as Solomon puts it, "the basic lesson of the *Phenomenology* is that our conceptions of experience . . . and the reality that we experience are inseparably one" (p. 326). In a formulation that anticipates Nietzsche, Solomon crystallizes Hegel's teaching: "*There are no uninterpreted experiences*" (p. 327).

This participatory dialectic of experience and expression, which will presently bring Hegel's gaze to the involvement of independent self-consciousnesses, is underlined also by Charles Taylor. Having concluded that the main theme of Hegel's first chapter "is a refutation of the claim of sensible certainty to be in immediate contact with sensible particulars,"[38] Taylor is quick to identify the positive moment of this *Aufhebung*: "The immediate is negated, but it is retained in mediated form" (p. 167). A "mediated immediacy" is the truth of sense-certainty; experience and knowledge essentially involve relation. In a passage that exposes the Hegelian seeds of both Heidegger's *Dasein*, "always already" involved with the world, and Heisenberg's quantum physicist, "always already" involved with his experiment, Taylor writes

> our experience of things is bound up with our interaction with them. . . . What we think of as conscious human experience is an awareness that arises in a being who is already engaged with his world. . . . From this point of view there is no level of experience that can be thought of, even as an abstraction, as pure receptivity. (p. 185)

Jacques Derrida has written extensively on Hegel, but it would be at least misleading to regard him as another "commentator" from whom brief exegetical or critical remarks might be surgically removed in order to graft them onto some semantic sore spot in Hegel's text. Derrida's own thought is much too developed; employing him as a hermeneutic nursemaid may only make the patient sicker. Furthermore, Derrida's reading(s) of Hegel, crucially influenced by both Heidegger and Nietzsche, necessarily form(s) a kind of locus around which any contemporary interpretation of the imperatives implicit in this history—this one, for instance—must at least circumlocute.

Nevertheless, in moving forward with Hegel from the point at which mediation is recognized to be already at work in the sense-certainty claimed by mere consciousness to the drama of an explicit mediation through which consciousness becomes self-consciousness, Derrida's attention to the otherness of the linguistic sign at once illuminates the transition and negates its implicit difference. Derrida's sensitivity to a certain "trick of writing" that pervades all texts is another step in isolating the metaphysical burden of a narrative tradition already implicit in Hegel.

The passage in the *Phenomenology* that Derrida—in writing about Heidegger's notion of "ontological difference"—unwittingly "deconstructs" is one in which Hegel, just as unwittingly, suggests that language, and in particular writing, has the "divine nature" of what Derrida calls "*différence*." "To the question 'What is Now?'" Hegel writes,

> let us answer, for example, "Now is Night." In order to test the truth of this sense-certainty a simple experiment will suffice. We write down this truth; a truth cannot lose anything by being written down, any more than it can lose anything through our preserving it. If *now, this noon*, we look again at the written truth we shall have to say that it has become stale. (para. 96; p. 81)

By writing, by manipulating linguistic signs, Hegel unites the universal 'Now' with the particular 'Night', the coexisting contents of this "example" (*Beispiel*) of sense-certainty. However, identifying the object of sense-certainty negates (defers) the particularity of the object while giving it meaning. By differentiating the "object" (in this case, 'Night') from its spatio-temporal context, by isolating "this particular thing" from the immediate presence that knows only universals, the linguistic sign forms a bridge between "Being in general" and the particular being meant by sense-certainty.

If the sign has the capacity of representing the object of sense-certainty (even if the truth of this representing is negated by time), it is because the conditions necessary for the sign, for writing, are already articulated in the "immediate" present. The differentiation of the object already contains the conditions necessary to overcome sense-certainty by making writing possible. Thus, thinking of Hegel when reading of Heidegger,[39] Derrida writes

> To come to recognize . . . that the sense of being is not a transcendental or trans-epochal signified (even if it was always dissimulated within the epoch) but already, in a truly *unheard of* sense, a determined signifying trace, is to affirm that within the decisive concept of ontico-ontological difference, *all is not to be thought in one go* [*tout n'est pas à penser d'un seul trait*]; entity and being...are, in an original style, derivative with regard to difference [*dérivés* au regard de la différence]. . . . Difference by itself would be more 'originary', but one would no longer be able to call it 'origin' or 'ground', those notions belonging essentially to the history of onto-theology, to the system functioning as the effacing of difference. It can, however, be thought of in the closest proximity to itself only on one condition: that one begins by determining it as the ontico-ontological difference before erasing that determination. The necessity of passing through that erased determination, the necessity of that *trick of writing* [*tour d'ecriture*] is irreducible.[40]

All is not to be thought in one go; the perpetual motion machine of dialectic immediately refutes what we mean to say. Language functions as a substitution, but a primordial substitution: consciousness for Hegel is *essentially* a dynamic differentiation, an ongoing process of differentiation that leads Spirit through its various historical shapes. In no one of those shapes is immediate certainty immune from difference.

The negativity of difference and its *Aufhebung* is possible only through "that trick of writing." The linguistic sign has significance in the Hegelian system precisely because it does not correspond to the particularity of the differentiated object, because it effaces difference. The antithetical function language serves is possible only because sense-certainty already contains the trace of a differentiating consciousness. A true immediacy can be established only on the order of the signifier: "A truth cannot lose anything by being written down."

At this beginning stage of sense-certainty, the distinction "within consciousness" between 'I' and 'This' dialectically anticipates the encounter with *otherness*, which motivates the drive of Spirit toward self-consciousness. Just as the object of sense-certainty is revealed to be a mediated immediacy, "the singular moment of consciousness is made up, in its very singularity, out of mediation, out of a relation of negation to its other."[41] The movement between distinguishable moments is already characteristic of self-consciousness, which Hegel describes as a return from otherness in general, but in the case of sense-certainty, "since what it distinguishes from itself is *only itself* as itself, the difference, as an otherness, is *immediately superseded* for it; the difference *is not*, and it [self-consciousness] is only the motionless tautology of 'I am I;' but since for it the difference does not have the form of *'being'* [die Gestalt des *Seins*], it is *not* self-consciousness" (para. 167; p. 134). The positing of an otherness that is different from consciousness is insufficient to create self-consciousness so long as it has not *being*; so long as it merely appears as difference, it halts the movement of self-consciousness. That "trick" of writing is thus a *tour* in another sense: a turn, even a return, from the other that is and is not the self, from the word that is and is not being.

CHAPTER TWO

Self and Other:
The Mastery of Mediation

The primacy of mediation, which Hegel shows to be implicit even in the simple relationship between 'I' and 'object' in "sense-certainty," is demonstrated once again in the analysis of intersubjective self-consciousness called "Lordship and Bondage." With the appearance of other selves, consciousness first comes upon the possibility of true self-knowledge. When the other is my object—but when, unlike any mere object, the other shows himself to be a dynamic agent like me—only then may I come to know that essence which I am. This mediation, by the other of my own essence, presenting self-knowledge in the form of other-knowledge, begins to reveal the content of Spirit; as Charles Taylor puts it, "mediation becomes a cosmic principle."[1]

But what has been sacrificed to gain this "cosmic principle?" The stubborn if seemingly innocuous linguistic turn of the first chapter has suddenly become appetitive and belligerent: the indifferent mediation of objective knowledge is, in the case of self-knowledge, heated by desire, and a profound and deadly struggle ensues. The immediate recognition of erotic and even pious love prove inadequate to the ideal of establishing an absolute accord beyond the negating power of time—rather, in place of the other whose desire we desire, Hegel will offer a timeless metaphysical principle, an other conquered by dialectic. In his bid for the other, Hegel always again finds the self—the ubiquity of which, the eternal return of which, will finally constitute absolute Spirit.

In Part I of this chapter, we will observe closely as mediation emerges between desire and its satisfaction to become the very engine of dialectical analysis. If there is to be history then there must be self and other, driven together by reciprocal desire but held apart by a still finite reflective understanding. The dramatic necessity of conflict is thus constituted metaphysically, just as it will be resolved metaphysically in the post-historical heresy of the absolute. But before that resolution may be examined in Chapter Three, Part II of the present chapter will explore the more mundane resolution of intersubjective opposition—love—that Hegel rejects. By calling upon the commentaries, Hegel's motives in this key phenomenological turning point may be isolated and evaluated.

PART I. SELF-CERTAINTY AND MEDIATION

1. The place of "Lordship and Bondage" in the structure of the Phenomenology

"But in point of fact self-consciousness is the reflection [Reflexion] out of the being of the world of sense and perception, and is essentially the return [Rückkehr] from otherness" (para. 167; p. 134). With these words, Hegel begins to set the stage for his famous analysis of "lordship and bondage" (Herrschaft und Knechtschaft)—a brief but lucid discussion of the primordial origins of self-consciousness. As such, this dialectic holds a privileged place in the Phenomenology. Whereas the preceding analyses have been concerned with mere consciousness, isolated, as it were, by abstract epistemological questions that arise from essentially artificial hypotheses—the ontological status of sense-certainty has been shown to be just this—Hegel now turns his attention to the social and historical structures in the context of which consciousness comes to know itself. We have already seen how the mediation of otherness is implicit in the claims of sensuous consciousness to immediate experience; in this chapter, Hegel will render this mediation explicit. And this move is of central importance, as it defines the spiritual essence of human history that characterizes Hegel's entire phenomenological project; even from the advanced perspective of Revealed Religion, its definitive significance is retrospectively re-affirmed: "Before it [i.e., the immediately posited individual self] can in fact be Self and Spirit it must first become an other to its own self" (para. 775; p. 537). In a word, with self-consciousness "we have therefore entered the native realm of truth" (para. 167; p. 134).

Because of the general importance of the appearance of self-consciousness in this dialectic, a few remarks about the structure of the Phenomenology as a whole are appropriate here. The elaborate and rather mystifying table of contents gives us too many clues, and these have sometimes been selectively exploited by tendentious commentators; with a better understanding of how "lordship and bondage" fits into Hegel's metaphysical plan, the otherwise puzzling, even apparently arbitrary progress of dialectic becomes surprisingly clear. It must be borne in mind, however, that such a sudden structural coherence is also a symptom: as we return to the pithy details of Hegel's account of human misunderstanding and struggle, the architectonic promise of an intelligible absolute lurks suspiciously behind the scenes in a most artfully dramatic fashion.

The seemingly straightforward problem of how to read the multiple divisions and subdivisions into which Hegel scattered analyses that pretend to be and, at least in some sense, clearly are "historical" has produced an abundance of strange suggestions. Klaus Hartmann,[2] embellishing on Hegel's own provocative imagery, describes the *Phenomenology* as a series of circles, such that the end of Reason marks a new beginning that is really a circular return in the form of Spirit, and Religion performs the cycle once again. But Paul Ricoeur, in an attempt to explicate paragraph 18 of the Preface as a highly condensed summary of the entire *Phenomenology*, observes that dialectical progress appears circular only from the standpoint of the absolute, that is, from *above*: from the temporal perspective of history, this circular ascent to the absolute appears as a spiral.[3]

Robert Solomon, on the other hand, sees the spiral with double vision: he describes a double helix, "two intertwined spirals, like a DNA molecule, one strand representing knowledge, the other ethics, culture, and religion."[4] This fanciful proposal is offered in the context of a slightly more extended argument, derived in part from "several noted German scholars," that "one *cannot* simply read this book as a linear progression of forms in any particular logical sequence. They are disrupted by Hegel's own confused view of his project."[5] Thus, although he rightly emphasizes the "historicist" dimension—according to which "forms of consciousness" are always to be understood as historically situated and "relative"—Solomon attempts an unwieldy re-writing of Hegel's structure that portrays the *Phenomenology* as a complicated "amalgam" of two books, "one more or less 'practical', the other 'theoretical'" (p. 218). Having thereby completely confused what needed to be clarified, he can only—and feebly—conclude that Hegel's text "could be a mistake, a disjointed, disrupted argument written in haste" (p. 220). In spite of what we know of the circumstances that brought the *Phenomenology* into being, it is Solomon's solution to the problem of organization, not Hegel's, that is "clumsy" (p. 217).

One further attempt to re-organize the *Phenomenology* deserves brief mention before we settle the matter by looking more closely at what Hegel himself has to say. Because of the superior insight afforded by his historical-materialist world view, Georg Lukács believes he sees very plainly "the basic structure of *The Phenomenology of Mind* that bourgeois scholars have never even noticed."[6] It is "due in part to their general hostility to theories of evolution in both nature and society" (p. 468) that these blinkered scholars have failed to recognize that "Hegel's historicism determines both the method and the structure of *The Phenomenology of Mind*" (p. 461). Accordingly, Lukács sketches an alternative to Hegel's architectonic labyrinth which at least enjoys the advantages of simplicity and intelligibility that had eluded Solomon—but unfortunately, it is not clear that Hegel's lauded historicism is thereby better served, nor can Lukács effect his reformulation without violence to the organic integrity of Hegel's own development. Insisting that "the road which each individual must traverse" in climbing the phenomenological ladder to the standpoint of science "is at the same time the road of human evolution in general . . . the abbreviated synthesis of all the experience of the human race" (p. 468), Lukács suggests a simple three-part division of the *Phenomenology*. Chapters I–V (Consciousness, Self-Consciousness, Reason) constitute section A, "Subjective Spirit"; section B, "Objective Spirit," contains only Chapter VI ("Spirit"); and finally Chapters VII–VIII (Religion, Absolute Knowing) together make up section C, "Absolute Spirit."

This proposal is immediately qualified, for it is obvious that the terms "Subjective," "Objective" and "Absolute" Spirit are proper to the *Encyclopedia*, but not to the *Phenomenology*. Although, as Lukács notes, Hegel already employs them in his Jena lectures, it remains the case that he "did not explicitly sanction the use of these terms as a conceptual framework" (p. 472). In itself, this would be no decisive difficulty if it were really the case that such a re-writing could "facilitate an analysis of the internal structure of the *Phenomenology*" (p. 472). On the contrary, however, the attempt to underline Hegel's historicism is now faced with a question Lukács himself unabashedly poses but unsatisfactorily answers: "Why is it that the entire course of history has to be traversed *three times*?" (p. 470). To this challenge, Lukács manages only to muster the explanation that Hegel ascribes three different stages to the individual's acquisition of the experience of the species—an answer that egregiously begs the question even as it confidently asserts that "there is no mystery about the threefold repetition of history" (p. 470). It does not help to be told that the individual must first assimilate history as his subjective essence, then again as the product of social praxis, and finally yet again as the recapitulation of the past: this reiteration remains apparently artificial, and it is precisely this that any clarification of the structure of dialectical progress in the *Phenomenology* must account for. With this proposal, we are therefore still no closer to grasping what is at stake in Hegel's serpentine strategy of repetition.

Nevertheless, it is clear that some sort of historicism is basic to Hegel's project. This is not so much a concession to Lukács as an acknowledgment of the obvious: Solomon also insists on this point, as indeed do all of the other commentators, bourgeois and otherwise, cited above. The problem is to explicate an impacted historical vision that critically returns on itself without thereby describing a strictly temporal repetition. Hegel is not Spengler, and the progress of Spirit from consciousness through self-consciousness to reason is not the epochal adumbration of some transcendent cultural morphology. What, then, is the meaning of this circuitous itinerary?

Turning to Hegel's own schematic, the most obvious solution to this riddle is as easy as A, B, C. Initiating speculation with purely theoretical questions of an epistemological nature (A., Consciousness) and proceeding from this abstraction to the concrete location of the object of study—consciousness—among others of its kind in a world that is always already social (B., Self-Consciousness), Hegel then turns to history properly so-called, to the long story of the deeds of Reason (C.). Sections A. and B. thus constitute an extended introduction to the principal task: they bring phenomenological speculation to the stage of self-consciousness, the analytically most primitive form of Spirit itself.

> With this, we already have before us the Notion of Spirit . . . 'I' that is 'We' and 'We' that is 'I'. It is in self-consciousness, in the Notion of Spirit, that consciousness first finds its turning-point, where it leaves behind it the colorful show [farbigen Scheine] of its sensuous here-and-now and the nightlike void [der leeren Nacht] of the supersensible beyond, and steps out into the spiritual daylight of the present [in dem geistigen Tag der Gegenwart einschreitet]. (para. 177; p. 140)

The importance of the chapter on "lordship and bondage" for Hegel's own project thus becomes clear: it is the "turning-point" (*Wendungspunkt*) of consciousness, the decisive moment when the Notion of Spirit first appears. And therein lies the reason for this excursus on the problematic structure of the *Phenomenology*: section C. is itself subdivided into an unprecedented four parts, in which the puzzling reiteration of Hegel's subtle historicism is worked out and *resolved*. This accomplishment entails more than Lukács is prepared to admit, for the teleological progress of dialectic ruthlessly imposes an interpretation on events at least as much as it is guided by them. The method and structure of the *Phenomenology* indeed *reflect* history, but they are hardly "determined" by it; rather, Hegel's motivation is *metaphysical*, and the *Phenomenology* is above all a work of speculative metaphysics. Just exactly what this means can only at last become clear, as we work our way through to the unprecedented fourth and final perspective that all along has controlled "our" gaze. Only the absolute can give content to the notion of "Spirit." But here, with the appearance of self-consciousness, the stakes of the discourse are already explicitly metaphysical, for it is the history not of "man" but of "Spirit" that Hegel is about to narrate. What or who is "Spirit"? How is Spirit related to and distinguished from self-consciousness?

2. *The dialectic of Desire: Self as relation*

Self-consciousness, Hegel tells us in paragraph 167 (p. 135), "is *Desire* in general [*Begierde* überhaupt]." With startling suddenness—and a consequent opacity—this provocative claim is offered by way of concluding reflections on the mutually definitive relationship between consciousness and its object-other.

The relationship is unbalanced and unstable, for there is an essential dynamism characteristic of consciousness that is lacking in the passive object; the latter, in fact, has shown itself to be but a mode of the former. Although in sense-certainty, "what is true for consciousness is something other than itself," the effort to make this otherness of immediate being *speak*, to give this truth some positive content, has failed. Rather, "what the object immediately was *in itself* . . . proves to be, in truth, not this at all; instead, this *in-itself* turns out to be a mode [eine Weise] in which the object is only for another" (para. 166; p. 133).

It is this being-for-another that will now emerge as the essence of self-consciousness. By initiating a new analytical turn that fixes on *certainty* instead of sense, Hegel shifts the locus of being—the essential ontological moment—from the object known, to the self which knows it. We have seen how certainty (*Gewissheit*) is decisively *aufgehoben* insofar as it pretends to be *sinnliche*, while sensuousness as such is left in dialectical limbo, held "in reserve" (as Derrida will say); but in moving from consciousness to self-consciousness, the proper domain of certainty is achieved, and "we have therefore entered the native realm of truth." Hitherto, the analysis has moved in the abstract and disembodied realm of positivistic empiricism; henceforth, the real world of social action and interaction will be the phenomenological stage. Whereas before, certainty and truth were alienated, divided by reflection into 'I' and 'object,' from now on "certainty is to itself its own object, and consciousness is to itself the truth" (para. 166; p. 133). But in what sense are we to understand "desire" in this context?

We can begin to see why Hegel speaks of self-consciousness as "desire" if we reflect for a moment on the consequences of this methodological transition away from an object-centered phenomenology. Self-consciousness, as has already been noted, is essentially dynamic; Hegel says that it is "movement" (*Bewegung*), a "return from otherness." Now, when otherness has the form of inert being, it is assimilated to (self-)consciousness according to the analysis provided in Chapter I: "Since what it distinguishes from itself is *only itself as* itself, the difference, as an otherness, is *immediately superseded* for it; the difference is not, and *it* [self-consciousness] is only the motionless [bewegungslose] tautology of: 'I am I'" (para. 167; pp. 134–35). Since this difference between (self-)consciousness and its object is illusory and dissolves upon reflection into mere self-identity, this (self-)consciousness "is *not* self-consciousness." Otherness is for it no more than a being (*als ein Sein*), which is to say a "distinct moment"—but this distinctness is assimilated dialectically: "there is also for it [consciousness] the unity of itself with this difference as a *second distinct* moment." In other words, so long as otherness takes the form of mere being, it is for consciousness no more than an aspect of itself, distinguished from itself only theoretically and inessentially; the sensuous object *belongs* to consciousness as proper to its own cognition. We can speak of consciousness as "self-consciousness" here only with qualification:[7] it knows itself as 'I' distinct from its object, but it equally recognizes the artificiality of this distinction, and so immediately returns to its "motionless" self-identity. As Hegel writes:

> With the first movement, self-consciousness is as consciousness, and the whole expanse of the sensuous world is preserved [erhalten] for it, but at the same time only as connected with the second movement, the unity of self-consciousness with itself; and hence, the sensuous world is for it an enduring existence which, however, is only *appearance* [*Erscheinung*], or a difference which, *in itself*, has no being. (para. 167; p. 135)

Since the essence of this antithesis between what *appears* to self-consciousness (i.e., the sensuous world) and its *truth* (i.e., the unity of self-consciousness with itself—and hence, also with the sensuous world, which is only appearance) *remains* its *truth*, the essence of self-consciousness must be the overcoming of the appearance of otherness. And this is Desire, the nature of which is "to abolish the otherness of the other," as Findlay puts it.[8] The object of consciousness as *self*-consciousness is now "doubled" (*gedoppelten*): "one is the immediate object, that of sense-certainty and perception, which however *for it* [self-consciousness] is marked with the *character of a negative*; and the second, namely *itself*, which is the true *essence*" (para. 167; p. 135). Consciousness thus distinguishes itself from itself by means of the thing, its other; self-consciousness is *derived* from this reflection of consciousness in the thing. And Desire "is this movement of consciousness which does not respect being but negates it, appropriating it concretely and making it its own."[9]

What is most important to notice here—although Hegel's difficult prose does not yet make this explicit—is that insofar as desire is *negated* by satisfaction, self-consciousness as desire would be merely *nothing* if the sensuous world were all that it knew. The "essence" of this antithesis is its "truth," Hegel tells us; but its truth—the unity of self-consciousness with its appearances—is already the overcoming of the otherness of the other, if the "other" is limited to these appearances. In distinguishing itself from itself by means of the thing, the difference remains for self-consciousness an *empty* self-identity. If there are only sensuous beings in its experience, then desire is satisfied with the tautology "I am I," and self-consciousness remains at the level of mere consciousness, isolated and alone among a plethora of objects from which it can learn nothing of itself nor of the satisfaction proper to itself.

But self-consciousness is not alone. "Desire," Paul Ricoeur explains, "seeks the internalization of otherness, the overcoming of the empty tautology 'I am I'; we want to join and abolish the other in self-identity."[10] The overdetermined word *Begierde* (Desire), so teasingly equated with self-consciousness in an almost offhand way toward the end of a page-long paragraph constipated with opaque dialectical elaboration, is not accidentally chosen. The essentially animate, even erotic implications of this term emerge through the analyses of life and struggle, domination and frustration which follow. For Spirit, whatever else it may be, is assuredly animate, and the vigorous process of history, initiated at this primordial moment when self-consciousness encounters another self-consciousness, is for Hegel the story of protracted strife, rooted in a desire not just for possession, but for mutual recognition. Not itself a mere thing, "*Self-consciousness achieves satisfaction only in another self-consciousness*" (para. 175; p. 139).

Thus, in a pithy passage characteristic of his lucid examination of the willful contention which will produce history and culture, Hegel warns that "Self-consciousness which is simply *for-itself* [*fürsich*] and which immediately marks its other with the character of a negative, or is first of all *desire*, will, on the contrary, learn through experience that the object is independent" (para. 168; p. 135). Of course, at this stage of the dialectic, self-consciousness is simply "for-itself": hitherto, it has encountered only things, dependent objects which *are* only insofar as they are for consciousness. It is therefore inevitable that the encounter with another self-consciousness will begin in misunderstanding. "Certain of the nothingness [Nichtigkeit] of this other, self-consciousness explicitly affirms that this nothingness is *for it* the truth of the other; it destroys [vernichtet] the independent object and thereby gives itself the certainty of itself" (para. 174; p. 139). But although consciousness can and does gain this self-certainty through the annihilation of the other, it is a barren victory. Such a self-consciousness remains self-enclosed in solipsistic futility; its negating activity, when the other is not a mere thing but rather another self-consciousness, is no more than impotent denial; its satisfaction from the encounter is still lacking.

Moreover, by remaining in the attitude of denial with respect to the other, self-consciousness is actually unable to supersede it: in order that any *Aufhebung* may take place, the other must first be recognized as such, it must be admitted to *be there*, it cannot simply be denied. Thus, "Desire, and the self-certainty obtained in its gratification, are conditioned by the object" and this futile self-consciousness, far from having done with the object in its simple denial, actually "produces [*erzeugt*] the desire as well" (para. 175; p. 139). In order to derive the desired satisfaction from this animated encounter with an essentially *independent* object, this object—the other self-consciousness—"must carry out this negation of itself *in itself*, for it is in itself the negative, and must be for the other what it is" (ibid.). The negativity of this peculiar new object is not passive and inert, like that of a mere thing; rather, like self-consciousness itself, it is dynamic, and it demands a new attitude from self-consciousness in its definitive negating activity. In short, this new object is *alive*: "self-consciousness is thus certain of itself only by superseding this other that presents [*darstellt*] itself to self-consciousness as an independent life; self-consciousness is Desire" (para. 174; p. 139).

Having asserted that the desire proper to and definitive of self-consciousness is necessarily a return from an other which is, like itself, vital and alive, Hegel has already anticipated the key event that will lead the dialectic to lordship and bondage: when the other resists, it will not do to kill him. The desire for the other that makes itself felt in the encounter between self-consciousnesses cannot be satisfied by a corpse. Accordingly, Hegel completes these preparatory pages with an analysis of Life. The new, doubled object of self-consciousness—the thing, on the one hand, and itself on the other—demonstrates *in itself*, by means of this reflexive movement, the principle of animation:

> Through this reflection into itself the object has become *Life*. What self-consciousness distinguishes from itself *as a being* [*als seiend*] has also, in so far as it is posited as being, not merely the character of sense-certainty and perception, but it is being that is reflected into itself [in sich reflektiertes Sein], and the object of immediate desire is a *living thing* [ein *Lebendiges*]. (para. 168; p. 135)

Now, it may seem that a rather limited understanding of "desire" emerges from these remarks. More bluntly, Solomon worries that it "is easy to dismiss this as a bit of sophistry" since, if we take the restriction of desire to living things literally, "what Hegel says is false, of course. Much of what we want are mere things—dead, inorganic, inanimate, lifeless—diamonds, sports cars, salt, pepper, and a glass of water."[11] With assistance from his then graduate student Eric Santner, Solomon interprets these passages in a Heideggerian fashion, insisting that, although not a "full-blown" animist, Hegel nevertheless attributes an essential vitality to all objects of desire. Observing that Hegel writes "*ein Lebendiges*" rather than "*ein Lebewesen*" for what Miller translates as "living thing," Solomon urges that the thing we desire is "itself a 'dynamic entity,' a 'vital being'" (p. 398). "The argument," he insists, "is that even in our dealings with things, they are seen by us not primarily as mechanisms nor as objects of knowledge, but rather as independent beings with a will [*sic*] of their own" (ibid.). He fills this argument out by describing how *angry* he gets at his car when it won't start in the morning on a day that he is already late for a lecture, comparing his example with Heidegger's discussion of the broken hammer in *Being and Time*, and he concludes that "in desire, one does indeed view objects as 'living beings,' in the sense just described" (p. 398).

However, this reading overlooks the fact that, insofar as the object of desire remains a mere thing, its otherness is immediately superseded (para. 167; pp. 134–35). Such a desire is at once satisfied by the empty self-reflection of consciousness, the simple "I am I," which cannot lead to self-consciousness properly so-called; it is the "desire" a beast feels for the grass and water it immediately consumes, "completely assured of its nothingness" (para. 109; p. 87). But if "self-consciousness is Desire" (paras. 167 and 174; pp. 135 and 139), then the object of desire, properly so-called, can *only* be an other that is also a self, in the return from which consciousness can come to know itself as such. For, as a return from otherness in general (para. 167; p. 139), self-consciousness is itself a mere thing if it desires only things.

The "psychological" insight afforded by this analysis in part atones for what surely remains a somewhat strained sense of desire. "You are what you eat" works only in German, where it has at least the appeal of a pun: "*Man ist was man ißt*"; it would be more correct to say "You are what you want." Thus, it is wrong on this analysis to speak of the "desire" for a glass of water—ultimately, this might more properly be called a "need," although the Stoic (as Hegel will show) manages to overcome even his bodily needs. As for diamonds and sports cars, the production of self-alienating desire by the "commodity culture" has come under analysis and attack by philosophers, psychologists, and even journalists; Solomon's example unwittingly reveals what has become a cliché of our times. Erotic desire, however, fits into Hegel's account very well: the relationship of domination called "lordship and bondage" can convincingly be read in sexual terms, and many ancient allegories of completion in sexual union describe how a self fully comes to itself only through loving contact with another complimentary self.[12] We will return to this theme presently.

But first, after all this has been said: *What does desire desire?* Hegel's preliminary answer, that "the object of desire is a *living thing*," decisively embarks dialectic on the complex and equivocal course of human history. "The endpoint of desire," Hyppolite explains, "is not, as one might think superficially, the sensuous object—that is only a means—but the unity of the I with itself . . . what it desires, although it does not yet know this explicitly, is itself: it desires its own desire. And that is why it will be able to attain itself only through finding another desire, another self-consciousness."[13] At this stage, self-consciousness does come to know explicitly that it desires another desire—it desires to be recognized, to be desired, by another self-consciousness. Only in the end will it come to understand that this other desiring self-consciousness is really itself. So, after a rather occult discussion of Life as "the simple universal fluid medium [die einfache allgemeine Flüssigkeit]" which "dissolves its development and in this movement simply preserves itself" (para. 171; p. 138)—that is, as the trans-individual principle of animation which preserves itself through an endless cycle of destruction and regeneration of individuals—Hegel concludes that "in this *result*, Life points to [verweist] something other than itself, namely to consciousness, for which Life exists as this unity" (para. 172; p. 138). The "extended introduction" to the history of social being—of self-consciousness—thus plays out what Lukács romantically describes as a "tragic breakdown" of the "self-deception" that consciousness can know itself by itself.[14] For in the end,

> A *self-consciousness* exists *for a self-consciousness*. Only so is it in fact self-consciousness; for only in this way does the unity of itself in its otherness become explicit for it. (para. 177; p. 140)

3. The dialectic of Lordship and Bondage proper

Anticipating the ultimate objective of absolute Spirit as already implicitly desired by a self-consciousness that encounters itself in its other, Hegel now sets out the metaphysical conditions for conflict and its eventual resolution. Recapitulating the claim that self-consciousness "exists in and *for itself* when, and by the fact that, it so exists for another," Hegel significantly adds that this means "it exists only in so far as it is recognized [es ist nur als ein Anerkanntes]" (para. 178; p. 141). The object—that is, the objective—of desire properly so-called, of the spiritual desire definitive of self-consciousness, is the other's desire: his (or her) recognition. It is a struggle for recognition, according to Hegel, that is at the bottom of all historical action, and that is unsatisfactorily resolved in the various structures of domination and servitude from which Spirit must finally be free.

Unfortunately, this freedom will be won by the improbable heroics of philosophy: from the metaphysical standpoint of absolute Spirit, there *is no* opposition, for just as the self loses itself in the other, it overcomes this otherness and "in the *other* sees its *own self*" (para. 179; p. 141). It is this methodological foresight that is responsible for the ambiguities in terminology. But we are ahead of the story; at this point, the abstract promise of absolute satisfaction merely lurks in the logic of the encounter, wherein "Each is for the other the middle term [die Mitte], through which each mediates itself with itself and unites with itself" such that "they *recognize* themselves as *mutually recognizing* one another" (para. 184; p. 143). We are not yet in a position to evaluate the potential pay-off of this promise, which looks so suspiciously bankrupt to post-Nietzschean eyes. At this crucial but still very early stage, Hegel's subtle sense of drama merely teases us with provocative suggestions about the already implicit mutuality of an encounter in which "the action has a double significance [doppelsinnig] not only because it is directed *against itself* as well as *against the other*, but also because it is indivisibly [ungetrennt] the *action of one* as well as of *the other*" (para. 183; p. 142). "We" are, as it were, already witnessing the miraculous synthesis of absolute Spirit; it remains only to be made manifest in appearances through the "labor of the negative" in the process of history. In the mean time, "We have now to see how the process of this pure Notion of recognition, of the duplicating [Verdoppelung] of self-consciousness in its oneness, appears to self-consciousness" (para. 185; p. 143).

The stage is set, then, with two actors, two independent selves, inexorably driven by a mutual desire they do not understand into a reciprocal action they cannot control. Like characters in a Beckett play—isolated in simple self-certainty, for which all otherness is the passive objective moment of their own subjective consciousness, yet thrown together on a cruel battlefield where the familiar passivity of mere being is suddenly, fearfully full of the same vitality as their own essentially negative selves—"one individual is confronted with another individual" (para. 186; p. 143).

As objectivity in general is negated in its otherness by the "absolute abstraction" of self-consciousness, in which all immediate being is mediated, the first move of each of these contending opponents is to attempt to demonstrate to the other that "it is not attached to any specific *existence* [an kein bestimmtes *Dasein* gekenüpft], not to the individuality common to existence as such [an die allgemeine Einzelheit des Daseins überhaupt nicht], that it is not attached to Life" (para. 187; p. 144). Like the special object of self-consciousness driven by desire, the action of this new encounter is also double: it is divided between what is demanded by the other as such, and what is demanded of self-consciousness itself. Thus,

> In so far as it is the action of the *other*, each seeks the death of the other. But in doing so, the second kind of action, *action on its own part*, is also involved; for the former involves the staking of its own life. Thus the relation of both self-consciousnesses is so determined that they *prove* [bewähren] themselves and each other through a life-and-death struggle [Kampf auf Leben und Tod]. (para. 187; p. 144)

Many readers of Hegel balk at the apparent necessity of so violent an origin of self-consciousness—the possibility of loving fellow-feeling seems to be rejected out of hand, even though it is something like this which, as "recognition," is clearly proclaimed as the ultimate goal. We will return to this question in Part II, where Hegel's own early writings on love will be considered in this context. But it is important first to look very closely at the terms of this "life-and-death struggle," for through it the metaphysical constitution of "Spirit" as the "essence of self-consciousness" begins to become clear, and we are afforded a glimpse of that singular entity—not merely "man," nor "consciousness," nor even "self-consciousness"—which is capable of the material metamorphoses we call history, and *also* of their absolute transcendence.

In order to be in a position to draw the "conclusion" that self-consciousness demonstrates, through this primordial encounter, that it knows itself—even if only "through a glass darkly"—to be more than mere animal being, Hegel begins his account of the metaphysical significance of war by underlining its necessity. Commentators sometimes point to Heraclitus as having influenced Hegel here, but the motivation of the latter dialectic has less to do with the ontologically constitutive inevitability of strife in general than with the hermeneutical consequences for self-consciousness of the willingness to risk death. "The individual," Hegel writes, "who has not risked [gewagt] his life may well be recognized as a *person* [*Person*], but he has not attained to the truth of this recognition as an independent self-consciousness" (para. 187; p. 144). Aggression toward the other is seen in part as the logical complement of this subjective risk—"similarly, just as each stakes his own life, so must each seek the other's death"—and in part as demanded by the alien externality of the other, in whom the self sees itself reflected: "Its essential being [Wesen] is present to it in the form of an other, it is outside itself and must supersede its self-externality" (ibid.).

That the essence of self-consciousness is something more than merely physical—that, as Spirit, self-consciousness is fundamentally metaphysical—follows, according to Hegel, as the only possible explanation for this extraordinary capacity of desire to reach beyond life itself for its satisfaction. Through the drama of the life-and-death struggle "it is proved that the essence [Wesen] of self-consciousness is not mere being [Sein],[15] not the immediate mode in which it comes on the scene, not its submergence in the expanse of Life, but rather that there is nothing present in it which could not be regarded as a vanishing moment" (para. 187; p. 144). Because, insofar as it is an individual living thing, self-consciousness is temporally (and spatially!) finite—and because it knows itself to be essentially more than such a mere accident of material manifestation—self-consciousness is capable of radically risking its own body, secure in the still only implicit certainty that there are worse fates than death. Like Kant, although for different reasons to be sure, Hegel regards freedom as a human possibility that decisively transcends human finitude, and "it is only through staking one's life that freedom is won" (ibid.).

With a keen eye once again for the dramatic potential of the scenario he has just described, Hegel next observes that the freedom won by the victor who *kills* his opponent is empty: the desire that motivated the encounter is not satisfied with a corpse. Rather, "just as Life is the *natural* position of consciousness, independence without absolute negativity, so death is the *natural* negation of consciousness, negation without independence, which thus remains without the required significance of recognition" (para. 188; p. 145). In killing his opponent, self-consciousness robs the other of precisely the element of independence that has aroused his desire. Even if death indeed demonstrates the metaphysical transcendence of the self-consciousness who risked it, it equally supersedes the entire relationship for those who survive the struggle: "*sie heben sich auf*," Hegel writes; they put an end to themselves by depriving themselves of the dialectical partner from whom they might have come to know themselves. "Their act is an abstract negation, not the negation coming from consciousness, which *supersedes* in such a way as to *preserve* [*aufbewahrt*] and *maintain* [*erhält*] what is superseded, and consequently survives its own supersession" (ibid.). With one of the actors dead, "the two do not reciprocally give and receive one another back from each other consciously, but leave one another free only indifferently, like things" (ibid.).

The lesson learned here involves acknowledging the necessity of precisely that which the metaphysical courage of self-consciousness had just shown to be inessential: life as such. Self-consciousness is, after all, embodied, spatio-temporal and finite, even if its as yet unrealized spiritual essence supersedes such dross. Thus, through this "trial by death," as Hegel now calls it, "there is posited a pure self-consciousness, and a consciousness which is not purely for itself but for another, i.e., as *existent* consciousness [*seiendes* Bewußtsein] in the form of *thinghood* [*Dingheit*]" (para. 189; p. 145). We are by now quite familiar with the "doubling" activity characteristic of self-consciousness, but in this instance, the theoretical duplicity of dialectic is manifest in the most concrete practical terms: the "positing" of these two "moments" of self-consciousness become "shapes of Spirit" in their own right, and the actors who will subsequently play out the spiritual drama of human history are born:

> Since to begin with they are unequal and opposed, and their reflection into a unity has not yet been achieved, they exist as two opposed

shapes of consciousness; one is the independent consciousness whose essential nature [Wesen] is to be for-itself, the other is the dependent consciousness whose essential nature is simply to live or to be for another; one is lord [*Herr*] the other bondsman [*Knecht*]. (para. 189; pp. 145–46)

Who is this "lord" and this "bondsman"? Are they historical characters? Archetypal heroes? Primal aspects of the psyche? Heuristic metaphors? Not surprisingly, the essential difference between these primordial socio-historical antipodes remains essentially metaphysical: the bonds of domination for Hegel have finally nothing to do with the merely political. The very possibilities of domination and freedom hold a theoretical significance for dialectic that points beyond their concrete manifestation in particular historical circumstances. For Hegel, the bondsman is not held in servitude by a cruel and overbearing lord; rather, this apparent situation serves as material for interpretation in terms of Spirit. On the evidence of his account of the life-and-death struggle, which had awarded mastery to the metaphysically courageous antagonist whose implicit (*an-sich*) understanding of his own spiritual essence had enabled him to risk bodily existence for the sake of a hoped-for recognition, Hegel now describes the bondsman as bound, by metaphysical cowardice, to *life*, to bodily materiality. The consciousness of the bondsman "is bound up [synthesiert] with independent *being* [*Sein*] or thinghood [*Dingheit*] in general"; "*a being* [*Sein*] *that is independent . . .* holds the bondsman in bondage; it is his chain from which he could not break free in the struggle, thus proving himself to be dependent, to possess his independence in thinghood" (para. 190; p. 146). Since the lord, on the contrary, having shown himself superior to mere being in his willingness to risk losing it, "is the power over this thing [dies Sein] and this again is the power over the other [the bondsman], it follows that he holds the other in subjection [unter sich]" (ibid.). The despotism of dictatorial *objectivity* is therefore most fundamentally constitutive of human bondage; the chains of slavery, on Hegel's analysis, are neither political nor racial nor psychical nor social—they are purely, crassly *material*. Things hold Spirit in thrall.

4. *Turning the tables on the lord and recuperating the bondsman*

It is this problematic relation with "thinghood" which is decisive for the dialectical turn Hegel will work on the dynamics of power between bondsman and lord. For it seems initially that the lord, whose courageous willingness to risk his own materially indispensable thinghood has won him the privilege of mastery over things—and over the bondsman, whose fear of death has reduced him to little more than a thing—the lord seems also to have achieved what desire first sought. Thanks to the mediation of the bondsman, who overcomes the simple otherness of corn and wheat by transforming them, according to the lord's idea, into bread,[16] the lord finds himself in the desirable position of a happy consumer. The bondsman's negating of the thing "cannot go the length of being altogether done with it [mit ihm fertig werden]" since, after working it to the point where it is fit to be consumed, he must then surrender it. But for "the lord, on the other hand, the immediate relation becomes through this mediation the pure negation of the thing, or the *enjoyment* [*Genuß*] of it; what desire failed to achieve, he achieves—to have done with it [the thing], and in enjoyment to satisfy himself" (para. 190; p. 146). The independence of the thing is mastered by the bondsman's labor—at which point, shaped and formed, dependent on a rational idea, it is turned over to the lord who negates it in consumption and enjoyment. Like the enlightened beasts in the Preface, although more sophisticated by virtue of the "means of production" imposed through the bondsman's servitude, the lord simply falls to and eats them up. The bondsman, enslaved by life, is not allowed to abolish mere being (*Sein*), he may only work on it, while the lord, by placing the bondsman between himself and the independence of things, receives being already mediated; free from work, he is also free to satisfy his animal desires.

But unfortunately for the lord, animal desires are not by themselves sufficient to constitute self-consciousness. The desire for recognition, through which the self of consciousness sees itself confirmed in its freedom, demands an other in all essential respects equivalent to the self—an other, that is, who also is free. Now, the lord does indeed receive the recognition of the bondsman, for whom he is everything desirable: "Here, therefore, is present this moment of recognition" (para. 191; p. 147). However, the circumstances render this slavish recognition incapable of satisfying what the lord really desires; the compulsion of such a radical inequality falls far short of mutuality. Thus, "for recognition proper [zum eigentlichen Anerkennen] the moment is lacking. . . . The outcome is a recognition that is one-sided and unequal" (ibid.).

Recalling that Hegel has defined self-consciousness as a return from otherness, and that here "the lord achieves his recognition through another consciousness" (para. 191; p. 147), that is, through the bondsman, we begin to see how the dialectic turns the tables on the lord. Although the bondsman's consciousness goes out to an other worthy of the aspirations of self-consciousness, the lord sees himself reflected in the thing-like consciousness of his bondsman:

> In this recognition the unessential consciousness is for the lord the object, which constitutes the truth of his certainty of himself. . . . What

now really confronts him is not an independent consciousness, but
rather a dependent one; he is, therefore not certain of *being-for-self* as
the truth of himself. On the contrary, his truth is rather the unessential
consciousness, and its unessential action. (para. 192; p. 147)

The truth of the lord's consciousness is the consciousness of the bondsman; just as the bondsman is enslaved by Life, by material being, the
lord is enslaved by his desire for recognition, which he seeks from the
other, his "subject" ("he holds the other in subjection [unter sich]").[17]
To be a lord, there must be a bondsman; the lord's freedom derives not
from the mutuality of recognition, but from the subjection of the other.
In short, the lord *depends* upon domination of the bondsman—a condition inherently unstable, as the bondsman sees his truth in the consciousness of the lord. An uncomfortable irony results: the bondsman,
slave to life, is really the master of the lord, whose freedom is wholly
dependent upon a condition of domination inconsistent with the true
nature of both consciousnesses.

Having thus stood the lord on his head—"the *truth* of the independent consciousness is the *servile consciousness*" (para. 193; p. 147)—
Hegel finally proceeds to recuperate bondage for the "inverted world"
of dialectic.[18] "We have seen," he writes, "what servitude is only in relation to lordship. But it is a self-consciousness, and we have now to consider what as such it is in and for itself" (para. 194; p. 148). Just as the
lord was shown to be "in truth" the slave of the bondsman, similarly
"servitude in its consummation [Volbringung] will really turn into the
opposite of what it immediately is" (para. 193; pp. 147–48). Having
been refused the animal satisfactions the lord enjoys, the bondsman is
"forced back into himself" (*zurückgedrängtes*) where, free of materiality, he can realize the independence of Spirit. The objective, apparent
independence of the lord is paradoxically (that is, dialectically) available
only to the self of the bondsman: it is his "truth," his self-conscious
essence returned from otherness.

Of course, "servitude is not yet aware that this truth is implicit [an
ihr] in it"—the bondsman remains a slave in fact, and must wait for history to liberate him in the absolute self-consciousness of Spirit. Nevertheless, all the constituents of freedom are here already present, "contained" within the servile consciousness: the "pure negativity" that is the
non-material, meta-physical essence of self-consciousness, has been
experienced (*erfahren*) by the bondsman in the primal moment of *fear*.

Once again, the negative potency of dialectic stands common sense
on its head. Anticipating Heidegger and post–World War II "existentialism," Hegel locates the bondsman's profoundest moment precisely
where he seems most vulnerable and thus most enslaved. Although it is

in his dread of the lord's deadly threat that the bondsman had initially failed to grasp Spirit as transcending mere life, he is now so utterly shaken by fear and trembling that everything stable (*Bestehens*) is melted away (*Flüssigwerden*), and he *experiences*, not merely imagines, the essential nothingness of his physical being. Distinguishing "absolute fear" (*absolute Furcht*) from "some lesser dread" (*einige Angst*) (para. 196; p. 150),[19] Hegel vividly describes the quaking slave, transported by his fear beyond the physical limits that factually constitute his bondage:

> For this consciousness has been full of dread [hat Angst gehabt], not of this or that particular thing or just at odd moments, but in its whole being [sein ganzes Wesen]; then has the fear of death, the absolute lord [des absoluten Herrn] been felt.[20] Therein is it [the servile consciousness] internally undone [innerlich aufgelöst], has it trembled [erzittert] through and through, and everything solid and stable [Fixe] has been shaken [gebebt]. (para. 194; p. 148)

Fear of death, "the absolute lord," thus vouchsafes the bondsman a metaphysical vision of an as yet only implicitly Christian character: ominously, but with obvious foresight, Hegel emphasizes that "fear of the lord is indeed the beginning of wisdom" (para. 195; p. 148).

To this negative moment of fear, which as we have seen reveals to the bondsman that there is nothing about his mere being "which could not be regarded as a vanishing moment" (para. 187; p. 148), Hegel finally adds the positive significance of *work*. "Through work," he writes, "the bondsman comes to himself" (para. 195; p. 148). On the one hand, the forced inferiority of slave labor, which must forgo the enjoyment of its own fruits, leads the bondsman to overcome his attachment to material existence; on the other, it achieves a permanence, through its formative activity, that the lord's immediately satisfied desire is denied. Thus, while labor provides a means for the bondsman to "destroy this alien negative" of thinghood before which he had trembled in fear, and to "posit *himself* as such [as negative] in the element of permanence" (para. 196; p. 149), it is simultaneously a "formative activity" which, compared to fleeting satisfaction, is "desire *held in check* [gehemmte Begierde], fleetingness *staved off* [aufgehaltenes]" (para. 195; p. 149). When we recall that, for Hegel, self-consciousness *is* desire, the picture is complete:

> Through this rediscovery of himself by himself, therefore, he [the bondsman] realizes that it is precisely in work, where it seemed he had only an *alienated meaning* [fremder Sinn], that he gains his *own proper meaning* [eigner Sinn]. . . . Without the discipline [Zucht: breeding, culture] of service and obedience [Gehorsams], fear remains at the formal stage and does not extend to the known real world of existence. Without the formative activity [Bilden], fear remains inward and mute, and consciousness does not become for itself. (para. 196; pp. 149–50)

In what appears almost as a qualifying afterthought, this prodigious chapter comes to a precipitous conclusion. Realizing the extent to which the negative power of dialectic has seemingly already recuperated the bondsman, but needing still to show how at this stage freedom remains only an idea, in order further to follow the progress of Spirit's unreconciled historical manifestations (the analyses of which constitute the largest part of the *Phenomenology*), Hegel at last calls attention to the limitations of the servile consciousness. In a few cryptic lines that turn on a pun (!), Hegel insists that the bondsman has not transcended his determinate existence by merely having mastered a "skill" (*Geschicklichkeit*): power over certain things is not "die allgemeine Macht," and the bondsman, merely by fashioning nature into consumable objects for the lord's desire, has not thereby conquered "the whole of objective nature." Rather, in such a presumption the bondsman's own proper nature (*eigne Sinn*) is no more than simple obstinacy (*Eigensinn*)!

PART II. THE SCRUTINY OF SELF-CERTAINTY: FURTHER MEDIATIONS

1. The fragment on "Love"; commentary by Freud, Solomon, and McTaggart

The drama of the struggle for self-consciousness in terms of domination and frustrated recognition is reiterated in many places throughout the Hegelian corpus, although nowhere is it so thoroughly developed or artfully staged as in the *Phenomenology*. It occurs toward the end of the *Encyclopedia*, in sections 424 through 439 of *The Philosophy of Spirit* (lord and bondsman are addressed with extreme brevity in section 433); reference is made to it in *The Philosophy of Right*; both series of lectures on the philosophy of spirit from the Jena period (1803–1804 and 1805–1806) provide nascent versions of the dialectic—and it may even be argued that, in his investigation into "The Positivity of the Christian Religion" (1795–1796 and 1800), Hegel's characterization of legalistic Judaism and the historical decline of Christian faith into a similarly spiritless obedience to the commands of Jesus prefigures his later account of authority and servility.[21] But none of these passages is potentially as revealing as is the brief fragment on Love,[22] which probably dates from late 1797 or early 1798—that is, nine years before the *Phenomenology* saw publication. For in this brief text, Hegel describes love in terms that seem to deliberately and explicitly answer the urgent call for recognition that issues from both lord and bondsman out of the failed resolution of desire through domination. Gentler natures may all along have been wondering why Hegel posits struggle and strife as the necessary consequence of a primitive encounter between self-consciousnesses; to such readers, the fragment on love may seem more profound and certainly more humane than the later, more famous and influential dialectic. Why does Hegel refuse to heed his own early "humanism"?

As if to underline the plausibility of this fragment's address to the lordship and bondage dialectic, Hegel, in another brief text written two years later ("Fragment of a System," 1800, in *Early Theological Writings*, op. cit.) describes object relations as dead oppositions in which for consciousness "no relation to an object is possible except mastery over it" (p. 308). In contrast to this lifeless mastery, love is described as a living unity, a "true union," which "exists only between living beings who are alike in power and thus in one another's eyes living beings from every point of view; in no respect is either dead for the other" (p. 304). Such a genuine love "excludes all oppositions" in a "duplicate of life" that transcends all reflection (pp. 304–305). Finally, in fanciful speculation that ironically anticipates Schopenhauer's remarks on the "metaphysics of sexual love," Hegel describes how, in lovers' contact, distinction of self is annulled, an "*Aufhebung*" out of which a living child is born as the enduring manifestation of this achieved unity (p. 307)! If lovers can achieve such a "true union," why must history suffer through the pangs of contentious desire—and why must we suppose belligerent opposition to be more fundamental for the development of culture than affectionate mutuality?

There are many different sorts of answer to this question. One might observe, first of all, that the idea of cultural history as a process of *Bildung* was very much in the air Hegel had long been breathing. Hölderlin, Schelling, Schiller, Goethe: they were friends and colleagues of Hegel's, and the wedding of the grand metaphors of *Bildung* and *Geist*—"the image of a universal spiritual force, which manifests itself in all things and uses them to its own purposes"[23]—could scarcely be avoided. Given this, the appearance of diversity and differentiation that history catalogues has to be accounted for; only discord between individuals marks them as first of all different from one another, and the temporally extended struggle for peaceful unity among these contesting individuals generates human history. If self-consciousnesses meet and fall in love, they don't need to make the world: like animals, they will simply fall to and. . . .

And the echo of psychoanalysis still inevitably reverberates for us whenever desire, aggression, and struggle are at stake in some developmental theory of human being. There has been much attention paid by philosophers to the Hegelian resonance in Freud's provocative speculations,[24] although admittedly the urgency of this attention has substantially passed into what sounds almost like platitude. Nevertheless, it is relatively easy to see a thematic parallel between Hegel's account of the emergence of self-consciousness and Freud's description of early psychosexual development. To begin with, the mere consciousness of sense-certainty, which does not yet distinguish among the objects of its world (although it implicitly distinguishes itself from its objects), is much like the "oceanic sense" of the narcissistic infant who, according to Freud, does not at first succeed even in identifying its mother's breast as again and again the same object. In the oral stage, the child develops an essentially pre-social understanding of its world in terms of appropriation and assimilation: displaying what Freud calls a "cannibalistic" relation to otherness, the year-old child is pure Hegelian Desire, seeking to abolish and overcome the other in self-identity. Even more specifically, as the child develops teeth and passes from sucking to biting, so that ingestion takes on a new and more overtly aggressive aspect in the "oral sadistic" phase, Hegel correspondingly describes a passage from Desire to aggression in the life-and-death struggle. Self-consciousness, frustrated by the identity and non-identity of the (of *its*) other, thus enters into the throes of an "identity crisis," in which this ontologico-personal frustration is expressed through the project of attempting to destroy the other. And as this struggle becomes fully embodied, an explicitly erotic dimension emerges: in lordship and bondage, self-consciousness has already discovered the father's power, and resolves its Oedipal complex by internalizing authority and recognizing the Master. Of course, this retreat from erotic ambition heralds the latency period for Freud—but similarly for Hegel, the Stoicism and Skepticism that attempt to resolve lordship and bondage represent two kinds of retreat which, as such, necessarily fail. "Unhappy consciousness" would then bear the psychoanalytic significance of repression, and indeed, the history of culture as the labor of unhappy consciousness toward a more adequate self-realization characterizes both Freud's "metapsychology" and Hegel's "phenomenology." And that adequacy, that therapeutic objective, is prerequisite to both projects, although it is an ideal that only Hegel actually claims to achieve. In the absolute, the neurosis of culture finally finds satisfaction and enjoyment—it is no coincidence that the last word of the *Encyclopedia* is *genießt*!

Spelling out the erotic dynamics of struggle with another kind of psychologically reflective finesse, Solomon points out that loving intercourse is always already a battle. Describing a scenario of erotic overtures that can misfire in various ways, eliciting unexpected responses that range from defensive to aggressive, Solomon wisely notes that the struggle for recognition manifesting itself as a struggle for power that Hegel describes in this chapter "might as well take place through love and constant approval—which Freud and Sartre rightly saw as just as manipulative as threats and disapproval." If the actors involved are both independent and compelled toward one another by desire, "then *any* such mutual process will appear to be confrontational and manipulative."[25]

But perhaps this account begs the question; after all, if "love" is, as Hegel writes, a "true union" that "excludes opposition," then the antagonistic emotional posturing Solomon describes begins to look more like a lover's quarrel than the warm glow of reciprocal recognition. Noticing this fallen aspect of "modern love" in order deftly to recuperate it in a chapter awesomely entitled "The Further Determination of the Absolute," J. M. E. McTaggart concludes that it is not love but *reason* that is or has "fallen"! Only perfection truly deserves the total abandoning of the critical faculties that the failure to differentiate—characteristic of the unqualified commitment of love—really requires. But everything and everyone we *might* love in this very imperfect world would then seem to be unworthy. That we *do* love nevertheless, McTaggart takes as proof that we embrace the perfect teleological essence of the other in our love. Beyond the merely positive—that is, commanded and authorized—love of the good in piety, and beyond even the articulate rational concord of discourse, "Reason cannot reveal—though in philosophy it may predict—the truth which alone can justify love."[26] At the heart of the absolute, for McTaggart, is therefore a mystical eros that *zieht uns hinan*, an ideal toward which even reason aspires: "when reason is perfected, love will consent to be reasonable" (ibid.).

Is love, then, finally the Hegelian absolute after all? Can we legitimately name this metaphysical unity with a sensual metaphor? Dare we drag Hegel's exalted speculation down to earth and into bodies, augmenting our libidinous litany with Hyppolite: "The concept is love" (op. cit., p. 147); "Love is the miracle through which two become one without, however, completely suppressing the duality" (p. 167)? Dare we join this romantic company ourselves? What would Hegel say?

Hegel's unambiguous response to these propositions must be to reject them. The love in real human relations, with all the attendant compromises of the human condition, is flawed even on its own terms,[27] and the higher spiritual love of the religious community lacks the conceptual mediation that would make it *knowledge*. Thus, in the *Lectures on the Philosophy of Religion*, Hegel writes that the "love of the man for the woman" and "friendship" are "characterized not as something evil, but as something imperfect; not as something indifferent, but as representing a state in which we are not to remain permanently, since they are themselves to be sacrificed."[28] Marriage and friendship are "to be sacrificed" to the truer manifestation of Spirit in piety, which "is directly mediated by the worthlessness of all particularity." But even this universal love remains inadequately "mediated." In the *Phenomenology*, Hegel insists that Christian love fails to posit the other as such; it is the *simple* unity of "a *loving* recognition in which the two, in their essence [Wesen], do not stand in an antithetical relation to each other" (para. 772; p. 536). The immediacy of Jesus' love, freely given if only asked for, "sinks into mere edification [*Erbaulichkeit*], and even insipidity [*Fadheit*], if it lacks the seriousness, the suffering, the patience and the labor of the negative" (para. 19; p. 20). Thus, although the appearance of the uniquely human desire for the other's desire in self-consciousness already puts us within the concerns of Spirit (para. 177; p. 140), the immediate reciprocity of love "does not dwell sufficiently on the tragic nature of separation,"[29] on the ravages of time.

It is in Hegel's attempt to grasp the absolute through the *Aufhebung* of the other that the material and physical reality of struggle is etherealized. The dialectic comes to an impasse rather than a resolution in "unhappy consciousness," but the very terms of this impasse reveal the promise of absolute synthesis negatively—a promise the constant deferral of which must be presupposed in order for phenomenological elaboration to be possible in the first place. "The desire for satisfaction," Stanley Rosen writes, "is a desire for complete self-consciousness. It is implicitly a desire for the Absolute Spirit."[30]

2. Two critical themes: The primacy of thinghood; self-knowledge is self-creation

There are two related themes that emerge with persistence among the very many excellent commentaries on this famous chapter,[31] and both of them struggle only half-consciously with the subtle, almost devious—but nevertheless, in "sense-certainty" already anticipated—move to mediation that Hegel makes decisive recourse to here. The first theme concerns the primacy of thinghood, of nature, in the dialectic: by arguing that slavery is most fundamentally the domination of Spirit by brute materiality, Hegel implicitly limits the scope of "revolution" to metaphysics. The second concerns the way in which the ontological constitution of self-consciousness is explicitly fictive; most incisively elaborated by Emil Fackenheim, this critical insight exposes the narrative structure of Hegelian self-*making* which will constitute the absolute, but which will itself come to self-consciousness only in Nietzsche's narrativizing textual strategies.

As remarked in Part I above, Hegel argues that it is because the slave fears for his life that he succumbs to the other, with whom he is in principle equal. The life-and-death struggle is the first test of Spirit: courage to risk death comes, Hegel tells us, from an as yet only feint understanding that *mere* biological life is not the ground of human striving, nor can it be the ground of its own meaning. But one of the contestants suffers a failure of nerve that Hegel interprets as metaphysical cowardice: not completely convinced of the illusory nature of his own body, he dares not risk it, and so he surrenders to domination by the other. What is important here is that the bondsman submits to domination out of his own lack of faith in what, to both contenders, is still a very dim and distant promise. His slavery, in other words, is the result of his own over-valuation of material existence, of the worth of his own body; it does *not* result from the superior strength or cleverness of his opponent.

There is a remarkable consensus among the commentators on this point, which is all the more remarkable for the fact that none seem perturbed by its audaciousness. Marcuse formulates the issue most bluntly; he writes: "It must be noted that according to this exposition, dependence of man on man is neither a personal condition nor grounded in personal or natural conditions (viz. inferiority, weakness, and so on), but is 'mediated' by things."[32] One might expect irony here—after all, this aspect of Hegel's argument "must be noted" precisely because it contradicts the most obvious facts about real circumstances of domination. But Marcuse merely describes an anomaly he does not himself seem to appreciate. And Hyppolite is even more carried away by Hegel's transcendental hat trick. Insisting that "the slave is, properly speaking, the slave not of the master but of life" (op. cit., p. 173), Hyppolite waxes eloquent, bloated with the kind of reverie that only a metaphysical resurrection of human finitude from the very brink of the abyss could inspire:

> Human existence, the existence of the being who is continually desire and desire for desire, breaks loose from the Dasein of life. Human life appears as of a different order, and the necessary conditions of a history are thereby posed. Man rises above life, which is nevertheless the positive condition for his emergence; he is capable of risking his life and thereby freeing himself from the only slavery possible, enslavement to life. (p. 170)

Liberation of the bondsman evidently has little to do with loosing of chains or a release from the enforced will of the other; indeed, the slave is particularly fortunate to be in such grim circumstances that his quaking fear shakes from him the now pathetic lust to live which, in its former intensity, overmastered his martial courage. Rising like a Phoenix of Spirit from the ashes of his own shame and dishonor, man-as-slave "rises above life" to create history, to labor, to make the world in his own image. The profound extremities, the fecund paradox of a conquered and crucified god, are definitive of man as well! As Fackenheim observes, the meek cowardice of the slave is the key to transcending a Faustian barbarism that would seek perpetual battle in order to win brief moments of selfhood through the recognition of a vanquished equal. It is possible to "pass beyond this condition," he writes, because "not all those desiring to negate nature risk life to satisfy their desires."[33]

So, contrary to appearances, Hegel reveals the slavery of an unsatisfied desire for recognition as constituted not by the flesh and blood of concrete individuals struggling with obscure passions in conditions of unequal power, but by flesh and blood *in general*: by the crude materiality of embodiment elevated to an abstract principle, "flesh and blood" as beatific synecdoches linking mundane man to the trials of God. With ingenious, almost Orwellian "double-think," dialectic thus reads divinity in degradation, and in so doing it resurrects finitude in the absolute freedom of thought. Kojève's unabashed idealism makes all this quite clear:

> The insufficiency of the Slave is at the same time his perfection: this is because he *is* not actually free, because he has an idea of Freedom, an ideal that is *not* realized. . . . And it is because he has an *ideal*, an *abstract* idea, that progress in the realization of Freedom can be completed by an *understanding* of Freedom, by the birth of the *absolute Idea*. (op. cit., pp. 49–50)

The creative power of nascent self-consciousness in the bondsman is therefore ironically *negative*: the original significance of desire remains the negation of otherness and, as Taylor points out, "the end of desire would be the end of man."[34] Since the "vocation of man," in Hyppolite's phrase, is "to make himself be" (op. cit., p. 167), servitude thus appears as the necessary condition of such a task: given being must fail to satisfy spiritual ambition. In short, the primal desire to be self-sufficient, stymied for the first time upon encountering another similarly motivated self, may now develop the possibilities implicit in the bondsman's situation: "The subject must make the world its own doing if it is to recognize itself as the only reality."[35] Since *the* element in the given world which does not correspond to this ideal is in fact the other, and since the self becomes self-conscious only through the other, the project of self-knowledge becomes a project of self-creation. It is this ontological dimension of the lordship and bondage dialectic that emerges from the commentaries as a second fundamental theme, preparing the ground for the imaginative elaboration of history as the self-unfolding of Spirit guided by the metaphysical telos of the absolute.

Interpreting the desire definitive of self-consciousness as an "attitude which seeks to *make* external things conform to our requirements, instead of merely seeking to *discover* that they do so"[36] is at once heroic and tragic. On the one hand, it suggests a willing optimism of truly infinite proportions—but at the same time, it is apparently quixotic. "To achieve self-coincidence as spiritual beings," Taylor insists, is "ontologically impossible" for opposed selves,[37] and yet to *be* a self requires such coincidence. That this situation is "tragic" has been abundantly noted;[38] these remarks and this chapter may finally be brought to a close with a look at the "unhappiness" of this consciousness that it will be the task of the absolute to make joyful.

Arguing that Hegel's "genetic" inquiry must pursue "the double process of self-making and self-knowing," Fackenheim[39] explains how the impossible desire to negate otherness as such—to assimilate the world as self—must fail of direct satisfaction: "a self as yet unmade is not one which is self and has desires; it is desire and as yet nothing else" (p. 40). However, as the "human power of self-making would be foredoomed to eternal frustration were it not for the possibility of *indirect* satisfaction," Fackenheim goes on to interpret Hegel's account of desire in terms of displacement. Since consciousness cannot in fact negate otherness as such, but since satisfaction can only come from the conquest and assimilation of all that is not the self, the encounter with another self-consciousness in the dialectic offers the alternative satisfaction of negating another hopeless desire. "Directly, then," Fackenheim writes, "this negating is of another desire to negate nature. Indirectly, however it is of nature *itself*, for each seeks to take the life of the other while risking his own" (p. 40).

What is important here is the "anti-nature" foundation of the desire for self-creation. Kojève calls it a "prestige battle"; it is, in Fackenheim's words, "a killing for the sake of killing, a risk for risk's sake, hence a negating—albeit indirectly—of nature *as a whole*" (p. 40). But it is a negation for the sake of creation—and the ironic objective of this creation is a recovery of the self which, by negating the other, was itself negated! In other words, the world created by Hegelian desire is a fiction: a fiction that begins with a refusal to be satisfied with the natural world, proceeds to elaborate in its place a human, historical world, and concludes by redeeming this parade of created shapes precisely by affirming its artificiality! The bondsman's labor according to the lord's idea "creates a real objective world, which is a non-natural world, a cultural, historical, human world"[40]—but it can come as no surprise that, originating in oppression and negation, this is a world of illusion. The "free self-made self" achieved in thought is "a *creation* out of nature become nihil" (Fackenheim, op. cit., p. 43): it is a prodigious performance like unto God's, which indeed usurps the creator's omnipotence in the annihilation of alienation that is the absolute.

In the meantime, however, consciousness is unhappy: having sacrificed the natural world to a rationalization, a fabrication in bad faith, consciousness must continue to seek itself through the historical creations of its own desire. Can this process of creative "externalization" (*Entäußerung*) reach fulfillment? Or is it rather the case that externalization and alienation (*Entfremdung*) are tellingly indistinguishable, that the very process of history is incompatible with the meaning of the absolute? Hyppolite writes "the being of life—is now dominated by a consciousness which is not content to negate it but discovers itself within it, and puts itself on stage within it as a spectacle for itself" (op. cit., p. 176). But when the play is over and the curtain falls, are stage and actors abolished? What does the absolute really have to teach us about the protean appearances that together make it up?

CHAPTER THREE

Absolute Knowing:
The End of Philosophy

A will to the thinkability of all beings: this *I* call your will! You want first to *make* all being thinkable, for you doubt with well-founded suspicion that it is already thinkable. But it shall yield and bend for you!
—Nietzsche, *Thus Spoke Zarathustra*,
Part II, "On Self-Overcoming"

The basic question to ask of *Das absolute Wissen* is posed out of the lordship and bondage dialectic: Does Hegel resolve the opposition of self and other that the history-generating but "unhappy" dynamics of domination had primordially established? Lordship and bondage is an unsatisfied condition, and Hegel has explicitly established the possibility of, and promised the realization of, satisfaction. What can it mean for the vital and contesting strife that has struggled to produce the historical *gestalten* of *Geist*, the very content of the present and of the past—what can it mean for all this to be *aufgehoben*? Is this possible, even on Hegel's own terms? How, for example, can the "philosophical *Begriff*" be persuasively distinguished from the "resolution in thought" that Stoicism and Skepticism achieve, and which the unhappy consciousness internalizes as the spiritual fallenness inevitable for finite man? What becomes of history itself if the present—Hegel's present!—has achieved the absolute and resolved all opposition? What becomes of the other, from whom alone the finite self came to know itself? And finally, what sense can we make of Hegel's bold step from finite self-knowledge, which is reflected from its other, to the infinite self-knowledge of the absolute, wherein both self and other as such are reinscribed?

In this chapter it will be necessary to look closely at what I will call the "epilogical" structure of Hegel's absolute. First, the initial "world-historical" resolutions of embattled opposition and domination demand attention: Stoicism and Skepticism do appear isomorphic with the move to the absolute Idea, even though Hegel claims that the truth of philosophy is no longer unhappy. And ironically, the famous and difficult *Vorrede* is also important in laying bare what Hegel believed to be unique in his absolute; written after the *Phenomenology* was completed, and thus after Chapter VIII, the Preface plants important clues for interpreting that final apotheosis. Thus, far from being the revolutionary transcendence it first appeared, "absolute knowing" has already been anticipated: its structure is recapitulative, revealing retrospectively its implicit role throughout the phenomenological analyses.

After inspection of these anticipatory pages, the great epilogue itself submits more easily to exegesis—a process that promises to make us "wise men" and to transform the world. Part I of this chapter performs this process. Turning to commentaries in Part II, we will find that Marx laments the absence of the same concrete reality Kojève absurdly describes the presence of. But both neglect to consider Hegel's conclusion in the context of speculative spirituality, a tradition of heterodox theology that at once situates Hegel's "philosophy" as beyond and within the concrete practice of religion. This situation, analogous to Nietzsche's in its historico-metaphysical dimensions, allows for a new evaluation of the status of the absolute as an end point that is still productive of a legacy.

In Chapter Four of this study, then, the interpretive confusion manifested in the critical antitheses of Kojève and Marx will be resolved through an analysis of the "Gnostic" eschatological narrative developed in Hegel's secular theology. As a repeated, heterodoxy-inclined gesture of transcendental epiphany, Hegel's final synthesis is neither the brazenly mundane political reality described by Kojève nor the inaccessably absolute abstraction pilloried by Marx. On the contrary, Hegel appropriates marginal and marginalized expressions of spiritual "anthropotheism" (to borrow a term from Kojève), marginalizing them still further merely by appropriating them, so that the authority of any deity is dissipated away. At the same time, Hegel's narrative borrows an aesthetic effect from those expressions of spiritual transcendence, almost as if the now denatured gesture resembled a musical crescendo. It is this transmogrification of a serious, dogmatic claim with high stakes into an aesthetic phenomenon that will establish the key for Nietzsche's further variations.

PART I. THE ABSOLUTE FROM BEGINNING TO END

1. Stoicism and Skepticism as retreats into thought

Because, for Hegel, nothing is what it is, the dialectic of lordship and bondage concludes, as we have seen, with the virtual—but not the actual—recuperation of the bondsman in the formative activity (*Bilden*) of work. Forced back into itself by the circumstances of domination, the bondsman's consciousness has at last the reflection of itself from the object it has formed to provide a basis for at least a rudimentary recognition of Self in Other. In short, the bondsman has a primitive but structurally complete self-consciousness. The autonomy that the lord embodies for the idealizing gaze of the bondsman finds its slavish counterpart in the reflective re-appropriation of Self in the Substance of the formed object. Although this reflective move will prove unsatisfactory, Hegel stresses that it is nevertheless of fundamental importance, for with it

> We are in the presence of self-consciousness in a new shape, a consciousness which, as the infinitude of consciousness or as its own pure movement, is aware of itself as essential being [Wesen], a being which *thinks* [*denkt*] or is a free self-consciousness. For *to think* does not mean to be an *abstract* 'I', but an 'I' which at the same time has the significance of being *in-itself*, of having itself for object. (para. 197; p. 151)

For both lord and bondsman, in other words, the rift between subject and object opened up by the novel problematic of self-consciousness results in a flight into subjectivity. Recall that Desire was identified as the essence of self-consciousness, and that the objectivity of what is desired must therefore be maintained. The lord, in spite of this, exercises the privilege of negating the objects he desires by consuming them, retaining only their form as a mode of his own consciousness.[1] Positing the desired object as outside of consciousness is immediately negated and overcome by the lord's assimilation of it in enjoyment; thus, the lord turns inward in this satisfaction, "subjectivizing" the relation with the other.

But the bondsman, for whom self-consciousness is "held in check" by the deferral of satisfaction through work and to whom the negation *in fact* of the desired object is denied—the bondsman turns inward as well. Recognizing what had originally been a wholly foreign object as the product of his labor, stamped with his own shape, the bondsman discovers the power of thought. And the world, he concludes, is no more irreconcilably other than was this land, these woods: the mutability of things, their plasticity, defeats the assumption that they are absolute in themselves. Rather, they have form and substance by virtue of thought, and are therefore inessential compared to it. "In thinking, I *am free* [Im Denken *bin* Ich *frei*]" (para. 197; p. 152)—so asserts the Stoic slave.

These two strategies of retreat from the otherness of the object—the lord's actual negation of substance in enjoyment, and the bondsman's virtual negation of substance in thought—both fail to achieve a real unity. As Charles Taylor puts it, "The basic problem is that man has achieved self-certainty [i.e., the stale subjective certainty of I = I] but only at the cost of retreating into himself."[2] The lord's gambit was the first to succumb: negating desire in immediate satisfaction, the lord forfeits self-consciousness itself, which is desire; furthermore, as the lord's very identity depends upon recognition from a bondsman, his apparent autonomy is specious. But the bondsman, who is the agent of history through his labor, accomplishes something profound in discovering the power of thought. Henceforth, it is the story of *thinking consciousness* that Hegel will tell, and the absolute promises a happy ending.

So, the appearance of thinking consciousness with what Hegel calls "Stoicism" needs to be carefully distinguished, if this is at all possible, from the Notion in which the absolute is thought. The "mind of his own," which the bondsman discovers in the products of his work and which Stoic and Skeptic deploy against the concrete domination of real chains, "is still enmeshed in servitude" (para. 196; pp. 149–50). And the inwardly divided "unhappy consciousness" to which these false distinctions between real and ideal inevitably lead must be clearly understood in order to evaluate the "happiness" offered by the absolute. If, as Jean Hyppolite writes, "the unhappy consciousness is *subjectivity*, which aspires to the repose of unity,"[3] what sort of maneuvers does Hegel employ to gain the epiphany of absolute Spirit, which transcends mere subjectivity to comprehend Self and Other together? Must not this achievement remain an aspiration, a project? Is the difference between unhappy consciousness and absolute knowing really intelligible? Or is it the case that, to remain a "difference," to preserve the other, the appropriative move of intelligibility itself must be refused?

Having thus sketched the possibility of freedom gained by thought—of transcending the "abstract I" of sense-certainty in a being-in-itself that is free in its self-certainty—Hegel goes on to characterize this move as it is actually carried out historically. "This freedom of self-consciousness," he writes, "when it appeared as a conscious manifestation [Erscheinung] in the history of Spirit has, as we know, been called Stoicism. Its principle [Prinzip] is that consciousness is essentially a being that thinks" (para. 198; p. 152.). For the first time in the *Phenomenology*—but hardly for the last—Hegel's analysis turns in a substantial way to real history;[4] from the ambiguously primal origins of self-consciousness as such in a conflict of wills, Hegel will now attempt to historicize the protean shapes that conflict has taken, drawing freely (and tendentiously) from the rough chronology of Spirit's developing self-consciousness that lies ready to hand.

But in spite of the historical attribution, Hegel here uses Stoicism—and the same will be true of Skepticism—as a conceptual exemplar: in the *Phenomenology*, no particular writer or doctrine is even mentioned, much less discussed in any detail. A fuller account can be had in the second volume of the *Lectures on the History of Philosophy*, where Stoicism and Epicureanism are both regarded as "dogmatic"; there, too, however, Hegel asserts that the principle of Stoicism "rests on the drive [Triebe] of self-consciousness toward self-satisfaction: it is the subject with which we are concerned."[5] In both texts, the subjectivizing inward turn of this thinking is emphasized and disparaged: Stoicism can arise historically, Hegel tells us, only in times of oppression, of "universal fear and bondage," since it itself stands in a negative relation to both lord and bondsman (para. 199; pp. 152–53). The positive fact that the Stoic retreats from the needy unhappiness of domination into *thought* is duly noted: the times of Stoicism are said to be rich in "universal culture [Bildung] which had raised itself to the level of thought" (ibid.). But the specific character of this thinking's error remains what Hegel must clarify.

Whereas Stoicism turns away from the unhappiness of the external world by asserting that virtue alone, attained through knowledge and reflection, is good—that real circumstances can be overcome by mastering the passions and emotions—Skepticism goes even further by denying the reality of the external world altogether. "*Skepticism* is the realization of that which Stoicism was only the notion [nur der Begriff]"; in Skepticism, "the wholly unessential and non-independent character of this other becomes explicit *for consciousness*; the thought [der Gedanke] becomes the total and complete negating thinking [vernichtenden Denken] of the being of the *variously determined* world" (para. 202; pp. 154–55). The promise held out by the Stoic discovery of thought is thus further developed by Skepticism: self-contained independence from the world through the negating power of thought, when augmented by dialectic, provides the Skeptic with a magic wand that makes the other "vanish"! Dialectic, Hegel admits, is the natural methodology of Skepticism; although naive consciousness tends to regard it as something extrinsic and external, a way of thinking that has consciousness "at its mercy,"[6] Skepticism takes to dialectic with gusto. "Difference," not to be oneself, the "determinate element," all vanish in Skepticism, and "self-consciousness thus experiences . . . its own freedom as given and preserved by itself" (para. 205; p. 156).

The rhetorical form of this Skeptical dialectic is not examined in any detail in the *Phenomenology*, but the amplification to be found in the *Lectures* is this time worth a closer look. Relying principally on Sextus Empiricus, Hegel specifies fifteen Skeptical "tropes" (*tropoi* in Greek, *Tropen* in German)[7] in which a purely negative dialectic labors to show that we cannot have knowledge: different animals perceive the world differently; the same man perceives the world differently at different times or in different psychological or physical conditions; judgments about physical objects are relative to position just as judgments of moral or legal values are relative to location—and so on. The Skeptical doctrine, insofar as it can be said that there is one, "consists in the art of demonstrating contradictions through these *tropes*" (*Lectures*, Vol. II, op. cit., p. 346; *Vorlesungen*, Vol. II, op. cit., p. 556).

However, it is too much to call this activity a "doctrine." Rather, the Skeptic wields the universal principle that every assertion is open to negation by its own proper other as if it were a club; Skeptic tropes are fragments, not even propositions, since they offer themselves as pure contingency and are unrelated to one another except by rhetorical negativity. Consequently, "in view of the nature of Skepticism, one cannot expect a system of propositions of it" (*Lectures*, p. 345; *Vorlesungen*, p. 555). For Hegel, this is a strong repudiation. Although dialectical in its methodology, Skepticism is reckless, an "*absolute dialectical unrest*" in which consciousness, "instead of being self-identical, is in fact only a plainly fortuitous perplexity, the dizziness of a perpetually self-engendered disorder" (*Phenomenology*, para. 205; *Phänomenologie*, pp. 156–57). Hegel compares this way of thinking to that of a contrary child (*ein Gezänke eigensinniger Jungen*), recalling the pun on *Eigensinn* with which the similar presumptions of the laboring bondsman were rebuked.[8] If a bilingual pun may be allowed to underline the judgment Hegel has reached of this inwardizing retreat into thought, the "self-consciousness" so far achieved is mere diffidence and embarrassment— not the self-consciousness of absolute Spirit, but rather that of a cowed servility too timid to really act.[9]

2. The internalized duplicity of unhappy consciousness

Thus, this consciousness is unhappy (*unglücklich*). Aware that it is itself responsible for the "confused medley" of its own contradictions and negations, it finally fails to convince itself of the negativity of the world *in itself*, and so becomes inwardly divided. On the one hand, it has the consciousness of itself as liberating and free, and yet, on the other, the world remains pure negativity for it. In Stoicism and Skepticism, consciousness has been fleeing the empirical, but—just as language was discovered to be "the more truthful" in the meaning-saying dialectic of "Sense Certainty"—[10] unhappy consciousness discovers that the deeds and words of these subjectivizing philosophies "always belie one another." The very pronouncement that the empirical other is not— itself *is*! The other is re-established by thought within consciousness itself, and "consequently, the duplication [Verdopplung] which formerly was divided between two individuals, the lord and the bondsman, is now lodged in one" (para. 206; p. 158). Substance and Subject are again distinguished within the alienated Subject itself: in Cartesian fashion, thinking implies thinking Substance, and so the thought that would deny Substance contradicts itself in its own essential being.

To further refine the details of this internal division and opposition, Hegel distinguishes the two selves of unhappy consciousness as essential or unchangeable (*unwandelbaren*), on the one hand, and changing or accidental on the other. The protean shapes of appearances speak against essence for the unhappy consciousness: only what is thought can have unchanging Being. Unfortunately, in drawing this distinction, unhappy consciousness has to recognize itself as changeable, full of contradictions—as the Skeptic tropes have already amply demonstrated. Yet at the same time, insofar as it thinks, unhappy consciousness is also a consciousness of unchangeableness and simple essential Being. And so it is trapped in the nihilism of self-opposition since "it must at the same time set about freeing itself from the unessential, i.e. from itself" (para. 208; p. 159).

In this struggle with itself, in which an ideal constituted in thought is opposed to the real vicissitudes of an existence structured by unreconciled domination, consciousness becomes its own enemy: to win the ideal is to lose the real self. This is the germ of religious thinking. By constructing allegories and mythologies in which the ideal is deferred but promised, in which redemption by the ideal is offered as a possibility following upon the loss of the real, religious thinking harnesses the futility of unhappy consciousness to a "beyond."

The Jewish Old Testament conception of God as absolutely other is the first moment of this dialectic:[11] "the unchangeable is opposed to individuality in general" (para. 211; p. 161). If it were to receive a definite form at this point, this would only more firmly establish the unchangeable aspect of the self as a *beyond*, and thus, as self-alienating: the hoped-for unity remains only a hope. But even the embodied individual Jesus Christ fails to heal the rift between man and God: for the unhappy consciousness, Jesus is not *this* individual, and so consciousness remains alienated from itself. In a passage that deserves to be quoted at some length, Hegel characterizes the attitude toward its own materiality of this frustrated religious consciousness:

> Consciousness is aware of itself as *this actual individual* in the animal functions. These, rather than being performed without affectation or embarrassment, as matters trivial in and for themselves which cannot possess any importance or essential significance for Spirit, are, on the contrary—since it is in them that the enemy [der Feind] reveals himself in his characteristic shape—the object of serious endeavor, and become precisely matters of the utmost importance. This enemy, however, renews himself in his defeat, and consciousness, in its fixation on him, far from freeing itself from him, remains forever with him, and forever

> sees itself defiled. . . . [W]e have here only a personality confined to its own self and its own petty actions, a personality brooding over itself, as wretched as it is impoverished. (para. 225; p. 168)

Der Feind is, as the rhetoric of the passage suggests, an expression for the devil. The sensuous temptations of embodiment are thus here given a theological interpretation, and henceforward consciousness will struggle to encounter its unchangeable aspect, which is Spirit, in embodied, incarnate form. To become "happy," unhappy consciousness must overcome the apparent alien reality of this form.[12]

The positive step in this direction is taken theologically in the sacrament of confession, an element of Christian practice to which Hegel finally turns his interpretive attention here by way of anticipating the future development of unhappy consciousness. Because the unchangeable has remained the thought of this divided consciousness, Hegel says that the misery of finite being is mediated by this thought: finitude is after all not immediately perceived as needy and tragic, but only in relation to the unchangeable. Now, in Christianity, this mediating thought is manifested concretely; it "is itself a conscious being" (para. 227; p. 169). 'It' becomes 'he', mediation becomes mediator, and the unhappy consciousness sacrifices its sinful finitude up to this mediator in confession, abandoning the freedom of self-certainty but at the same time relieving the burden of responsibility.[13] Through this self-negation something is achieved, however, that has so far been steadfastly refused since the life-and-death struggle: the other, which both lord and bondsman had internalized and thereby evaded, is finally posited. Thus,

> the surrender of one's own will is only from one aspect negative; in *its* Notion, or *in itself*, however, it is at the same time positive, namely the positing of will as the will of an other, and specifically, of will not as individual [einzelnen], but as universal will. (para. 230; pp. 170–71)

3. Toward the Begriff, the form of absolute synthesis

In moving beyond the inwardly divided religious consciousness toward the unity of absolute Spirit, Reason emerges as the dialectical residue of an original self-certainty; at this stage, the idea (*Vorstellung*) of Reason takes shape out of "the certainty that, in its particular individuality, it [i.e., consciousness] has being absolutely *in itself*, or is all reality" (para. 230; p. 171). This is the "truth" of religious consciousness, and also the truth of philosophy: but whereas the former defers this truth to a beyond in which the finite individual is completely absent, Hegel will now argue that the form of philosophical expression—an *Entäußerung* in terms of the *Begriff*—captures the immanence of the finite individual along with the transcendent universal in a simultaneous unity that overcomes the oppositions whose forms are Time and Being.[14] A substantial accomplishment, if it is possible. How does Hegel attempt to carry it out?

We have already seen how consciousness turns away from its embattled other in the sequence of subjectivizing moves that culminate in unhappy consciousness. Thinking here fails to win a freedom that is not lacking the "fullness of life": freedom in thought alone is "only the Notion [nur der Begriff] of freedom, not the living reality [lebendige] of freedom itself" (para. 200; p. 153). *Only* the Notion?! In the same paragraph, Hegel characterizes the general terms of Stoicism—the True, the Good, Wisdom, Virtue—as merely "uplifting": *erhebend* but not yet *aufgehoben*. The rhetoric of such passages underlines the close proximity of Spirit to these early experiments in thought even as it qualifies their value.[15] But just what can paradoxical limitations on the absolute such as are suggested by locutions like "only the Notion" really mean?

Hegel's elliptical answer at this early dialectical stage is concise but mysterious: "unhappy consciousness . . . brings and holds together pure thinking and particular individuality, but has not yet risen to that thinking *for which* consciousness as a particular individuality is reconciled with pure thought itself" (para. 216; p. 163). The legacy of unhappy consciousness flowers luxuriantly in the rich peat of history, but religious thinking remains impeded by a formal obstacle. "Philosophy has been reproached with setting itself above religion," Hegel writes in the *Lectures on the Philosophy of Religion*, but this "is false as an actual matter of fact"; rather, philosophy "sets itself merely above the form of faith; the content is the same in both cases" (op. cit., Vol. III, p. 148). *Vorstellungen*, the media of pious myths, allegories, images, are not themselves of the same form as thought, and so their mediation remains obtrusive, resisting the unity required by the absolute. Spirit is seeking a form of expression, of *Entäußerung*, that is simultaneously true to the objectivity of its content and to the subjectivity of its ground. How and why do *Vorstellungen* fail to answer this need?

In historically concrete terms, the *Vorstellungen* of religious dogmatics (Lutheran versions of which Hegel assays in paras. 774–79, pp. 536–40) are interpreted as forms of otherness: the *Kenosis* and externalization of Substance by Subject is "represented" by the "emptying" of God the Father into the Son, the Son into the Spirit, the Spirit into the believing Soul.[16] But the being of the absolute is not a meaning, not something abstract, pure thought—it is what is *actual*. The otherness of religious *Vorstellungen* is only a difference, and not yet a world, it is a "pure othering of itself." Thus, such thinking fails in its implicit task: to recover the presence of Christ. Christian faith is grounded in revelation, and the sermons of Jesus actually took place. But there is a tension between the immediateness of the incarnation and the memory (that is, the re-presentation) of the religious community. The immediacy of God's presence in the living Christ is, like all immediacy, vanishingly negligible; the living man-part, in any event, surrendered its particularity many centuries ago. History itself intervenes to mediate this presence for the understanding—but unfortunately, "*Remoteness in time and space* [*Vergangenheit* und *Entfernung*] is only the imperfect form in which the immediate mode [weise] is mediated or posited as universal" (para. 764; p. 531). The apparatus of piety implicitly longs for this vanished historical event and explicitly anticipates its return: that is to say, it distinguishes itself in the here-and-now from the perfection that was or is not yet, and thus it "is still burdened with an unreconciled [unversöhnten] split into a Here and a Beyond" (para. 765; p. 532). An incomplete mediation frustrated by the impossible externality of history and the unbridgeable gulf of time, Hegel reiterates that "its satisfaction therefore itself remains burdened with the antithesis of a beyond" (para. 787; p. 548). For the unhappy religious consciousness, reconciliation is always deferred, always future.

The theological imagination which makes of the absolute something tangibly objective, which expresses or externalizes Spirit in the "picture thoughts" of sacred mythology,[17] condemns its own conception to the unhappiness of a divided consciousness. For the unhappy consciousness, the nullity of what is not self kills the God of religious *Vorstellungen*: having lost Substance through the subjectivizing retreat into thought initiated in Stoicism, unhappy consciousness cannot tolerate what is other, even if it be posited as absolute. Thus, because the religious form of expression falsely reifies the absolute, "consciousness misunderstands its own nature, rejects the form and also the content and, what amounts to the same thing, loses the content to an historical representation [Vorstellung] and to an heirloom handed down by tradition; in this way, it is only the purely external [Äußerliche] element in belief that is retained and as something therefore that is dead and cannot be known" (para. 771; p. 535). In short, Hegel implies (as Nietzsche will affirm) that religious thinking, because it formally alienates consciousness from its own true content, leads inevitably to nihilism.

The positive moment in this dialectic initiates Hegel's final move to the philosophical *Begriff*. For philosophy, the death of the divine mediator heralds the death of an abstraction or projection. Against the nothingness of the other, consciousness opposes its own self-certainty: the abstract lifelessness of the merely "objective" is thereby ruled out at the beginning, leaving open the possibility of knowing a living other in the living certainty of consciousness itself. Hegel calls this penultimate subsumption of Substance by Subject "the *inbreathing of Spirit* [*Begeis-*

tung]" (para. 785; p. 546). When Spirit breathes out again, that living internalized Substance is externalized (*Entäußsert*) as history—actuality is recuperated in the movement of Spirit through its own dialectical phases and shapes, and this movement is its Life. What moves is more than abstract, and "what moves itself, that is Spirit; it is the Subject of the movement and is equally *the moving* [*das Bewegung*] itself, or the Substance through which the Subject moves" (para. 786; pp. 546–47). The "dead opposition" that Hegel had already lamented in the early "Fragment of a System" (1800) is finally resolved in a "living unity" anticipated in the fragment "On Love" (1798), but not realized until the philosophical *Begriff* makes this formally possible. What are the specific characteristics of this important new form? What, in other more grandiloquent words, is the structure of absolute knowing?

4. The structure of absolute knowing

The first explicit clue tellingly appears in paragraph 197 (p. 152), at the very outset of the Stoicism dialectic: "in *thinking* the object does not represent itself in representations or forms and figures [Vorstellungen oder Gestalten] but in *Notions* [*Begriffen*]." The paragraph goes on to explain, with rare lucidity, that whereas *Vorstellungen* posit the object as outside of consciousness, a determinate difference from consciousness, *Begriffen* are at once one with consciousness and with the objects of which they are the Notions. In the case of *Vorstellungen*, the object is represented as a figure or entity and accordingly has "the form of being something other than consciousness"; consciousness must "specially bear in mind that this is its representation" in order not to lose itself in Substance—but, bearing this in mind, it negates Substance instead, subsuming it into itself. With Notions, on the contrary, being-in-itself and being-for-consciousness immediately coexist without mutual exclusion, for a Notion is at once "*something that is* [ein *Seindes*]" and "for me immediately *my* Notion." Thus, when thinking is in the form of Notions, knowing subsumes being: since Self is possible ontologically only as a *knowing* of Self (as Sartre will put it, "The being of consciousness is the consciousness of being"), then when the object of that knowing is absolute Spirit, self-consciousness in that moment *is* absolute. Individual self-consciousness becomes absolute self-consciousness when it takes the form of the (adequate) understanding of the Notion of absolute self-consciousness.

It is perhaps surprising to find so clear an account of Notional thinking in preparation for an analysis of Stoicism, Skepticism, and the unhappy consciousness since, as we have already seen, these attitudes represent a retreat into thought that flees the domination of Substance without reconciling itself as Subject with this oppressive externality. But in fact, the foundation of the absolute is laid even earlier. The famous Preface, which Hyppolite notes has intentions similar to those of Chapter VIII,[18] already anticipates such formulations in spite of Hegel's claims that they may be intelligible only in conclusion. Thus, although we are warned that "the real issue [die Sache selbst] is not exhausted merely by stating it as an *aim* [*Zwecke*]" (para. 3; p. 11), nevertheless the circular structure of the absolute—"It is the process of its own becoming, the circle that presupposes its end as its goal, having its end also as its beginning" (para. 18; p. 20)—at the same time allows an early access that is in no simple way merely preliminary. Indeed, the absolute is to such an extent constituted by reiteration and recapitulation of the forms already so elaborately surveyed that it is possible to assert, following Solomon, that Hegel's "finale is philosophically unsatisfying," to insist "what is most remarkable about the concluding chapter of the *Phenomenology* is how little it says, how empty it is, and how many questions it leaves unanswered."[19]

Now, although it is also probably true, as Taylor glibly remarks, that "[Hegel's] actual synthesis is quite dead . . . no one actually believes his central ontological thesis, that the universe is posited by a Spirit whose essence is rational necessity,"[20] such dismissals fail to take into account their own interpretive consequences. If the absolute returns us to the beginning, if its content is nothing other than the historical shapes that produced it in the phenomenological narrative somehow gathered together in the omega point of self-reflection, then rejecting the absolute would appear to reject "the process through which it came about" as well—a standpoint uncomfortably ironic for productive scholarship! Like the mystic's manual of enlightenment, which is to be discarded once it has accomplished its task of transforming consciousness, the *Phenomenology*—read backwards from the absolute—would seem to claim practical results altogether inaccessible to the limits of theory within which the pedant is confined. The absolute may thus be "philosophically unsatisfying" or "unbelievable" precisely because it is philosophically heretical! But the *Phenomenology* as a whole would then in retrospect be similarly heretical: citing Hegel's own imagery, which significantly anticipates this conclusion from the very beginning and which strikingly evokes the rhetoric familiar in texts of mystical theology, the *Phenomenology* is described as a "ladder" to the "standpoint of Science" (para. 26; pp. 24–25).[21] The absolute at the threshold of this standpoint can appear "empty" only if one remains on the ground, merely admiring the ladder.

We need, then, to look still more closely at the peculiar character of the "speculative proposition" that formally distinguishes the absolute from its constituent shapes in order to evaluate the nature of Hegel's accomplishment. This will involve the very difficult question of the relation between thought and action as well as the even more obscure but essential relation between the *Phenomenology* as a temporal-historical *process* and its outcome, which is atemporal. What kind of circularity is at stake in the recapitulative movement of *Erinnerung*? And what are the consequences for philosophical reflection of Hegel's realizing the all-inclusive comprehension of absolute knowing?

The inwardizing movement of thought which, as we have noted, initially rescues the oppressed bondsman from the unreal chains of pure, unmediated otherness, and which anticipates the decisive form of the absolute in spite of its inadequacy to that very otherness it negates, must now be distinguished from thinking in terms of the Notion. For although "determined thoughts have the 'I', the power of the negative, or pure actuality, for the substance and element of their existence, whereas sensuous determinations have only powerless abstract immediacy, or being as such" (para. 33; pp. 30–31), these particular and determined thoughts succeed in overcoming the abstraction of simple otherness only with the abstraction of a simple self, an 'I' whose self-identity is finally a stale and empty certainty. The tautology of 'I = I', although irrefutable, lacks any content, and the consciousness which thus opposes self to other remains stuck in an attitude that can only regard both moments as unconditioned and absolute. When, however, the mutual determination of self and other is recognized, when lifeless stasis gives way to the fluid movement of dialectical interrelation, thinking finally becomes properly Notional: "Through this movement the pure thoughts become Notions, and are only now what they are in truth, self-movements, circles, spiritual essences, which is what their substance is" (para. 33; p. 31). The individual self-consciousness of an empty self-certainty becomes the spiritual fullness of universal self-consciousness in and through the synthetic power of a new form.

For it is a mistake, Hegel insists, "to suppose that cognition [das Erkennen] can be satisfied with the in-itself or the essence [Wesen], but can get along without the form" (para. 19; p. 20). Just as the static contentless certainty of self-identity fails to account for the shapes of otherness that constitute the history of externalized Spirit, "the divine essence" is expressed as an actuality only when its essential immediacy is mediated by "the whole wealth of its developed form" (ibid.). Since "The power of Spirit is only as great as its expression [Äußerung], its depth only as deep as it dares to spread out and lose itself in its exposition [Auslegung]" (para. 10; p. 15), the problem of form is finally identified as the very locus of absolute knowing itself. Hegel's metaphysical apotheosis is neither more nor less than a formal innovation, a matter of style.

Whereas the thinking of Skepticism, according to the careful analysis offered in the *Lectures on the History of Philosophy*, is capable only of fragmentary "tropes" and not yet even of "propositions" (Sätze)—much less of a philosophical system—[22] Hegel also repudiates the propositional "argumentation" (*Räsonnieren*) of subsequent philosophizing. Such thinking assumes an attitude of arrogance toward its own content, as if the form that represents it were merely an abstraction: in returning always to "the vanity of its own knowing," argumentation understands its content in terms of "Accident and Predicate" (*Akzidens und Prädikat*) in relation to the self-certain 'I' (paras. 59–60; pp. 48–49). But rather than this formal opposition of subject and predicate in propositional stasis—an opposition which reduces the actuality of content to a mere modification of the subject—the "speculative proposition" (*spekulativen Satz*) merges the distinction into a harmony without thereby effacing the difference figured in the form. Thus, in expressions like "God is being," or "the actual is the universal," the subject-predicate distinction imposed by form is at the same time overcome in the unity of form and content, and the dialectical movement between these moments in the speculative proposition itself supplants the "proof" of argument. "The *proposition* should express [ausdrücken] *what* the True is," Hegel writes, but since "essentially the True is Subject . . . as such it is merely the dialectical movement, this course that generates itself, going forth from, and returning to, itself" (para. 65; p. 53). It is this extraordinary dynamism of the speculative philosophical proposition which accounts, Hegel adds, for popular objections that philosophy is unintelligible; in failing to apprehend the peculiar demands of speculative language, such misunderstanding hinges on inappropriate habits of reading:

> The philosophical proposition, because it is a proposition, leads one to believe that the usual subject-predicate relation obtains, as well as the usual attitude toward knowing. But the philosophical content destroys [zerstört] this attitude and this opinion. We learn by experience that we meant something other than we meant to mean; and this correction of our meaning compels our knowing to go back to the proposition, and understand it in some other way. (para. 63; p. 52)

The error of argumentative, propositional thinking finds its mirror-image counterpart in the "picture thinking" of religious *Vorstellungen*, as Hegel notes in the Preface (para. 58; p. 48) but does not explicitly develop until Chapter VIII. If argumentation neglects the actuality of content by presuming the form of expression to be inessential, thereby subsuming all otherness in the self-identity of consciousness, in the case of *Vorstellungen* the otherness of what is represented remains hopelessly incorrigible: form obtrudes itself as a determinate difference from consciousness, becoming the very medium of an irreconcilable alienation. Since the appearances of Spirit, the plethora of its historical determinations, are regarded as external in Time and Space by the religious consciousness, Spirit itself is subsumed by "the form of objectivity" (para. 788; p. 549) and thus lost to the self of self-consciousness. Although the unification of consciousness and self-consciousness, of being-in-itself and being-for-itself, has already occurred *in principle* in religion, it has not yet been achieved "according to the proper form" (para. 795; p. 553); the content, in other words, has been exhibited, but the simple unity of the Notion is still lacking. It is only through the *action* of dialectic in speculative thinking that the concrete existence of Spirit can be recovered from the passive objectivity that is its own externalization: the dynamism of dialectic, its movement in process through Time, lies at the beating heart of Hegel's absolute presented in the form of the Notion. The dialectical unrest that has driven philosophical speculation through the phenomenology of Spirit's many shapes comes at last to be isolated analytically as the essence of Hegel's special method and practice. How, then, are thought and action finally reconciled at the end of this long historical process in an atemporal conclusion whose form is Time itself?

The first step involves a "spiritualizing" of the object which remained an alienated other for the *Vorstellungen* of religious consciousness. Since simple immediacy "*does not act* and is *not actual*" (para. 796; p. 555), the multiplicity of object determinations which make up the experience of consciousness already "establishes the object as *in itself* a spiritual being [zum geistigen Wesen]" (para. 788; p. 550). Hegel's famous claim in the *Philosophy of Right* that "what is rational is actual and what is actual is rational" is illuminating here, just as the passage with which we are concerned reciprocally illuminates what is often misconstrued as a reactionary justification of the status quo: the philosophically apprehended history narrated by the *Phenomenology* has been revealed in terms of its intelligible *telos* as an actuality (*Wirklichkeit*, from *wirken*, to work or effect) that is distinct from what simply exists (*Dasein*). The "world" of consciousness, as well as the history of this world, is in fact the *product* of consciousness, and thus the object, which was irrevocably alienated in its externality by religion and its representational thinking, "does truly become a spiritual being for consciousness when each of its individual determinations is grasped as a determination of the self" (para. 788; p. 550). Objective determinations are, as it were, traces of action, and since it is "only through action that Spirit *is* in such a way that it is *really there*" [daß er *da ist*] (para. 796; p. 555), the externality of objectivity, rather than alienating consciousness from otherness, in fact establishes the spiritual unity of self and other as a reality. By recognizing the participation of consciousness in shaping the world—a principle first realized by the working slave, but then lost to the inward turn which culminated in the proto-religious asceticism of unhappy consciousness[23]—the alienated otherness of the true content common to both religion and philosophy is overcome: "What in religion was *content* or a form for presenting an *other*, is here the *Self's* own act" (para. 797; p. 556).

Since this has, from the outset, always implicitly been the case, what "we phenomenologists" have done in following out the teleology of Spirit's development concealed in the traces of its historical manifestations is no more than "simply to *gather together* the separate moments" (para. 797; p. 556); nothing new is added by making explicit the interpretive structure whose form retroactively clarifies the meaning of these moments. The "logic" of absolute knowing is thus an "epi-logic": passive and dependent, lying outside the content of its own development as an almost extraneous gesture belatedly laid upon the *Versammlung* of historical shapes that always already manifest it, Hegel's final chapter is not so much a conclusion as an epilogue. In absolute knowing, the content of religion merely receives the shape of the self such that certainty and self-certainty finally coincide; self-knowing Spirit "is the *certainty of immediacy*, or *sense-consciousness*—the beginning from which we started" (para. 806; p. 563). More precisely, it finally becomes explicit for consciousness that the content of experience always had this shape. In this final move, the circle is closed with a return to certainty, this time a *mediated* immediacy that knows itself in its object, and Spirit

> at the same time gives its complete and true content the form of the Self and thereby realizes its Notion as remaining in its Notion in this realization—this is absolute knowing; it is Spirit that knows itself in the shape of Spirit, *or speculative knowing [begreifende Wissen]*. (para. 797; p. 556)

With this pronouncement, only one question remains to be answered. Since dialectical understanding is *essentially* temporal, a "movement" (*Bewegung*) between past and future that reveals the Real as a present in process, what is the temporality of absolute knowing? Even given its epilogical status within the structure of the *Phenomenology*, the absolute remains a result, and as such it would seem to arrest or terminate the animating movement of Time in the empty static abstraction of pure theory. Hegel's initially mystifying resolution of this difficulty is to assert that in fact the Notion *is* Time, a claim whose manifest circularity is the essence of its profundity. Opening a Pandora's box of revealing interpretive difficulties that exercise the commentaries in extravagant ways to be evaluated in Part II of this chapter, the problem of Time will again appear in Chapter Five—eternally returning as the central thought of Nietzsche's *Zarathustra*. In portentous anticipation, then, this study of the *Phenomenology* may provisionally conclude with a timely riddle as heavy with consequence as the Sphinx's.

In effect, Time for Hegel is at once the medium in which Spirit, "recoiling in horror" from the abstract unity of Stoic self-certainty, externalizes itself historically "in the sphere of culture"—and, precisely as a medium or form, the very substance of Spirit itself. Hegel describes this dialectic in the long and exceedingly difficult paragraph 803 (pp. 559–61) by densely summarizing the entire course of Spirit's phenomenology.[24] "Frightened" by the otherness of Substance, consciousness flees into the certainty of self-identity only to react against this contentless negativity which excludes everything that is not self by recognizing the self as a "pure difference"; against this difference stands the self-identity of the 'I' which, "as pure and at the same time objective to the self-knowing self, has to be expressed as Time." What can this admittedly dark saying mean?

The clue is to be found four paragraphs later in a passage that sets up the final discussion of recollection (*Erinnerung*) as the inwardizing movement of absolute Spirit in terms meant to distinguish it from the inward turn made by consciousness when it first—unhappily—began to think. "The self-knowing Spirit," Hegel writes, "knows not only itself but also the negative of itself, or its limit [Grenze]" (para. 807; p. 563)— that is to say, unlike the simple self-identity of 'I = I' which excludes all otherness in principle, self-conscious Spirit has proceeded through the various forms of its otherness to a recovery of itself, and has thereby come to know these forms as well. By realizing itself in these forms at last, "Spirit displays the process of its becoming Spirit in the form of *free contingent happening*, intuiting [anschauend] its pure Self as Time outside of it, and equally its Being as Space" (ibid.). The process of Spirit's externalization is thus also the path back to itself: the 'I' of absolute knowing "is not merely the Self, but the *identity of the Self with itself*; but this identity is complete and immediate otherness with self, or this *Subject* is just as much *Substance*" (para. 803; p. 560). Were it not for Time, the process of Spirit's historical externalization could not unfold, and were it not for this substantial manifestation, the being of Spirit could have only the form of abstract self-identity, an empty tautology divided against itself.

Nevertheless, although Spirit necessarily appears in Time, yet "it appears in Time just so long as it has not *grasped* [erfaßt] its pure Notion, i.e. has not annulled Time" (para. 801; p. 557). As its "destiny and necessity," Spirit appears in Time only in order "to set in motion the *immediacy of the in-itself*—the form in which Substance is present in consciousness" (ibid.). But absolute Spirit is not in Time; rather, as the immanent synthesis of Being (its self-externalization) and Time (its self-mediation), absolute Spirit transcends both of these forms of finite determination. As Nature, Spirit is "emptied out" into Space while "the other side of its becoming, *History*, is a *knowing* self-*mediating* process—Spirit emptied out [entäußerte] into Time" (para. 808; p. 563). Significantly, then, Time rescues the Notion from abstraction: engendered by Desire, by the telos of what does not yet exist, Spirit plays itself out as real History, becoming concrete and substantial in Space and Time.

But with the satisfaction of Desire in the reconciliation of the absolute, for which all that is or can be is Spirit, the passage of Time is finally annulled through its complete assimilation. Although enduring in Time paradoxically means that every present moment is immediately annihilated in the past, the preservation of what thus disappears is accomplished by the Notion: *Erinnerung* (recollection, memory) as *Er-Innerung* ("inwardizing") overcomes both the otherness of the other and the absence of the past in a fulfilled present of self-knowing. As Herbert Marcuse writes, "the force which accomplishes the conquest of time is remembrance (re-collection) . . . Being is no longer the painful transcendence toward the future but the peaceful recapture of the past."[25] By grace of the passage of Time, the inward turn of absolute Spirit does not exclude the concrete reality of historical events, as Stoicism had done, but rather includes and incorporates this reality such that "the *inwardizing recollection* [Er-Innerung] of that experience has preserved it and is the inner being [das Innere], and in fact the higher form of Substance" (para. 808; p. 564). Spirit thus "absorbed in itself" (*In seinem Insichgehen*) is "sunk in the night of its self-consciousness"—but this is not an absolute of undifferentiated unity, a "night in which all cows are black," such as Hegel had already repudiated in the Preface. Rather,

> in that night its vanished existence [sein verschwundenes Dasein] is preserved, and this transformed existence [dies aufgehobene Dasein]— the former one, but now reborn of the Spirit's knowledge—is the new existence [das neue Dasein], a new world and a new shape of Spirit. (para. 808; pp. 563–64)

PART II. RE-READING THE ABSOLUTE: A NEW BEGINNING

Having reached and read through the recapitulative epilogue of "Absolute Knowing," completing the hermeneutic circle that was begun in the anticipatory Preface, a certain thrill of metaphysical giddiness is palpable. A profound secret has been won through arduous effort, and the secret claims nothing less than to be of absolute consequence. This is Wisdom, the comprehension of reality, the absolute truth, and we philosophers have become wise by studying it. This, at any rate, is apparently what Hegel means to tell us, its grandiose optimism notwithstanding. And no one has better or more boldly spelled out just what that optimism implies than Kojève:

> The fact that a man has decided to read the *Phenomenology* proves that he loves Philosophy. The fact that he *understands* the *Phenomenology* proves that he is a Philosopher, since, by reading and understanding it, he actually makes the consciousness he had of himself *grow*. As a Philosopher, he is interested in himself and not interested in all those who are not Philosophers—i.e., those who, from *principle*, refuse to read the *Phenomenology* and hence to extend their self-consciousness. Leaving them to their own fate and returning to himself, the Philosopher learns through the *Phenomenology* that, being a Philosopher, he is a "lover [amateur] of *Wisdom*," as it is defined in and by this book. This is to say that he learns that he wants to be a *Wise Man* [un *Sage*]: namely, a perfectly self *conscious* man, fully satisfied by this coming to consciousness, and thus serving as the model for all his "colleagues." And, by seeing in the Wise Man the human *ideal* in general, the Philosopher attributes to himself as Philosopher a human value without equal (since, according to him, only the Philosopher can become a Wise Man).
>
> The whole question reduces to knowing if the Philosopher can truly hope to become a Wise Man. Hegel tells him that he can: he claims to have attained Wisdom (in and by the *Phenomenology*).[26]

This is an extravagant, audacious passage, but it is only one of many that result from Kojève's Hegelian partisanship. Like the fundamentalist who disbelieves the great antiquity of fossils because Carbon 14 contradicts the Bible, preferring instead the disingenuous subterfuge that a Brontosaurus bone is really a divine test for the faithful, Kojève scrambles to account for Hegel's claims as if they were a sacred revelation to be taken literally. He thus represents an approach to Hegel's unbounded optimism perfectly antithetical to that of Karl Marx. For Marx, the very objective of self-consciousness is already an abstraction that fails to account for the "real man of flesh and blood"; even if the sort of "wisdom" Kojève exalts is possible, it remains a charade, for "philosophical mind is nothing but the alienated mind of the world conceiving of itself and thinking inside its self-alienation, i.e. abstractly."[27] For Marx, the convoluted evasion of Hegelian complacency is flattered ludicrously by the term "Wise Man"—"wise guy" would be more appropriate!

The fundamental issue, then, remains in question as we turn from Hegel's text to the commentaries. It would seem that either the absolute is possible—but then philosophy itself is transcended[28]— or else it is impossible, in which case absolute idealism is at best a charade, at worst a vice.[29] Hyppolite notes that "unhappy consciousness is the fundamental theme of the *Phenomenology*,"[30] recalling Hegel's statements that, with the appearance of this unsatisfied condition, we are nevertheless already "in the native realm of truth" and close to the Notion of Spirit (*Phenomenology*, para. 177; *Phänomenologie*, p. 140). Resonating with Sartrean language, Hyppolite adds that "most contemporary thinkers deny the possibility of such a synthesis of the in-itself and the for-itself. . . . They generally prefer what Hegel calls 'unhappy consciousness' to what he calls 'spirit'" (op. cit., pp. 204–205).[31]

In order to evaluate these alternative attitudes toward absolute knowing, so dramatically opposed to one another in their judgments of Hegel's success, a closer look at Kojève's faithful literalism and at Marx's critical materialism will be useful. Is it necessary to take a stand on one or the other side of this hermeneutical dispute, as it were for or against Hegel? Or do both Kojève and Marx go too far? What remains of Hegel's claims if we recognize that they must at least be qualified by materialist objections?

1. The Hegelian fundamentalism of Kojève

Kojève's attempts to read Hegel into contemporary history—or rather, post-history—are the extreme consequence of a tendency among French commentators to emphasize and develop the "realist" side of Hegel. Now, with the sort of realism which holds that universals *exist*, and that indeed they exist before things, Hegel has clearly much in common. Ontologically, the reality of thought is presupposed by the phenomenological project, and epistemologically, the dialectical analyses Hegel performs are intended to give a true account of knowledge about things and events in the real world. But Hyppolite and Kojève make this potentially intellectualist sympathy into a full-blown existential realism to which the assertion of mind over matter, of universals *ante res*, begins actually to look strange. Since, after all, Hegel's absolute is not "the night in which the cows are black," Hyppolite (op. cit., p. 578) argues that, like all knowledge, even the absolute is grounded in experience. The *Phenomenology* seems to support this suggestion; paragraph 802 (p. 558) insists that "nothing is *known* that is not in *experience*, or, as it is also expressed, that is not *felt to be true*, not given as an *inwardly revealed verity*," reaffirming what Hegel had already said in the Preface: "consciousness knows and comprehends only what falls within its experience" (para. 36; p. 32). Hyppolite accordingly concludes from such passages that Hegel's onto-logic answers the objection of dry abstraction squarely and unproblematically:

> With Hegel, the reduction of philosophy to logic does not at all lead to formalism or even to the intellectualism (i.e., the idea that he constructs the universe a priori with only his thoughts) for which he has often been reproached. Rather, it leads to a spiritualization of logic. (op. cit., p. 575)

But Hyppolite's generous reading of the absolute appears niggardly compared to what Kojève makes of such clues. "Hegelian absolute Idealism has nothing to do with what is ordinarily called 'Idealism,'" he confidently proclaims; rather, "if terms are used in their usual senses, it must be said that Hegel's system is 'realist'" (Nichols, p. 150; Queneau, p. 427). For Kojève, the *Phenomenology* demands a "realist metaphysics" by the fact that Subject and Object originally stand opposed and in need of dialectical reconciliation: the very notion of opposition "is meaningful only if one supposes the existence of an object properly so-called [proprement dit]—that is, an Object external to and independent of the Subject" (Nichols, p. 152; Queneau, p. 428). Although he acknowledges that synthesis is "effected inside the subject" (ibid.), Kojève nevertheless insists that Hegel remains an "ontological dualist."

Holding, then, that the distinction between Subject and Object is real, important consequences follow from this dualism Kojève attributes to Hegel. Analogously distinguishing Self from Being, Kojève goes on to associate Self with History, which the Self generates through Action—while Being is simply "the Real," objectivity as such. Citing Maine de Biran, and anticipating Sartre, Kojève says that the Real is what "resists." However, this independent otherness, this wall through which I cannot pass my head, nevertheless does not resist *thought*. In a graphic footnote whose brutal literalism is at the verge of the excess in which he is about to indulge, Kojève writes:

> Indeed, if I say I can pass through this wall, the wall by no means resists what I say or think: as far as it is concerned I can say so as long as I please. It begins to resist only if I want to realize my thought by Action—that is, if I actually hurl myself against the wall. And such is always the case. (Nichols, p. 156; Queneau, p. 433)

Since a "realist" philosophy already grants that Being is, Kojève reasons that Action and History must now be at the center of concern. Consequently, he turns to analyses of Self and Time; "Man," he avers, is Action and Time—hence, change—hence, error. With this Marx-inspired first step, however, Kojève proceeds with alarming rapidity to leap from the concrete incarnation of Hegelian *Geist* in "Man" (*l'Homme*) to speculations about what it might mean to "overcome Man"—along with Time and History—in the Absolute:

> [W]hen specifically human error is finally transformed into the truth of absolute Science, Man ceases to exist as Man and History comes to an end. The overcoming of Man (that is, of Time, that is, of Action) in favor of static Being (that is, Space, that is, Nature), therefore, is the overcoming of Error in favor of Truth. (Nichols, p. 156; Queneau, p. 432)

Having reminded us that Hegel already accomplished "the definitive annihilation of Man properly so-called," Kojève extends these speculations about "post-historical animals of the species *Homo Sapiens*" in two long and exceedingly strange footnotes to which is appended an even longer and stranger editorial addendum that blithely begins: "The text of the preceding note is ambiguous, not to say contradictory" (Nichols, p. 159)! In the preceding note, Kojève defends realism by elaborating a bizarre hypothetical in which the revealed reality "dog" subsumes the being of the consciousness to whom it is present such that "we would be faced with the *dog* that is conscious of *itself*, and not a *man* who is acquiring knowledge *of* the dog . . . in this case we would be faced with a true dog (a *natural* being) and not a *man* in canine form" (Nichols, p. 157; Queneau, p. 433).[32] The note concludes with the claim that, although the end of History implies also the end of Action, nevertheless it will only be wars and philosophy that will really cease: "all the rest can be preserved indefinitely; art, love, play, etc., etc.; in short, everything that makes man *happy*" (Nichols, p. 159; Queneau, p. 435).

But the real pearls of Kojève's post-Hegelian, post-Historical Wisdom are nestled in the "Note to the Second Edition"—a text that is perhaps mad in its imaginative lack of restraint, but that accordingly shows, with the clarity of overstatement, what consequences follow from naively assuming Hegel means what he says.[33] There is no point in summarizing Kojève's fantastic conclusions—his own account is inimitable. Somewhat extended citation, therefore, seems best suited to sketching this fundamentalist Hegelian scenario of Spirit after Life and History:

> [I]t would have to be admitted that after the end of History, men would construct their edifices and works of art as birds build their nests and spiders spin their webs, would perform musical concerts after the fashion of frogs and cicadas, would play like young animals, and would indulge in love like adult beasts. But one cannot then say that all this "makes Man *happy*" [*this* is Kojève's reason for finding the preceding note "ambiguous, not to say contradictory"!]. One would have to say

that post-historical animals of the species *Homo Sapiens* (which will live amidst abundance and complete security) will be *content* as a result of their artistic, erotic and playful behavior, inasmuch as, by definition, they will be contented with it. . . . Animals of the species *Homo Sapiens* would react by conditioned reflexes to vocal signals or sign "language," and thus their so-called "discourses" would be like what is supposed to be the "language" of bees. (Nichols, pp. 159–60)

The note goes on—for three more pages—to describe how contemporary events may be reinterpreted in terms of what is now called "the Hegelian-Marxist end of History." Kojève boldly explains such diverse phenomena as "the sovietization of Russia and the communization of China," "the democratization of imperial Germany (by way of Hitlerism)," the Japanese Noh play and kamikaze warrior—even "the accession of Togoland to independence, nay, the self-determination of the Papuans" (Nichols, pp. 160–62)! He finally concludes with vertiginous observations of "superpower" socio-economic relations:

One can even say that, from a certain point of view, the United States has already attained the final stage of Marxist "communism," seeing that, practically, all the members of a "classless society" can from now on appropriate for themselves everything that seems good to them, without thereby working any more than their heart dictates. . . . [T]he Russians and the Chinese are only Americans who are still poor but are rapidly proceeding to get richer. I was led to conclude from this that the "American way of life" was the type of life specific to the post-historical period, the actual presence of the United States in the World prefiguring the "eternal present" future of all humanity. (Nichols, p. 161)

2. The materialist critique of Marx

If Kojève's "realism" drives him to the absurdity of accounting for post-Hegelian events as consequences of history's having concluded itself in the absolute, Marx's "materialism" takes Hegel's next step just as seriously. For the *result* of the *Phenomenology* is the *presupposition* of the *Logic*: the 'I' of absolute knowing becomes the *Begriff* of logic such that "the element of existence of the Spirit is no longer the Dasein of consciousness, but the concept" (Hyppolite, op. cit., p. 581). But this means that the real element of existence of the Spirit, conceived of as "thought returning to its birthplace," is abstraction.[34] The *Phenomenology*, with all its apparent empirical content, moves ultimately beyond a mere examination of the appearances of being to consciousness: it takes us to the standpoint of Science, to the verge of the *Logic*, wherein Being-in-itself is examined, the opposition of Self and Being having been resolved in absolute knowing. Thus, it would seem that the final chapter of the *Phenomenology* is indeed decidedly "idealist," Kojève's implausible apologetics notwithstanding: synthesis of Self and Other appears to reduce the 'I' to a pure logical category, a formal abstraction. This, at any rate, is Marx's objection. How does he argue the point?

In the "Economic and Philosophical Manuscripts" of 1844, Marx alleges that "the only labor Hegel knows and recognizes is abstract, mental labor" (Marx in McLellan, op. cit., p. 101). Recognizing the Hegelian strategy for recuperating objectivity through a realization of *Geist* in the products of labor, Marx observes that "man" is not mere *Geist*, nor merely the Hegelian abstraction of "self-consciousness." The "real man of flesh and blood," he insists, is an "objective being" that "is by origin natural" (ibid., p. 103). Since "a non-objective being is a non-being" (ibid., p. 104), Marx concludes that "the being that Hegel transcends in philosophy is not actual" (ibid., p. 108).

The first move in Marx's critique thus involves a doubt about what we may call the dialectical premise of Hegel's absolute: that the object of labor, although external, can be rescued from alienation by recognizing the trace of Spirit, of the bondsman's formative activity, which distinguishes it as a created thing. Nature is transformed by the bondsman's labor, and to this extent it is recoverable by dialectic. But it is recoverable only as non-natural: besides being a *formed* object, Nature is also the bondsman's opponent, "it exists outside him, independent and alien, and becomes a self-sufficient power opposite him . . . the life he has lent to the object affronts him, hostile and alien" (ibid., p. 79). The objective being "man," who "is by origin natural,"[35] thus knows his thought to be impressed upon the object he has formed, but he equally knows that the object has a natural being which distinguishes it—qua object—from himself. Attempting to hide this knowledge in self-deception would be tantamount to what Hegel calls "unhappy consciousness"—yet, Marx insists, this is just what Hegel has done in absolute knowing. Accordingly, it is with Chapter VIII of the *Phenomenology*, wherein these premises draw to conclusion, that Marx is principally concerned (ibid., p. 101).

And the consistent thrust of his concern is leveled at the abstraction of Hegel's final apotheosis. Man for Marx is "a directly natural being" like a plant or an animal, a being with real objective needs that cannot be satisfied by even absolute ideas. Unlike trans-individual Spirit, the disembodied abstract agent of history, man "as a natural, corporeal, sensuous, objective being is a passive, dependent and limited being . . . the objects of his instincts are exterior to him and independent of him and yet they are objects of his need" (ibid., p. 104). To be real is to be sensuous, to be an object and to have objects outside oneself, to be needy—and "To be sensuous is to suffer [Sinnlich sein ist leidend sein]" (ibid.). Hence, to be *real* is to suffer, and the very ambition of eternal satisfaction in absolute reconciliation and recognition is already suspiciously "idealistic." The transcendence of alienation would imply the transcendence of objectivity, such that man would be reduced to "a non-objective spiritual being" (ibid., p. 102)—but "a non-objective being is an unreal, non-sensuous being that is only thought of, i.e., an imaginary being, a being of abstraction" (ibid., p. 104).

Without making explicit reference to the passage in the Preface that discusses the "speculative" or "philosophical" proposition,[36] Marx also attacks this formulation as straightforward formal evidence of abstraction. Since any process must have an agent, Marx notes the oddity of history's agent appearing only at its end, coming into being as a *result*. Thus, "Real man and real nature become mere predicates or symbols of this hidden, unreal man and unreal nature"; subject and predicate are "completely inverted" in relation to one another, and the unreal—the ideal—becomes essential (ibid., p. 109). Absolute self-knowing Spirit, a "mystical subject-object" that creates the world with the divine word of its self-externalization—and which "is therefore God"—nevertheless remains trapped in "a pure and unceasing circular movement within itself" (ibid.).

Consequently, Marx concludes that what Hegel transcends in moving from finite to absolute Spirit "is not actual religion, state, nature, but religion as itself already an object of knowledge, dogmatics; and similarly with jurisprudence, political science, natural science" (ibid., p. 108). Only interpretations are at stake here, not the realities themselves, and Hegel's gesture is just one more interpretation, relative to intellectual parameters and accordingly "absolute" in a very qualified sense. "Thingness" can *only* be externalized as self-consciousness for Hegel because "it is not real man as such . . . that is made the subject, but only self-consciousness, the abstraction of man" (ibid., p. 103). And thus, it is only the abstraction of man that is transcended, while real men of flesh and blood remain in circumstances of unhappiness and oppression.

What, on the contrary, Marx is willing, even eager, to credit in Hegel is his vision of the "self-creation of man as a process" through the dynamic principle of dialectic (ibid., p. 101). Even if Hegel's conception of dialectical negation is not adequate to "the real history of man," it nevertheless does describe "the history of the act of creation" in a profound and incisive way (ibid., p. 98). Furthermore, the formal abstraction of Hegel's final overcoming of historical, "externalized" Spirit confirms in practice the very concrete manifestation it transcends in theory. Thus, Marx concludes his critique by locating the drama of opposition and expression as the domain proper to human life:

> [F]or Hegel the process of self-creation and self-objectification as self-externalization and self-alienation is the absolute and therefore final manifestation of human life which has itself for aim, is at peace with itself and has attained its true nature. (ibid., p. 109)

CHAPTER FOUR

Anticipatory Repetition:
Heterodox Spirituality and
Hegel's Philosophical Eschatology

> It would perhaps have done more credit to us and to mankind if
> no matter what heresy, damned by council and creeds, had risen
> to become the public system of belief, instead of the orthodox sys-
> tem maintaining the upper hand.
> —Hegel to Schelling, Aug. 30, 1795

Characterizing absolute Spirit from Marx's materialist perspective as a "mystical subject-object" that, like God, creates its own ideal self-reconciled world at once invokes the theological underpinnings of Hegel's thinking and the heterodox intellectualism of his philosophical ambitions.[1] The rational-conceptual epiphany of absolute knowing, although it represents a decisive formal step beyond the "picture thinking" of religious *Vorstellungen* as we have seen, tellingly concludes with borrowed poetic images that conjure up the absolute as King of a realm of Spirits, set upon the throne of Calvary and drinking from the chalice of infinitude (*Phenomenology*, para. 808; *Phänomenologie*, p. 564).[2] Even if it is through the speculative proposition and the absolute Idea that Hegel claims to have achieved the synthesis of finite and infinite Spirit, philosophy is more than empty idealism because its concepts are grounded in real presence, in a revelation that functions as the endpoint of interpretations.[3] As Emil Fackenheim insists, the *Aufhebung* of religion must preserve what is overcome: "critics, in short, have paid insufficient heed to the fact that nothing is further from Hegel's intentions than the dissipation of human life—life in general and religious life in particular—into philosophical thought."[4]

Nevertheless, the "pure consciousness" of devotional feeling that lies at the heart of religious fervor—the disciple's conviction that he is recognized by the absolute—remains at the level of simple immediacy. Accordingly, in Hyppolite's blunt words, Hegel "viewed Christianity as one of the great forms of unhappy consciousness."[5] The manifest spiritual unity of Jesus contrasts significantly with the separation and consequent duplicity of finite consciousness, a self-alienation initiated by the disciples' physical distance from Jesus and perpetuated to the present by the intervention of time. Although the sensuous immediacy of the incarnation is first overcome through the universality of spiritual resurrection in the traditions and memory of the community,[6] its recovery in mediated form is beyond the grasp of religious thinking.

Since, however, the *Begriff* is equal to this task while its content remains identical with the content of revealed religion, Hegel's absolute seems to flirt with traditions that may broadly be called "Gnostic" and which, when they appeared in earlier times, were fiercely repudiated by orthodox Christianity as heretical.[7] More specifically, taking the theologoumenon of apocalypse as a favored topos of heterodox theologies which proclaim a spiritual dispensation that functions as a surrogate eschatology, the "genre of Hegelian apocalypse," in Cyril O'Regan's phrase,[8] displays a manifest Gnostic resonance.

Now, the overlap of Hegelian and apocalyptic thought generally is well documented in the literature;[9] indeed, "Hegelian ontotheology evidences almost all the features of Judeo-Christian apocalypse or apocalyptic."[10] However, the ways in which Hegel departs from the traditional catalog of apocalyptic topoi are consistent with precedents in Valentinian Gnosticism:

> Valentinian Gnosticism not only evidences a narrative span that is absolutely inclusive, it shows eminent signs of suggesting that the divine loudly asserted to be immune to change and becoming is in fact a divine that undergoes a process of perfecting as it traverses the drama of fall, exile, and return. Valentinian Gnosticism, therefore, seems to supply the first instance of this nonapocalyptic kind of apocalypse that finds later instances in Boehme and Hegel.[11]

The analytical emphasis of O'Regan's interpretive position here significantly focuses on the narrative dimension as constituitive of the pattern of influence in Hegel,[12] the special relevance of which will concern us directly in tracing through the consequences of Hegel's eschatology below, for the transition to *Begriffen* from the *Vorstellungen* of revealed religion is achieved by means of narrative structuration that recalls Gnostic ontotheology. The premise in any case is that "the genre of Hegelian apocalypse is the genre of *Gnostic apocalypse* in contradistinction to Judeo-Christian apocalypse or apocalyptic" insofar as "Revelation, or *apokalypsis* in the Greek sense, is, at once, the sign of the new age and testimony that within the age of Spirit disclosure is fully transparent, thereby undercutting the necessity of the distinction between faith and knowledge."[13]

But it is with the twelfth-century abbot Joachim of Fiore that Hegel's phenomenological project is most revealingly allied.[14] Joachim's interpretation of the Trinity in anticipation of a future but nonetheless *historical* access to the eschaton, although by no means "Gnostic" in any strict sense (Joachim was in fact initially legitimated by three popes), proclaimed an intellectualist monachism openly sympathetic to the Eastern Basilian tradition—itself a less extreme alternative to Gnostic eremeticism. Joachim describes the course of history as proceeding according to three dispensations, corresponding to the three persons of the Trinity. The first dispensation was associated with the Father, and characterized by the rule of Law; the second, properly Christian age of the Gospel was mediated by the Son. But the last, the third dispensation, the age of Spirit risen out of the Letter, will endure for a millennium in order finally to bring all the ages and time itself to an end in the Last Judgment.[15] This trinitarian structuration is adumbrated, interpreted, represented, and conceptualized in various ways throughout Joachim's major writings; indeed, the linguistic and extra-linguistic demands imposed by an unmediated, absolute knowing of the divine presence will concern us insofar as such demands are precisely those which Hegel, too, struggles under and claims to meet. In any case, what must be successfully expressed is nothing less than the manifold promise of a culminating and consummating *Bildung* implicit symbolically in the very structure of the Trinity itself. A characteristic and synoptic passage appears in Joachim's *Concordia*:

> The mysteries of Holy Scriptures point us to three orders [states or conditions: *status*] of the world: to the first, in which we are under the Law; to the second, in which we are under grace; to the third, which we already imminently expect, and in which we shall be under a yet more abundant grace. . . . The first condition is therefore that of perception, the second that of partially perfected wisdom, the third, the fullness of knowledge. The first condition is in the bondage of slaves, the second, in the bondage of sons, the third in liberty. The first in fear, the second in faith, the third in love. The first in the condition of slaves, the second of free men, the third of friends. The first of boys, the second of men, the third of the aged. The first stands in the light of stars, the second in the light of dawn, the third in the brightness of day. . . . The first condition is related to the Father, the second to the Son, the third to the Holy Spirit.[16]

These ideas were to provide a basis for several of the most influential medieval heresies,[17] and Joachim's influence in European and particularly German metaphysics has had a long and strange history since then—a history that arguably includes the Aryan millennialism of National Socialism. In this context, the secularization of Christian eschatology in Hegel's absolute has famously been interpreted by Karl

Löwith as the realization of a heretical impulse whose time had finally come. "Hegel," Löwith writes, "completes the history of the spirit in the sense of its ultimate fulfillment, in which everything that has taken place hitherto or has been conceived is comprehended in a unity; but he completes it also in the sense of an eschatological end, in which the history of the spirit is finally realized. . . . [H]e pronounces the end of the history of the Christian logos."[18]

. . . After which, however, "the Logos" (to repeat, in quotation marks, a now anachronistic name) finds a new language, yet another expressive shape: meta-reflections on its own form as such at first, and then further experiments in and permutations of that form. For the bold discourse of Truth called metaphysics, caught in the circle of its own self-contradictory repetition, is dispersed in a myriad of metafictions from that alpha-point of self-understanding. Thus, in anticipation of Nietzsche's further revaluations of this post-apocalyptic legacy to be examined in the next chapter, we must first situate Hegel's "secular theology" within the history of speculative spirituality it occupies and appropriates—as an anticipatory repetition. This situation is twofold: ontological (or ontotheological) and linguistic. For subsequent to Hegel's proclamation of having achieved the standpoint of the absolute—an idea that orthodox theology cannot accept and that real history mocks—there remains (only) the performing utterance, an aesthetic fact, the first (but already repeated) instance of which the *Phenomenology* itself is.

1. Hegel and Joachim: A fateful syzygy (Löwith)

The so-called secularization hypothesis championed by Löwith and others has its opponents, it should be noted,[19] but the balance of scholarly opinion recognizes an essential, organic link between Hegel's metaphysical "knowing" and the revelatory impetus of Christian eschatology. It is uncontroversial, to begin with, that Joachimite ideas informed the radical Reformation[20] and that, more specifically, Gottfried Lessing's *The Education of the Human Race*—which evokes Joachim's "eternal evangel" in section 87, "The Three Ages of the World" in section 89, and the dubiousness of Joachimite prophesy in section 90—was known to Hegel.[21] O'Regan even affirms that "The Lutheranism reprised by Hegel . . . is a mystical Luther that has undergone something of a Joachimite contamination between the sixteenth and early nineteenth centuries" and that, "Morphologically, . . . Hegel's eschatological position more nearly resembles the position of Joachim than that of Lessing, and historically Hegel can be regarded as representing a deeper and more comprehensive retrieval of a tradition that bears a Joachimite stamp."[22] On this latter point Michael Murray concurs, noting that Lessing's "secularization" is "thinner" than Hegel's because it lacks an explicit concern with the Trinity and with an eschatological telos.[23]

Joachim's interpretation of history is, like Hegel's, compellingly teleological in character. In order to understand the past and present it becomes evident that one must know the future, since both the individual's and the race's fates are defined in terms of a future *telos*. Like a good dramatic plot according to Aristotle's influential analysis in the *Poetics*, meaningful history must have a beginning, a middle, and an end; as the ancient Greek proverb advises, "Call no man happy until he is dead."[24] And in Joachim's case, as subsequent developments were to make all too clear, the proverbial takes the form of apocalyptic prophesy. The world, Joachim suggested and those he inspired loudly proclaimed, had reached the threshold of the final dispensation: a life of divine contemplation could now become universal as the hierarchy of the church "effaces itself in the third age before the order of monks, the *viri spirituales*. The entire world will become a vast monastery on that day, which will be the resting season, the Sabbath of humanity."[25]

Joachim's scheme went far in making vast historical epochs of human striving seem intelligible, meaningful, fulfilled, but that his ideas had to lead in unacceptable directions is evident. The obvious incompatibility of the pure spirituality he described with the elaborate mosaic of power and wealth that was the church logically required the supersession of that now archaic institution. For prophesy based on a teleological narrative suffers from a peculiar paradox: we can understand the past only if we are in possession of a clear knowledge of its *telos*—that is to say, only if history is now over and we know its end. The intelligible, purposive eschatological pattern Joachim described was compelling only because the contemporaneous rise of mendicant orders seemed to correspond to the hoped-for end of a redeemed life close to God. As Löwith writes, the passionate followers of Joachim "attempted indeed the impossible: to realize the laws of the Kingdom of God without compromise in this *saeculum*."[26] For such heresy—which could not be reconciled with the orthodox Augustinian view that "the Kingdom of God had been realized, so far as it ever could be realized on this earth, at the moment when the Church came into being, and that there never would be any Millennium but this"[27]—Joachim's followers were cruelly persecuted, his writings and the writings he inspired burned.

Although Löwith is by no means the only scholar to have asserted that more than coincidence is at work in the parallels between Joachim's millennial eschatology and Hegel's *Aufhebung* of faith by reason,[28] in pushing the parallel further than others have dared he sketches a modern apocalypse in which Hegel plays "prophet in reverse" of the last dispensation to Nietzsche's Antichrist. Emphasizing the transcending moment of Hegel's final *Aufhebung*, Löwith argues that, since orthodox theology has failed in the task, "philosophy has to vindicate the Christian religion by demonstrating God's execution of his purpose in history."[29] The "cunning of reason" works to "translate theology into philosophy and realize the Kingdom of God in terms of the world's real history" (ibid., p. 58). Like Nietzsche, who praised the Greek gods for having provided the only satisfactory theodicy ever invented by living life themselves, Löwith insists Hegel's phenomenological dialectic demonstrates that "the history of the world is the true theodicy" (ibid., p. 57). Reconciling finite and infinite, immanent and transcendent, in the *Gnosis* of rational speculation, the here-and-now becomes Absolute: a consummation once devoutly to be wished is blasphemously achieved. But "the interpretation of history thus necessarily becomes prophesy" (ibid., p. 150),[30] and from it demons issue forth. While the Franciscan Spirituals had taken Joachim for a new John the Baptist, heralding Saint Francis as the *novus dux* of the last dispensation, Löwith hears in Hegel the echo of apocalypse "taken over five centuries later, by a philosophical priesthood"[31] which heralds the advent of *il Duce* and Hitler, the Third Reich and the Third International—a new dispensation whose uncanny spirit is incarnated in Nietzsche's flagrant usurpation and inversion of Christian values. Since the Enlightenment, those values had been losing their hegemony until, with Hegel's secular appropriation, the metaphysical power of Unity is loosed from its clerical bonds altogether—only to be seized by fascism, and wielded catastrophically, the enactment of a metanarrative alienated as far as possible from the soteriological divine. "The Joachite 'transition,'" writes Frank Kermode, augmenting Löwith's speculations with a similar conclusion, "is the historical ancestor of modern crisis."[32]

But how can there be any new crises after the end? If Time is a linear progression that concludes eschatologically, as Christian orthodoxy promises—but as Joachim heralds and Hegel finally realizes—then how is our present possible?

The answer lies concealed in the structure of Hegel's absolute, and it will be explicitly revealed in Nietzsche's idea of eternal return. The *Phenomenology* begins at the end, anticipating what is to come from the perspective of having achieved it, while the final chapter epilogically recapitulates what has gone before. We have already examined this curious circularity, but its significance as a philosophical legacy only becomes clear in the context of eschatology and its consequences—in the context, that is, of Hegel's own eschatological repetition. If Desire engenders the future, then Desire must be re-affirmed whenever it is threatened with satisfaction, for satisfaction has no future. The circularity of the phenomenological project, which begins as it were "again" and proceeds at every step guided by a vision of the end, implies a temporality of return, a cyclical process which makes every end a new beginning. This, too, is a heretical idea, and far be it from us, writes Augustine, to believe it: "The wicked walk *in a circle.*"[33]

But far be it from us, sings Zarathustra, to deny it: "*Doch alle Lust will Ewigkeit. . . .*"

2. Narrativity and Repetition: A textual resurrection (O'Regan and Murray)

We shift now—inevitably, in the wake of yet another failed *parousia*—from the domain of ontotheology to that of hermeneutics. By definition, apocalypse cannot be repeated, standing as it does at the teleological end of history and time; but Hegel repeats it nevertheless, as we have seen. It is natural as a consequence to withdraw ontological credulity from our engagement with what is variously, and in descending order of reverential valorization, called "Scripture," "Gnosis," "the Absolute," "the Notion," "the text." What remains to us—the revelation that however does not take place (to paraphrase Borges)—remains (only) as an *aesthetic* fact: from the conjunction of metaphysics and real history, we reap (only) metafictions.[34]

Hegel's absolute, being structured by Gnostic apocalypse, manages to evade the traditional Christian *Vorstellungen*, which it should properly overcome, by means of a subterfuge: opting for a heterodox model. Since the embracing of an eschatology of immanence carries with it the promise and burden of imm[a][i]nent realization, eschewing as it does the deferral of full revelation that is faith, we want to know how this was to have been carried out, after it, too, is read from a distance as yet another chapter in the history of Gnostic apocalyptics. Heeding Hegel's warning in the Preface—"we find that what in former ages engaged the attention of men of mature mind [den reifen Geist der Männer beschäftigte], has been reduced to the level of facts, exercises, and even games for children" (para. 28; p. 27)—we should also heed Michael Murray as he reasonably turns this principle upon itself, affirming that "this truth must be applied likewise to us late readers of Hegel; the *Phenomenology* itself enters into the past we recollect, and to which the 'Preface' alludes, so to speak, in retrospect."[35] Thus, we now need to see how Hegel is guided by narrative structures, intrinsic to the Gnostic ontotheology by which he was inspired, which, willy nilly, compose his text. For Joachim, the immanent *parousia* is hermeneutically revealed:

"Since Joachim accepts the two Testaments as the departure point, though not the end, for interpretation of history, that interpretation can immediately be seen as modelled on the interpretation of a literary work."[36] Even the sacraments are subjected to a realist reading that makes of them signifiers of historical actuality.[37] And Hegel's thought, as in Joachim's case, may be called "apocalyptic" precisely insofar as "vision or revelation is a function of a specific kind of hermeneutic (i.e., anagogic, futural) of scripture."[38] This parallel definition of "apocalyptic," linking Joachim and Hegel by means of their significantly similar strategies of linguistic and textual focus, is offered by Cyril O'Regan, whose research will decisively support and assist the interpretation developed here. How, then, do signs and symbols assume an unmistakably narrative structure by means of which Hegel's ontotheology presumes to transsubstantiate the concrete actuality of revelation into the medium of philosophical concepts?

First, given the context of a "strong analogy" between theology generally and Hegel's logic,[39] the heterodox "swerve" characteristic of Hegelian ontotheology[40] provides important clues that will direct our attention to the constituitive function of linguistic, and especially narrative, elements. Whereas traditional trinitarian discourse "gives unhappy testimony to the reifying activity of the understanding, which changes moments into entities and transforms processes into static relations between entities," Hegel's insistently developmental narrative impulse, O'Regan reminds us, "demands that the dominant be process rather than entity."[41] Indeed, although the tendency to affirm as immanent what tradition leaves as transcendent powerfully links Hegel with heterodox theologies that verge on the heretical, nevertheless Hegel criticizes "many so-called heresies" precisely for failing to do justice to the dynamism of philosophical understanding: "The resolution [die Auflösung]" of the impasse resulting from a speculative turn that "hypostatizes" the universal as "abstract" for the heretic, Hegel writes, "consists in the fact that Spirit is the Totality, and the first moment itself is grasped as first only because, to begin with, it has the determination of the third, of activity [Tätigkeit]."[42]

The difficulty, of course, is, as ever, one of expression, and the "resolution" to which Hegel alludes must ultimately be worked out linguistically. What is required is a form in which simultaneity and succession can co-exist without cancelling one another out—a repetition of the same impacted paradox that manifests itself historically in Hegel's repetition of heterodox ontotheology and formally in the anticipation of the absolute present already in the *Vorrede*. Traditional logical "syllogisms" are inadequate for this task, as we have already seen; the "speculative propositions" of philosophy must be employed in their stead.[43] But in fact, the revelation of the divine constituitive of Christian discourse encountered this problem too, even as the *Vorstellungen* of Christian *Logos* similarly fail to meet the challenge. Thus, the quintessence of Hegel's metaphysical project is located at, and arises out of, the very interstices separating—and uniting—the epistemological scruples of logic and the ontological ambitions of theology. O'Regan aptly summarizes the decisive *aporia*:

> Predicates are the best available discursive gestures for disclosing the divine, but, in a strict sense, all language and concept as finite is riddled with opacity and is forever surpassed by the reality it would name. Hegel, who makes much more ambitious claims for language as well as concept and thought, recommends a shift from understanding to reason[,] from *Verstand* to *Vernunft*, in which shift non-nominalistic predication of the divine becomes not merely possible but actual and the spectre of agnosticism—the subjective correlative of the evocation of the Unknown God—is exorcised.[44]

Hegel's attempt to carry out this "shift" is characterized by what O'Regan calls the "centrality of narrative, its perdurance in the logical space of the concept."[45] Although the alienated relationship between consciousness and the objectivity of Christian *Vorstellungen* is overcome by means of the special character of philosophical *Begriffen*, whereby the latter are shown to be united with—and, at one and the same time, markers of a determinate difference from—consciousness, nevertheless intelligibility would seem to presuppose that ground-consequent relations of some kind remain intact. After all, the simultaneity of the concept, for which there can be no before and after, no ordered sequence, would be incompatible with the nature of discursive understanding—hence, the necessity of Hegel's shift from *Verstand* to *Vernunft*. We have previously examined Hegel's exposition of the Notion as Time; it is in virtue of this conceptual *Aufhebung* of temporality that Notions are capable of recursively accounting for their own presuppositions, thus establishing the autonomy of philosophy as truly "presuppositionless science" beyond the threat of relativism.[46] But it is not yet clear what specific strategies are applied in Hegel's hermeneutics in order to accomplish what must seem to be an impossible, even self-contradictory synthesis of elements cognitively distinct yet ontologically united. "The issue is crystalized," O'Regan writes, "in the question whether narrative relations of anteriority-posteriority are dismantled in the elevation to the level of logical relations with their requirement of reciprocal determination."[47]

Indeed, a principle contribution of O'Regan's interpretation of heterodox influences on Hegel's ontotheology consists precisely in his

attempt to isolate and analyze what he calls "denarratizing operators," whose function is to "traject symbolization into the sphere of
the concept proper."[48] It is by means of these "operators," O'Regan
argues, that Hegel manages to preserve in philosophical form the
dynamism that drives the Christian narrative account of the divine,
thereby accomplishing a true *Aufhebung* of *Vorstellungen* in which
what is overcome is not abolished but rather raised to a higher level of
articulation. O'Regan's efforts are ingenious and illuminating of deep
structures within narrative as such, but he does not address the issues
of influence and continuity raised by noticing that the same strategies
are already evident in the traditional, orthodox theologies of Augustine and Aquinas. Thus, without by any means abandoning the claims
of a Gnostic tendency in Hegel's demonstrated affinity with heterodox
theology and the essential demythologizing of the divine consequent
upon it, the final lesson of the Hegelian usurpation will force upon
us—upon the legacy of Hegel's thought—a full realization of the linguistic turn which had long lurked implicitly within the structure of
the discourse of transcendence as the immanence of expression and
intelligibility.

The "denarratizing operations" that O'Regan identifies in Hegel's
text are divided into two "groups," the first consisting of three "operators," and the second of a single but more radical demand that stands in
need of a tactical resolution, which O'Regan also reveals. The first of
these strategies, the "antipunctiliar or antiepisodic operator" (exemplified by *Encyclopedia* sections 565 and 571), removes any temporal distinctions from descriptions of divine actions; specifically, terms like
"first," "then," "and then" are removed from the discourse by means of
its application. Functioning in a similar fashion, the second "operator"
"effects the erasure of contingency, deconstructs the language of happening and accident"; O'Regan cites *Encyclopedia* sections 1 and 9 as
instances. Rounding out this first "group," the third "operator" "erases
the tendency in representation to construe divine activity in terms of discrete acts of will."[49]

The more radical second "group" of denarratizing operators, consisting of a single member, and exemplified by *Encyclopedia* section
574, affirms that "a condition of the possibility of the move to *Begriff*
is the subversion of the narrative order of posteriority-anteriority"—a
condition, however, which would "amount to a radical destruction of
the narrative character of the Inclusive Trinity to which Hegel gives general support and endanger any and all claim that Christianity, albeit in
a highly swerved form, is the presupposition of Hegelian philosophy."[50]
The passage at the end of the *Philosophy of Mind* that O'Regan cites,
which elliptically proclaims that "science has gone back to its beginning:

its result is the logical system but as a spiritual principle," may seem scant textual support for so strong an interpretive claim, but these few words could easily be augmented by other passages from the Preface and Chapter VIII of the *Phenomenology*, which constitute instances of or moments in what Tom Rockmore calls "Hegel's circular epistemology," and which affirm that the end is already in the beginning.[51] In any case, O'Regan finds such an apparent abolition of temporality a threat to the central presupposition of Hegel's engagement with Christian theologoumena in general—a threat he cannot allow to go unanswered. And so, in response, O'Regan concludes his analysis of Hegel's "denarratizing operators" by rescuing the move to the *Begriff* from any thoroughgoing denarrativization!

This final hermeneutic feat is accomplished by distinguishing between what O'Regan designates "ontotheological structuralization" and "perspectival structuralization." The former, by suggesting that the "master religious syllogism" Universality-Particularity-Individuality (U-P-I) "can be broken and the terms made free-floating and susceptible to rearrangement," threatens to annihilate the determinate content of Christianity. The latter, in contrast, by suggesting that the different philosophical syllogisms PS1 (U-P-I), PS2 (P-I-U), and PS3 (I-U-P) "represent perspectives on the master religious syllogism, with only PS1 directly translating it," offers a discursive medium that would not destroy the content of Christianity but rather "represent different entrées into the shared narrative of religion and philosophy."[52] In effect, O'Regan attributes to Hegel's transformation of Christian *Vorstellungen* a "perspectivist" move strikingly anticipatory of Nietzsche's similar epistemological "operator," by means of which the "transvaluation of all values" will be carried out—a resonance O'Regan does not comment on and which we must set aside for now. "The upshot of all of this," O'Regan concludes, "is that, far from abolishing narrative, *Begriff* is a witness to its perdurance in a form that escapes, on the one hand, the inhospitable friendship of popular religious imagination and various classical as well as modern forms of theology and, on the other, the hospitable enmity of rationalism and atheism."[53]

However, such "denarratizing operations" in Hegel's ontotheology are not exclusively to be found in the heterodox context, despite the extent of Hegel's demonstrated swerve from traditional Christian thinking. In *The City of God*, for example, in one of several passages that resist the heresy of eternal return (Bk XII, Chap. 17: "What defense is made by sound faith regarding God's unchangeable counsel and will, against the reasonings of those who hold that the works of God are eternally repeated in revolving cycles that restore all things as they were"), Augustine admonishes:

He can act while He reposes, and repose while He acts. He can begin a new work with (not a new, but) an eternal design; and what He has not made before, He does not now begin to make because He repents of His former repose. But when one speaks of His former repose and subsequent operation (and I know not how men can understand these things), this "former" and "subsequent" are applied only to the things created.[54]

The problem of intelligibility with respect to expressing the nature of an active principle whose essence transcends time is faced squarely in these words, just as it is unambiguously affirmed that what O'Regan calls "antipunctiliar or antiepisodic operators" must be invoked ("this 'former' and 'subsequent' are applied only to the things created") when speaking of the divine.

Nor is Augustine the only precursor within mainstream Christian theology of Hegel's strategies of "denarratizing" the discourse of the divine. Although the theologoumena that make up the Trinity are central to O'Regan's interpretation, and although he cites *Summa Theologica* at least eight times in the course of his book, the opening pages of Aquinas's "Treatise on the Trinity" appear to belie O'Regan's dismissive claim that Hegel's "punctiliar critique also applies to . . . Aquinas."[55] In the first of five articles on "The Procession of the Divine Persons" (Q. XXVII), Aquinas writes:

As God is above all things, we should understand what is said of God not according to the mode of the lowest creatures, namely bodies, but from the likeness of the highest creatures, the intellectual substances; although even the likenesses derived from these fall short in the representation of divine objects. Procession, therefore, is not to be understood from what it is in bodies, either according to local movement, or by way of a cause proceeding forth to its exterior effect, as, for instance, like heat from the agent to the thing made hot. Rather it is to be understood by way of an intelligible emanation, for example, of the intelligible word which proceeds from the speaker, yet remains in him. In that sense the Catholic Faith understands procession as existing in God.[56]

Here intelligence, and particularly language, are offered as models of the sort of ontological medium in which narrative sequence and simultaneous "intelligibility" can coexist, as they are supposed to do in the divine—and in the *Begriff*.

That Augustine's discussion of the temporality of the divine should arise within what will be the quintessentially Nietzschean topos of eternal return, even as O'Regan's attempt to resolve the second "group" of "denarratizing operators" anticipates Nietzsche's "perspectivism," promises to be revealing: the ontotheological problematic that comes to a head in Hegel—but which had always already lain implicitly within the heart of "traditional" speculative metaphysics—ever more compellingly emerges as the special site with which the discontinuity of postmodernity will share its topography of rupture.[57]

The heterodox swerve from the tradition, however—not so much an exception that proves the rule as a more extreme and explicit form of the tradition's own essence—remains the crucial clue that leads us to this site. And once again, it is most vividly in Joachim that the ambiguous relationship between *Vorstellung* and *Begriff* qua narrative is prefigured.

In the Hegelian context, this instability can be read in the symptomatic ambivalence of O'Regan's term "denarratizing operations" in light of his governing conviction that there remains a "perdurance [of narrative] in the logical space of the concept": "narrative not only is tolerated by logico-conceptual space but is intrinsic to it," O'Regan insists, such that "it is not woefully inaccurate to think of Hegelian logical space as a kind of contracted narrative."[58] This formal equivocation may also be noted in O'Regan's persistent attribution of the *Bildungsroman* genre to the *Phenomenology*, whereby Hegel's text is described as a "narrative model" that "sums up for Romantic Idealism the ontogenetic and phylogenetic aspects of *human* becoming."[59] What Hegel demands of philosophy as the inheritor of the truth already imperfectly expressed in Christianity is nothing less than a new language[60]—but a new language that, far from being "denarrativized" and static, exalts narrative dynamism even as it proclaims the simultaneity of synthesis.

These same paradoxical imperatives drive Joachim's attempts to devise a means for realizing what he took to be the promise of Scripture—and "[f]or articulating this purpose a new language and new concepts need to be forged."[61] As Murray puts it, "Joachim's own work on Scriptures could be described as an effort to de-mythologize its language, that is, to translate into another and more adequate language what is said by the two Testaments."[62] This tendency to modulate the discourse of the divine in the direction of the sensuous and graphic dimensions of language is common to, even characteristic of, medieval theology generally,[63] but the radical turn it takes in Joachim is—like the radicality of his prophetic historicism itself—especially apposite in conjunction with Hegel. Reprised here is the very question central to this chapter as a whole: How can a formal innovation answer to an ontological problem? Just as the *Phenomenology*, after overcoming *Vorstellungen* by means of a re-inscription of the narrative impulse characteristic of that lower form of expression, concludes with a (mis)quotation (that is, a repetition, but with a difference) of Schiller's vivid poetic *Vorstellungen*, so Joachim turns decisively to images in order to convey the very simultaneity-in-differentiation the structural polyvalence of which is supposed to motivate Hegel's move to "philosophy."

I dare here only to speculate briefly on the curious parallel between Hegel's puzzling evocation of Christian images via the borrowed words that close the *Phenomenology* and Joachim's turn to figures and diagrams as "picture-thoughts" expressing various features of his system.[64] In particular, a pair of diagrams[65] show three consecutive interlocking circles, representing each of the persons of the Trinity and each of the respective epochal *status* associated with them; Joachim's adaptation of the Tetragrammaton, given as "IEVE,"[66] is inscribed upon these circles such that "I" appears within the outermost domain of the circle of the Father alone, "E" within the intersection of the circles of Father and Son, "V" within the intersection of the circles of the Son and the Holy Spirit, and "E" within the the outermost domain of the circle of the Holy Spirit alone. The narrative-conceptual unfolding of the unity of the Trinity is thus simultaneously represented as a sequence of discrete elements and as the unity of the single divine name—itself composed of parts (letters) which, however, as they name the un-nameable, are not sounded in the medium of time but rather comprehended instantaneously as a meaning.[67] Thus, the synthesis of unity and diversity, of sequence and simultaneity, which Augustine had despaired could be made accessible to human understanding, is here conveyed by means of a new kind of writing that partakes of both conceptual and pictorial elements. The "divine nature" of this new language, as the *Phenomenology* might be said to have subsequently described it, has the power of "not letting what is meant get into words at all" (para. 110; p. 89). At stake here is the very mystical union of *Sinn* and *Gestalt* which Hegel himself had evoked in verse years earlier: "Sense approaches the image of eternity, / wedding it with Form—[Dem Sinne nähert Phantasie das Ewige, / vermählt es mit Gestalt—]."[68]

3. Conclusory transition

Taking stock of the implications of these reflections, we find Hegel still wanting a resolution of the seeming paradox of time and eternity: the "mystery" of progression in the Trinity is repeated in the "dialectical shuttle" between concept and representation driven by O'Regan's "operators."[69] But this shuttle must cross borders into very foreign territory, where the same mechanism may not function, and it is not clear that it can ever arrive. "Metaphoric discourses have purposes that philosophy cannot serve,"[70] O'Regan admits; the bluster of Hegel's dynamic logic notwithstanding, a remainder—immediacy, revelation—remains.

This remainder is the germ of the romantic yearning for lost innocence, and not surprisingly it leads to speculations about the sensuous (and thus supposedly immediate) use of language in poetry as superior to the dead ossification of concepts. This was a path the very young Hegel, still in league with Hölderlin and Schelling and reading Schiller, had pledged himself to, and O'Regan refers to the text obliquely in proffering the claim that "the failure of standard versions of the Christian narrative point to a need for the construction of a mythology of reason that is, at the same time, a mythology for reason."[71] The text, however—the so-called "Earliest System Program of German Idealism" written in Berne, probably (but not certainly!) by Hegel[72] in 1796—is insufficient to justify the suggestion that the quaint notion of a "mythology of reason" is central to Hegel's later philosophical project. Indeed, his naive protestations about the originality of an idea that "so far as I know, has never occurred to anyone else" notwithstanding, Hegel there sketches an apt *précis* of the then-rampant literary romantic credo.[73] That timely desideratum of "mythologizing reason" requires the suspect lyrical alchemy of poetic diction (an awkward fact in the context of his mature thought which, however, Hegel unabashedly affirms in the "Earliest System Program" fragment): even religion can be a "mythology" only when its constituent *Vorstellungen* are artfully *narrativized*.[74] But, as Jürgen Habermas pointedly puts it, "Hegel begins to doubt the aesthetic utopia almost immediately";[75] already in the *Differenzschrift* of 1801 we hear no more of it, and the opening chapter of the *Phenomenology* dispatches the fantasy of romantic immediacy forever. Thus, to the extent that Hegel himself openly urged a regression to (a repetition of) poetic *Vorstellungen* in the name of realizing the ideal, he did so only as a youth; the adaptation of Schiller that closes the *Phenomenology* is not so much a retrograde step as the stumbling of a sleepwalker. In these strange final lines, Spirit becomes "he," the revelation of Spirit becomes "Calvary," and "he" sits on a "throne" of truth, actuality and certainty drinking from a "chalice" the *foamy head* of immortality ("*aus dem Kelche dieses Geisterreiches/schäumt ihm seine Unendlichkeit*")! The wine of the Eucharist has been transmogrified into beer, that most Teutonic of celebratory beverages, aided by the already achieved secularization of Schiller's lines and the audible echoes of the *Ewigkeit* which closes Goethe's archly Teutonic *Faust* (and which will continue to resound in Nietzsche's "*Alle Lust will Ewigkeit*" and Mahler's parting incantation in "*Der Abschied*": "*ewig, ewig . . .*"). It is a short step from this chalice "foaming forth" to Zarathustra's overfull cup of wisdom; no wonder that Nietzsche would ultimately complain "The German spirit is an indigestion" (*EH*, "Why I Am So Clever, sect. 1).

But a retrograde step is precisely what is here called for, a step back into the "free contingent happening" of history as the only possible source of truth or being for any given present. Between the demythologizing of the divine in Joachim, and the re-mythologizing of reason in Hegel, "the speculative becomes onto-theology *of history*." Murray, noting that "Joachim's concept of *transire* already contains the basic sense of Hegel's *Aufheben*," goes on to conclude:

> History becomes the mode of the being of the knower and at the same time what is known. So that the transcendent and the transcendental rather than being in opposition as eternity versus time come together in the conception of transcendence as history. From this it follows that speculative metaphysics must come to an end in onto-theology of history.[76]

The repetition of the figures of apocalypse at the level of philosophical thinking severs the metaphysical claim from its ground in faith even as it places its authority under erasure; uncovering this repetition "thus opens the way to personal perceptions of spirit that transcend recognized and accepted boundaries."[77] The proud philosophical pretension of speaking the Truth about the Real is revealed as just another metafiction, and "eschatology" thereby becomes a trope for the tradition of philosophy itself: it tells its own end by being parasitic upon the faith that such is possible! The highest and central questions of philosophy themselves exceed the limits of philosophical discourse; they are swallowed up in a whirl of repetitions. The sublime irony of Hegel's metaphysical accomplishment is thus a call for the abolition of philosophy with all its teleological hubris, and its resurrection in the very form of repetition itself, the content of which is history.

Going forward, beyond the "modern" transcendence of religious transcendence, requires the retrograde step of recognizing the anticipation of the same in what Hegel pretended to overcome by repeating, and thus of denying a superior place to philosophy—which loses its privilege when it is seen to share the same linguistic foundation, together with all its aspirations and aporias, as that which it would surpass. More, such a move will involve not the abrogation of history but rather its celebration, and its celebratory repetition. It remains only to learn how to make that retrograde step.

> *A few steps back.*—One, certainly very high level of culture has been attained when a man emerges from superstitious and religious concepts and fears and no longer believes in angels, for example, or in original sin, and has ceased to speak of the salvation of souls: if he is at this level of liberation he now has, with the greatest exertion of mind, to overcome metaphysics. *Then*, however, he needs to take a *retrograde step*: he has to grasp the historical justification that resides in such

ideas, likewise the psychological; he has to recognize that they have been most responsible for the advancement of mankind and that without such a retrograde step he will deprive himself of the best that mankind has hitherto produced.—[. . .] The most enlightened get only so far as liberating themselves from metaphysics and looking back on it from above: whereas here, too, as in the hippodrome, at the end of the track it is necessary to turn the corner.[78]

CHAPTER FIVE

Eternal Return:
Re-Telling the End

[W]hat finer achievement would there have been in my life than to write a work of great benefit to mankind and to bring the nature of things to light for all men? I do not, however, think the attempt to tell mankind of these matters a good thing, except in the case of some few who are capable of discovering the truth for themselves with a little guidance.

—Plato, *Letter VII*

Do as I do. Thus you also learn from me. Only the doer learns.
—Nietzsche, *Thus Spoke Zarathustra*, Part IV

There can be no doubt that Hegel's absolute has "failed": repeating the claims of Judeo-Christian ontotheology in the form of "philosophy" can no more realize the unity of the soul with the infinite than could the orthodox and heterodox discourses that had already attempted to "mediate the immediate" for a suffering, mortal humanity that thinks beyond itself. As we previously noted, Charles Taylor reports with neither surprise nor regret that Hegel's actual synthesis "is quite dead"; in an off-hand manner whose lack of gravity seems obtusely at odds with the significance of what he is saying, Taylor easily affirms that "no one actually believes his central ontological thesis."[1] And Fredric Jameson concurs with this judgment against Hegelian fundamentalism, insinuating further that the absolute has become something of a laughing stock: "the rhetoric of totality and totalization that derived from . . . the Germanic or Hegelian tradition," Jameson writes in a preface about postmodernism, "is the object of a kind of instinctive or automatic denunciation by just about everybody."[2] Even Robert Solomon, writing "In the Spirit of Hegel," devotes only five pages to the absolute in a book about the *Phenomenology* almost six hundred pages long, admitting that he finds Hegel's finale "philosophically unsatisfying," "empty," lacking in the revolutionary new content that had been dangled like a carrot before the nose of the eager reader.[3] It would seem that such a reader, a philosopher, a lover of wisdom, must have been crassly seduced by extravagant promises!

But if Hegel is Don Juan of the Mind, why are his seduced and cheated conquests so unruffled by the deception? Doesn't it matter whether or not we accept Hegel's conclusions? Or is it rather the case that philosophy "can afford us no guidance as to the next step to be taken at any time"?[4]

The great Scottish Hegelian J. M. E. McTaggart put it that way, but he did not thereby imply a criticism of Hegel for being impractical. McTaggart's insight into the irrelevance of questions about whether or not the Hegelian absolute—or any other philosophical ideal—is realizable in the here-and-now affords a glimpse of a new perspective on the meaning of philosophical ideals. Particular actions in the real world can only be guided by the "particular circumstances which surround us at the moment," since the ideal is "so enormously distant that the most perfect knowledge of the end we are aiming at helps us very little in the choice of the road by which we may get there" (ibid.). With great lucidity, but lacking the desperate note of apology that the collapse of Hegel's grandiose ambitions would seem to demand, McTaggart neatly formulates a post-Nietzschean Hegelianism:

> The result seems to be that philosophy can give us very little, if any, guidance in action. Nor can I see why it should be expected to do so. Why should a Hegelian citizen be surprised that his belief as to the organic nature of the Absolute does not help him in deciding how to vote? Would a Hegelian engineer be reasonable in expecting that his belief that all matter is spirit should help him in planning a bridge? . . . The use of philosophy lies not in being deeper than science, but in being truer than theology—not in its bearing on action, but in its bearing on religion. It does not give us guidance. It gives us hope. (ibid., pp. 195–96)[5]

It is the project of the present chapter to explore this "truer theology," which the unsatisfactory claims of Hegelian science left as the legacy of philosophy. Responding to the hopeful urgency of the question of value left unresolved by the pretensions of reason, Nietzsche's "countermyth" of Zarathustra provides just such a "gospel of the future" that proves to be decisively resistant to the empty repetition of disciples and other asses. Chastened by a mistrust of the universal utterance with its "divine nature," Nietzsche maintains a skeptical attitude toward truth; like the meaning/saying dialectic in "Sense-Certainty," he admits only the most tenuous leap of faith, founded in forgetfulness, to join these distinct spheres of being. But whereas Hegel claims to resolve the ontological alienation of mere propositions in the linguistic alchemy of a dialectical absolute, Nietzsche never pretends to achieve freedom from personal perspective. Nor does he expect a cessation of opposition, the engine of life and movement, especially in its familiar form of agonistic competition. Interpersonal relations, the place of the individual in society, and the proper role of pedagogy are defined, for Nietzsche, by a dynamic of perpetual struggle like the adversarial structure of master and slave, primal conditions for the exercise of the will to power. The dialectical inversion of the master's fortune is an Hegelian lesson which Zarathustra struggles until the end to come to terms with;[6] and failing the mystical recognition of a harmonious transsubjective *Geist*, the old sage finally returns to his solitude in retreat from his hearers (and readers), having tried to provide an example instead of a doctrine.

A process of *Bildung*, so irresistible to the nineteenth-century mind, is thus also apparent in Nietzsche's "teachings." Zarathustra first attempts to address a crowd of idlers gathered for an entertainment, but discovering that not everyone is disposed to learn from him, he seeks disciples instead. Readers who get further than the Prologue are in effect invited to join this select group of "higher men." But here again, a false Hegelian apotheosis is denied, and the truest student's final lesson closes the circle in the solitude from which Zarathustra's wisdom originally issued.

Whether or not Zarathustra succeeds in his pedagogical midwifery depends upon the extent to which the infants he delivers remain dependent on him—and for Nietzsche's readers, the key to independence is the eternal return. A mock-Hegelian metaphysic of time that makes "buffoons and barrel organs" out of unimaginative disciples who can only learn by rote, the eternal return is at once tragic in content and comic in form: tragic and heroic for him whose special cross it is to bear, but comic in the repertoire of truths held dear by would-be philosophers. For the eternal return is an absurd doctrine, "not even a point of view" as George Bernard Shaw's well-placed wit gaily rants: "It is an absolutely fictitious hypothesis."[7] But because of the place it holds in the explicit claims Nietzsche makes for his philosophy, its fictitious improbability serves an important role in the pedagogical *Bildung* of the Übermensch. If the *Phenomenology* is a ladder to a higher perspective, then it is dispensable, and Zarathustra courageously kicks it away—while demanding the same courage of those who would follow him. He bolsters that courage with self-mockery and laughter, but although they have been shown the writing on the wall by the jokester who put it there, and even though *Thus Spoke Zarathustra* ends with the worship of an ass, the higher men remain in thrall to the irreverent graffiti they take to be a gnomic god's script. Too few have understood the joke—and fewer still, appreciating the daunting challenge it implies, have dared to laugh.

PART I. AFTER THE END OF PHILOSOPHY:
THE PERSPECTIVE OF AN AESTHETIC ATTITUDE

1. Nietzsche contra Hegel

In favor of criticism.— Now something that you formerly loved as a truth or probability strikes you as an error; you shed it and fancy that this represents a victory for your reason. But perhaps this error was necessary for you then, when you were still a different person—you are always a different person—as are all your present "truths," being a skin, as it were, that concealed and covered a great deal that you were not yet permitted to see. What killed that opinion for you was your life and not your reason: *you no longer need it*, and now it collapses and unreason crawls out of it into the light like a worm. When we criticize something, this is no arbitrary and impersonal event; it is, at least very often, evidence of vital energies in us that are growing and shedding a skin. We negate and must negate because something in us wants to live and affirm—something that we perhaps do not know or see as yet.— This is said in favor of criticism. (*GS*, section 307)

A great deal is relevant to the task of interpreting this aphorism—in fact, more than the mere "rumination" (*das Wiederkäuen*) Nietzsche himself proclaims is demanded for artful reading.[8] Besides the worldly wisdom that speaks in these words, describing what everyone may observe in reflecting on his or her own development, there is also a wincing autobiographical reference to Lou Salomé and the only serious romantic involvement of Nietzsche's life, which occupied his correspondence and his thinking during the summer of 1882 while *The Gay Science* was being completed.[9] Although reductive from a literary critical point of view, the autobiographical dimension is of particular importance in Nietzsche's work; this has long been recognized, but only recently incorporated significantly into theory. And section 307 resonates with other passages in such a way that its aphoristic independence and isolation begin to dissolve in the larger contexts of the particular work and, in turn, the place of that work in Nietzsche's overall development. Thus, for example, the reference to "habits" (*Gewhonheiten*) which constitute everyday life in section 308 is a clue that encourages reading section 307 with 295, in which Nietzsche praises "brief habits" as "an inestimable means for getting to know *many* things and states."

This repudiation of final solutions, this Faustian preference for perpetual change which can never be permanently satisfied with the passing moment, which chooses danger over safety (*GS*, section 342), guessing over deducing (*TSZ*, Part III, "On the Vision and the Riddle"), suggests a methodology that is conspicuously anti-Hegelian in its bias. Dubbed "perspectivism" by Nietzsche's epigones, it is an attitude with which absolutes are incompatible; although the process of position and revision looks dialectical, it lacks the teleology which, as we have seen, implicitly constrains the movement of phenomenology.[10] Lacking any such explicit *telos*, Nietzschean *Bildung* leads to no definite conclusion (unless it be the acceptance of there being no conclusion); it is an education that is not and cannot be fulfilled in the mastery of a teachable truth. "What is novel about the position we take toward philosophy," Nietzsche writes in an unpublished note from 1881, "is a conviction that no prior age shared: *that we do not possess the truth*. All earlier men 'possessed the truth,' even the skeptics."[11]

Although direct references to Hegel are comparatively rare in Nietzsche's writing, he nevertheless makes it clear that Hegel is an important target when he practices the sort of "criticism" that rests uneasy with assumed truths. For all truths, not just those of the heart, have their origin and ground in personal prejudices, in the moralizing presumption of imperatives—even those that speak with the critical voice of reason. "Both tendencies," Nietzsche writes, "culminate in Hegel: at bottom, he generalized German criticism and German romanticism—a kind of dialectical fatalism, but in honor of the spirit" (*WP*, section 422; *KSA* 11, p. 531). The *enduring* philosophical habit of searching for truths solid and eternal as stone is twice mistaken: submission to "matters of fact" is already an unacceptable fatalism that becomes offensive in Hegel's "faith in the greater reason on the side of the victorious . . . his justification of the actual 'state'" (*WP*, section 95; *KSA* 12, p. 442).

The larger context of these objections is Nietzsche's sustained critique of traditional moral values, of moral valuation itself; the "genealogy" of such convictions, he discovers, reveals their roots in the dynamics of domination and servitude, and undermines our naive tendency to suppose that they are properly and impartially justified. "Let us not be deceived," he therefore urges, "either in the Kantian or the Hegelian manner: we no longer *believe* in morality, as they did, and consequently we have no need to found a philosophy with the aim of justifying morality" (*WP*, section 415; *KSA* 12, p. 163). Instead, Nietzsche allows himself a new perspective, gained by critical distance, on the rationalizing pantheism[12] of Hegel:

> Deeply mistrustful of the dogmas of epistemology, I loved to look now out of this window, now out of that; I guarded against settling down with any of these dogmas, considered them harmful—and finally: is it likely that a tool is *able* to criticize its own fitness?—what I noticed was rather that no epistemological skepticism or dogmatism had ever arisen free from ulterior motives—that it acquires a value of the second rank as soon as one has considered what it was that *compelled* the adoption of this point of view.

> Fundamental insight: Kant as well as Hegel and Schopenhauer—
> the skeptical-epochistic attitude as well as the historicizing, as well as
> the pessimistic—have a *moral* origin. (*WP*, section 410; *KSA* 12, pp.
> 143–44)

The details of Nietzsche's critical genealogy of moral valuation have
become less important than the epistemological lesson they imply for the
rather curious reason that it has proved to be far easier to accept the specific significance of the death of God than it has been to grasp its more
general consequences. "Concern" is no longer regarded as a sophisticated response to the collapse of the Judeo-Christian tradition: as Cornell West quips in his Afterword to the aptly titled volume of essays
Post-Analytic Philosophy, "The shock effect of Catastrophic nihilism is
now boring and uninteresting."[13] Nor is he alone in yawning before the
abyss: the "tiresome celebrity" Nietzsche has given to the death of God
implies, writes Maurice Blanchot, an analysis that "can no longer move
us, so familiar has it become. What would nihilism be? A mere humanism!"[14] And for Nietzsche himself, the advent of nihilism has a positive
significance: it heralds the exhaustion of the "moral interpretation of the
world, which no longer has any sanction after it has tried to escape into
some beyond" (*WP*, section 1; *KSA* 12, p. 126). Nihilism is thus the
necessary prelude to a "countermovement" of new values, to a "gospel
of the future," because "we must experience nihilism before we can find
out what 'value' these values really had" (*WP*, Preface, section 4; *KSA*
13, p. 190—see also the Preface to *GM* from the same date). Zarathustra celebrates the "last man": like a heavy drop of rain, his fall heralds
the lightning of the overman.

Although the Judeo-Christian God and his various attendant dogmas were already under siege at least since the Enlightenment, the most
pervasive and subtle form of the old faith, its most amorphous and
durable deity, is "truth" itself: the hypothesis that some ultimate reality
lies behind the polymorphous play of appearances. But Nietzsche
regards Hegel's rationalism as pantheist just because it represents a "will
to deify the universe and life in order to find *repose* and *happiness* in
contemplation and in getting to the bottom of things" (*WP*, section 95;
KSA 12, p. 443). "German philosophy," he writes in *The Antichrist*, "is
at bottom an *insidious* theology" (section 10). And ironically, it is the
moral valorization of "truthfulness" that proves in the long run to be
incompatible with a dogmatic belief in "truth"; the cultivation of truthfulness "eventually turned against morality, discovered its teleology, its
partial perspective—" (*WP*, section 5; *KSA* 12, p. 211). Nietzsche sees
his "perspectivism" as the inevitable historical consequence of moral
thinking turned inward on itself, as a step beyond the nihilism which
still longs for the certitude of absolute truths.

The epistemological conclusions of Hegel's dialectical examination of sense-certainty thus correspond to the premises of Nietzsche's perspectivism: contradiction implicit in the presumption that the truth of saying is unproblematically adequate to the meaning of being comes to light as a necessary consequence of its self-revelation through its own proper history. In a famous passage from the early unpublished essay "On Truth and Lies in an Extra-Moral Sense," Nietzsche traces out the discontinuous sequence of associations and relations that inevitably mediate for consciousness what was naively presumed to be immediately given:

> What is a word? A representation of a nerve stimulus in sounds. . . . A nerve stimulus is first transferred into an image: first metaphor! The image again copied into a sound: second metaphor! And each time there is a complete overleaping of one sphere, right into the middle of an entirely new and different one.[15]

As we have already seen, the alienation of form and content characteristic of sense-certainty is overcome for Hegel in the rational *Begriff*. For Nietzsche, however, any such resolution is doubly impossible: the evasive metaphoricity of language is, first of all, unreducible, but further, "reality" is itself always already appearance. The "divine nature of language," whereby meaning and saying are distinguished in principle, is here reinterpreted. As Paul de Man writes, "The metaphor does not mean what it says but, in the last analysis, it says what it means to say" because "not only is it the representation of an event and not the event itself, but the event itself is already a representation, because all empirical experience is in essence fantastic."[16] A quasi-dialectical "negation of the negation" animates this move, but with very different consequences: the "constructed" immediacy which results affirms above all its synthetic character, and Nietzsche admonishes all philosophers that "they must no longer accept concepts as a gift, nor merely purify and polish them, but first *make* and *create* them, present them and make them convincing" (*WP*, section 409; *KSA* 11, 486–87). Thus, the assumption of perspectivism follows from the exhaustion of values and the nihilism to which that exhaustion gives rise, while it implies a general imperative to create, to give voice to one's own perspective.

2. Regression to Vorstellungen: *The pervasiveness of metaphor*

From a formal point of view, Nietzsche's celebration of metaphor suggests a return to the *Vorstellungen* Hegel's conceptual absolute had supposedly superseded—a "regression" anticipated in the Christian image of the overflowing cup. The borrowed words from Schiller which close the *Phenomenology* evoke a "chalice" (*Kelche*) which "foams forth" to

"him" (*schäumt ihm*) whose Spirit is become absolute; as if consequently, the image with which *Thus Spoke Zarathustra* begins is one of
fullness and overfullness: "Bless the cup [*Becher*] that wants to over-
flow. . . . Behold, this cup wants to become empty again" (*TSZ*, Prologue, section 1).[17] And the association of *Vorstellungen* with religious
discourse is explicit in both thinkers as well, albeit with very different
rhetorical intent. Whereas for Hegel, the revealed religion contains the
same truth as philosophy expressed in an obfuscating medium, Nietzsche recognizes the persuasive power of religious mythologizing and
harnesses it for his own ends. Thus, although both philosophers affect a
superior posture with respect to religion, Hegel reveres the content Nietzsche repudiates while Nietzsche appropriates the form Hegel rejects![18]

Which is not to say that Nietzsche approves of religious mythologizing in any of its available forms: indeed, the theological habit of
devaluing the world of the senses meets with his fiercest invective. "To
invent fables about a world 'other' than this one has no meaning at all,"
he writes in *Twilight of the Idols,* "unless an instinct of slander, detrac-
tion, and suspicion against life has gained the upper hand in us" ("'Reason' in Philosophy," section 6). Unfortunately, philosophy, with its distinction between 'being' and 'becoming', is one of these available forms
of "monotonotheism" (ibid., section 1): since whatever becomes cannot
have being according to this antithesis, philosophers have blamed the
senses for the impasse. The senses can provide access only to appearances; accordingly, philosophers have looked elsewhere—in particular,
to Reason—when they quest for Reality and Truth. This is why Nietzsche regards Plato as the first Christian.

The senses, however, do not lie in making appearances available to us;
on the contrary, Nietzsche insists that "they do not lie at all" (ibid., section
2). Again taking up a position very much like Hegel's in the sense-certainty
dialectic, Nietzsche reverses the traditional philosophical valuations: "what
we *make* of their testimony, that alone introduces lies. . . . 'Reason' is the
cause of our falsification of the senses" (ibid.). It is only when sense-certainty is forced to speak that it speaks falsely about the immediate experience it means. But whereas Hegel proceeds from this starting point with a
promise to return to it, having made the long phenomenological detour
through Spirit's appearances in order to craft at last a language capable of
expressing the Real, Nietzsche refuses the "crude fetishism" of a supersti-
tious faith in the metaphysical presuppositions of language or reason: "I
am afraid we are not rid of God because we still have faith in grammar"
(ibid., section 5). "The 'apparent' world is the only one," he boldly proclaims; "the 'true' world is merely added by a lie" (ibid., section 2).

Although he thus praises the senses while he condemns philosophers for preferring "concept-mummies" to the reality of experience,

Nietzsche is not an "empiricist." For he also abandons the traditional habit of epistemology: the apparent world may be the only one, but that does not mean appearances "give" us knowledge. Rather, appearances are the stuff out of which *we make* knowledge; science and system represent uniquely human efforts to organize appearances into coherent schemas, but to pretend that these constructed and imposed orders correspond to some transcendent reality would be as foolish as to feign surprise at finding something behind a bush that one had previously put there oneself.

> Everything which distinguishes man from the animals depends on this ability to volatilize perceptual metaphors in a schema, and thus to dissolve an image into a concept. For something is possible in the realm of these schemata which could never be achieved with the vivid first impressions: the construction of a pyramidal order according to castes and degrees, the creation of a new world of laws, privileges, subordinations, and clearly marked boundaries—a new world, one which now confronts that other vivid world of first impressions as more solid, more universal, better known, and more human than the immediately perceived world, and thus as the regulative and imperative world.[19]

Nietzsche was uncannily true to this insight. Observing that the rational structure of the world results from the rationalizing activity of mind is not, in itself, un-Hegelian; indeed, Nietzsche admits that this second-order world appears "more solid" and "better known" than the vivid but mute plethora of sensations out of which it is built. However, the fact of intellectual participation in the constitution of that world signals for Nietzsche an emancipation from the constraints of any given reality: if the world is what we make it, if we are "artistically creating subjects" instead of passive observers of an already complete creation, then "A painter who wished to express in song the picture before his eyes would, by means of this substitution of spheres, still reveal more about the essence of things than does the empirical world."[20]

Hegel's "fatalism," the retrospective justification of the status quo in terms of the necessary historical development of emerging Spirit, is thus linked with Nietzsche's critique of nihilism. When "the highest values devaluate themselves," when "truthfulness" has progressed so far as to deconstruct "truth," then justification *is* rationalization: objective standards are no longer tenable and the rhetoric of values has lost all grounding. The apparent world is the only one, but appearances, constructed out of sensations by reason, are always already lies. "This antagonism—not to esteem what we know, and not to be *allowed* any longer to esteem the lies we should like to tell ourselves—results in a process of dissolution" (*WP*, section 5; *KSA* 12, p. 212). But this process of dissolution "is only a *transitional stage*" (ibid., section 7; *KSA*

13, p. 50); if nihilism means that everything is permitted, this is only because the authority of any particular doctrine of appearances has been undermined. "Such a spirit who has *become free* stands amid the cosmos with a joyous and trusting fatalism, in the *faith* that only the particular is loathsome, and that all is redeemed and affirmed in the whole—*he does not negate any more.* Such a faith, however, is the highest of all possible faiths: I have baptized it with the name of *Dionysus*" (*TI*, "The 'Improvers' of Mankind," section 49).

The creative affirmation of this "faith" has come full circle, redeeming the loathsome particular in the fullness and self-sufficient completeness of Dionysian rapture. But if we "have measured the value of the world according to categories *that refer to a purely fictitious world*" (*WP*, section 12B; *KSA* 13, p. 49), then it follows that we are now free to create new values even as we recreate the world. Only the "monotono-theism" that lies about a "true world" has been dissolved by nihilism; deconstruction is the prelude to reconstruction, and the death of God is a tragedy only for the poor in spirit who would remain children, who lack the strength to become fathers and mothers in their own right by making their own worlds. Nietzsche's "regression" to the dialectically superseded form of *Vorstellungen* is a retreat toward the immediacy of lived experience from the abstraction of concepts—a retreat which, however, fully recognizes the gulf between experience and our "knowledge" of representations. Reality is always already appearance and so, as De Man writes, "the detour through the metaphorical realm of appearances is necessary."[21] In place of meek acquiescence to a faith in given truths that has become unstable anyway, Nietzsche—"the first perfect Nihilist of Europe who, however, has even now lived through the whole of nihilism, to the end, leaving it behind, outside himself" (*WP*, preface, section 3; *KSA* 13, p. 190)—proposes instead the creative invention of a second childhood,[22] a return to the beginning where nothing is given, with a cheerful "aesthetic attitude" (*ästhetisches Verhalten*) that can reconstitute the world and its value as well.

> The true world—we have abolished. What world has remained? The apparent one perhaps? But no! *With the true world we have abolished the apparent one.*
>   (Noon; moment of the briefest shadow; end of the longest error; highpoint of humanity; INCIPIT ZARATHUSTRA.) (*TI*, "How the True World Finally Became a Fable," section 6)

3. No facts, only interpretations: The world is a kind of fiction

So *Zarathustra* begins only after the "true" world has become a fable—a starting point which corresponds to the methodological premise of Hegel's *Phenomenology*, for both celebrate language's "divine nature of not letting what is meant *get into words* at all" (para. 110; pp. 88–89). For Nietzsche, the nature of language is "divine" because it is creative: the world is not something passively observed, something simply available to immediate intuition, but rather the product of a creative *aesthesis*; even the "apparent" world is thus abolished insofar as we presume it to be simply given. As Alexander Nehamas has most tellingly argued, Nietzsche "looks at the world in general as if it were a sort of artwork; in particular, he looks at it as if it were a literary text."[23] Saying is always fictional, and Nietzsche's dictum "facts is precisely what there is not, only interpretations" (*WP*, section 481; *KSA* 12, p. 315 [see also *KSA* 12, p. 149]) could ironically stand as the motto for Hegel's intellectual *Bildungsroman*.

But if Hegel's premise and method accord with the spirit of Nietzsche's *ästhetisches Verhalten*, the dogmatism of his absolute conclusion emphatically does not. Compared with the optimistic Hegelian claims of universal finality that have so troubled devoted exegetes, *Thus Spoke Zarathustra* is a tragedy. The passage cited above from *Twilight of the Idols* is an intertextual clue that recalls the end of the first edition of *The Gay Science*, where the opening paragraphs from *Thus Spoke Zarathustra*, transcribed almost verbatim, are headed "*Incipit tragoedia*" (*GS*, section 342). The "book of the eternal return" thus begins with a repetition, a recycled conclusion, that is in tension with its own valorization of creative originality, and it ends with Zarathustra's rejection of his disciples, the "higher men," who have learned only to repeat, who blaspheme with devotion: the universality Hegel sought is anathema to Nietzsche. At the same time, however, the pessimistic resonance of "tragedy" is itself dissonant with an "*active* nihilism" that is "partly destructive, partly ironic" (*WP*, sections 14 and 22; *KSA* 12, p. 353 and 350). It is important to remember that "tragedy," as an historical art form, dates from the heroic pre-Socratic age; it expresses what Nietzsche, in *The Birth of Tragedy*, called "a *strong* pessimism" (Preface, section 1). Thus, whereas Hegel's Napoleonic optimism, deriving from the hubris of "absolute knowing," was undone by the inevitable advance of history, Nietzsche's ironic optimism springs from the positive historical potential of nihilism, from the rich compost of exhausted European decadence. And whereas the legacy of Hegel's dialectical heroism, culminating in the self-proclaimed Wisdom it was the philosopher's traditional task merely to seek, foreclosed on the future with the sterility of a spiritual Elba, Nietzsche's grim announcement of the death of God—like the funeral march in the Eroica Symphony—is not a tragic finale but rather a bold invitation to new invention, a formal iconoclasm that initiates a new way by burying the old.

Zarathustra is the exemplar of this new way. But if Hegel's apotheosis is stifling because it subsumes all possible subjective individuality within an historically terminal absolute Spirit, Nietzsche's anti-systematic iconoclasm is daunting for exactly the opposite reason. "Perspectivism" finally means that *every* perspective, including Nietzsche's own, is partial and ought not be privileged with impunity. The enlightened critical approach to Nietzsche which emphasizes the literary character of his "philosophy" must face up to its own consequences: an exhortation to create is not and cannot be a doctrine, and so a didactic engagement with Nietzsche's "teachings" runs obvious risks. "I have set up the most difficult ideal of the philosopher," Nietzsche writes in an unpublished note. "Learning is not enough! The scholar is the herd animal in the realm of knowledge—" (*WP*, section 421; *KSA* 11, p. 153). And when Nietzsche asks for readers who "ruminate" over his aphorisms in the Preface to *On the Genealogy of Morals*, he describes them as cows—hardly a favorable image in his allegorical menagerie. Just what, then, *is* Nietzsche trying to tell us? What sort of example does Zarathustra provide? Why is *Thus Spoke Zarathustra* a "tragedy," and what roles do irony and comedy play in defining the difficult pedagogical relationship between Nietzsche/Zarathustra and his readers/disciples? Finally, what will it mean for "philosophy" and "scholarship" if we heed this laughing soothsayer's admonition: "He shall be greatest who can be loneliest" (*BGE*, "We Scholars," section 211)?

PART II. DISCIPLESHIP AND ETERNAL RETURN

1. Zarathustra's "going under": Self-knowledge is deception

The question of originality, problematized for Hegel in the complex of problems arising out of the sense-certainty dilemma, emerges most profoundly in Nietzsche's writing through Zarathustra's struggle with the conflicting imperatives of discipleship and pedagogy. "With the characters [Zeichen] of the past written all over you, and these characters in turn painted over [überpinselt] with new characters: thus have you concealed yourselves perfectly from all interpreters of characters" (*TSZ*, Part II, "On the Land of Education")—thus spoke Zarathustra to "the men of today." But Nietzsche was himself a man of today, a palimpsest of signs and characters historically derived, which point to a concealed self that does not exist: "Are you genuine [echt]? Or only an actor [ein Schauspieler]? A representative [Ein Vertreter]? Or that which is represented? Perhaps in the end you are only a copy of an actor" (*TI*, "Maxims and Arrows," section 38). Heavy with the private burden of eternal return, Zarathustra wishes to share the conviction of his wisdom—but Zarathustra is also a mask, even as he badgers the men of today: "How should you be *capable* of any belief, being so dappled and motley [Bunt-gesprenkelten]—you who are paintings [Gemälde] of all that men have ever believed?" (*TSZ*, Part II, "On the Land of Education").[24] Zarathustra, the motley mask of Nietzsche's own face, is his most convincing disguise, and the words that cloak the "thoughts behind his thoughts," giving them a deceptively tangible form, are merely garments which still hold the imprint of an absent body.

Zarathustra's first gesture is one of abundance and generosity: "like a bee that has gathered too much honey" (Prologue, section 1) or a cup that "wants to become empty again" (ibid.), he is driven from the seclusion of his cave, where he has spent ten years "gathering honey." Having "gone over" at the age of 30—gone over man, spiritually and physically, into high mountains—Zarathustra is finally ready to "go under" again, to reverse the self-imposed apartness from man that began at that overdetermined age.

Zarathustra's "going under" is associated with the sun—that is, with a natural process full of mystery and grandeur. The descent to man is as inevitable as a force of nature. But "going under" also has an Hegelian echo: it would appear to be the antithetical movement of dialectic that opposes the all-important, forward-driving *Aufhebung*.

Correspondingly, then, Zarathustra's *Aufhebung* is his move to the mountains—thus, his initial retreat and his final return to seclusion. The honey-gatherer Zarathustra, going down to man overfull of wisdom, no longer seeks *himself*—his going under is a parody of Hegel's struggle between fundamentally equal warriors, and Zarathustra becomes a "stranger to himself" (that is, he *loses* self-consciousness) through contact with the mere "men" he encounters. Indeed, for Nietzsche self-knowledge is a *deception*, since there is no self to be known—only a collection of masks and attitudes; Zarathustra may be a "man of knowledge" in his cave, but in solitude he knows nothing of himself. The fiction of a substantial subject is the very ground for the urgency of imperatives to be original or "authentic."

The bee metaphor is a clue here; another intertextual reference, this time to *On the Genealogy of Morals*, sermonizes on the meaning of Zarathustra's metaphor:

> We are unknown to ourselves, we men of knowledge—and with good reason. We have never sought ourselves—how could it happen that we should ever *find* ourselves? It has rightly been said: "Where your treasure is there will your heart be also"; *our* treasure is where the beehives of our knowledge are. We are constantly making for them, being by nature winged creatures and honey gatherers of the spirit. . . . So we are necessarily strangers to ourselves, we do not comprehend ourselves,

> we *have* to misunderstand ourselves, for us the law "Each is farthest
> from himself" applies to all eternity—we are not men of knowledge
> with respect to ourselves. (*GM*, Preface, section 1)

Displaying his learnedness in the conventional way—by quoting
scripture (Matthew 6:21)—the self-revealed "man of knowledge" in this
passage quasi-Socratically admits to a *lack* of *self*-knowledge.[25] Learning
has always distracted him from life so that, sitting up startled and noting that the clock has just struck, he thinks back and tries to count the
hour, the "trembling bell-strokes of our experience, our life, our
being"—but alas, he (he says "we") miscounts (Preface, section 1).
Thus, the irony of claiming *any* knowledge if one does not first know
oneself complicates this passage with an unmistakable affect of self-con-
tempt, as if Nietzsche lamented his own unbreakable habit of—as it
were—"quoting scripture." To quote is to don a mask; as Zarathustra
will say: "Verily, you could wear no better masks, you men of today,
than your own faces! Who could possibly find you out?" (*TSZ*, Part II,
"On the Land of Education"). To speak is always to re-use words, to
place a foreign medium between the speaker and his own experience, to
render the uniqueness of that experience universal.[26]

But Nietzsche's irony runs to a still deeper level in these passages. In
criticizing the idea of an immediate, perspectiveless truth, it is not only
the naive certainty 'This' 'Here' 'Now' that succumbs to the retrospectively recognized inevitability of mediation; the naive self-certainty of a
simple 'I' is just as unstable. Where Hegel undermines this subjective
certainty by revealing the dialectical "trick of writing" that utters the
universal pronoun when the particular and personal is meant, Nietzsche—analogously but more elaborately—argues that the very notion
of a "subject," a doer behind the deed, is a confusion. It is "only owing
to the seduction of language (and the fundamental errors of reason that
are petrified in it) which conceives and misconceives all effects as conditioned by something that causes effects, by a 'subject,'" that we are
inclined to be persuaded by Cartesian sophistries. In fact, however,
"there is no such substratum; there is no 'being' behind doing, effecting,
becoming; the 'doer' is merely a fiction added to the deed—the deed is
everything" (*GM*, I, section 13). Nor is this an occasional or marginal
view in Nietzsche's work, as the implied irony of juxtaposing the
scholar's regrets about self-ignorance with this "refutation" of any self
to be known might suggest.[27]

The heaviest, but also the most hidden irony that haunts Zarathustra's apparently innocent bee metaphor thus implicates Nietzsche's oft-
repeated and polemically insistent critique of the subject *against* the possible quasi-Hegelian objection to solitude: that it is only from others that

we may come to self knowledge. Even if "It was only as a social animal that man acquired self-consciousness," there is in the last analysis neither self nor consciousness apart from the conventions of linguistic practice that emerge out of the need for communication by "inventing signs" (*GS*, section 354). Zarathustra "goes under" to others not to find the "self" hidden from him in and by the isolation of his cave—there is no "self" to hide or to hide from. Rather, he descends to man like the sun sets, like the overfull cup overflows, without a goal "unless the joy of the circle is itself a goal" (*WP*, section 1067; *KSA* 11, p. 611)—although he does not yet know this explicitly.

What he—that is, Zarathustra—*thinks* he knows, the (still incomplete) lesson learned from his miscarried attempt to speak to the crowd gathered to watch a tightrope walker, is that he must seek listeners not among the multitude, but only among like-minded "companions" and "followers" (Prologue, section 9).[28] "I am not the mouth for these ears," Zarathustra observes in witnessing his failure before the crowd (section 5); rather, amid the ripe field of corn that is man, Zarathustra "lacks a hundred sickles: so he plucks ears" in commencing the harvest of the overman (section 9). The "herd" is *hostile* to new and original ideas, to the iconoclasm of value-skepticism—a lesson philosophy learned from the fate of Socrates, and that Zarathustra learns from the "motley jester," who warns him that "you are hated by the believers in the true faith, and they call you the danger of the multitude" (Prologue, section 8).

2. The tightrope walker and the motley jester

Since this lesson, Zarathustra's "insight" into a "new truth"—a truth which the following four books of Zarathustra's speeches and adventures will test and finally reject—is recounted in an allegorical manner, some exegetical clarification is needed to reveal what is at stake in the project thus begun. Who are the tightrope walker and the motley jester? What have they to do with Zarathustra?

Textual clues suggest that both the tightrope walker and the motley jester *are* Zarathustra, the opposed "moments," as it were, of Zarathustra's exemplary self-overcoming. As a rope or bridge spanning an abyss between beast and overman (Prologue, section 4), as both the "heavy drops" that perish and the "lightning" of which such drops are the heralds (ibid.), Zarathustra is "the mean between a fool [Narr] and a corpse" (section 7): he is both and he is neither.[29]

The tightrope walker is associated with Zarathustra is several ways. First of all, the crowd to which Zarathustra addresses his first speech has gathered to see the tightrope walker's performance, and in fact, they respond to Zarathustra's words as if they were a mere introduction to the exciting spectacle: "one of the people cried: 'Now we have heard enough about the tightrope walker; now let us see him too!'" (section 3). Furthermore, at the end of this same section, the tightrope walker hears the crowd's laughter and, "believing that the word concerned him, began his performance." After the jester humiliates him and the tightrope walker falls, the crowd rushes for cover—and the body lands at Zarathustra's feet. Praising the tightrope walker for having made danger his vocation, Zarathustra finally takes responsibility for the corpse, promising to bury it.

But there is also evidence that links Zarathustra with the jester; indeed, the reader is first and most of all inclined to associate Zarathustra—who talks of surpassing and overcoming—with the jester's superhuman agility. And Nietzsche is careful to make this connection plausible. On his way out of town with the corpse, Zarathustra meets the motley jester, who tells him that he had "talked like a jester" before the crowd (section 8). And using the same challenging rhetoric with which the jester had threatened the tightrope walker, Zarathustra says of himself that he shall leap over those who lag behind: "Thus let my going be their going under" (section 9).

Nevertheless, the key passage, which discourages any temptation to identify Zarathustra with the jester (even in spite of clues that, contrarily, link him with the tightrope walker), follows the warning to heed Socrates' fate: before he vanishes, the jester threatens to leap over Zarathustra if he lags behind by staying in town (section 8). If "leaping over" is a trope for overcoming, and Zarathustra *is* simply the jester, then why is this a threat? Why is it not rather a promise of self-overcoming?

Of course, Zarathustra is *not* simply the jester: he is also the tightrope walker, and he has not yet overcome the corpse of his own dead self when he meets the jester. Zarathustra still believes he has an ethical mission in "going under": he is a bridge to the overman, not himself the overman. Even though this ethical mission is interpreted aesthetically—as jester and tightrope walker, Zarathustra wants to dance on the rope at this dangerous crossing—and even though he realizes that the scope of his mission is limited, that he must seek disciples instead of the multitude, he has not yet had nor come to terms with the "difficult thought" which will be "the climax of his whole philosophy."[30]

3. Eternal return as shibboleth for discipleship

Textual clues once again link Zarathustra's decisive insight to limit the scope of his teaching to a few disciples with what Nietzsche himself, writing of *Thus Spoke Zarathustra* in *Ecce Homo*, called "The fundamental conception of this work, the idea of the eternal recurrence, this highest formula of affirmation that is at all attainable." For the tightrope walker and the jester resemble the dwarf from the third book who, in "On the Vision and the Riddle," first tellingly formulates the eternal return.[31] The dwarf is called "the spirit of gravity"—citing an earlier passage, it is "through him all things fall" ("On Reading and Writing," section 1)—and the tightrope walker plunges even faster than his pole (Prologue, section 6), as though overfull with the spirit of gravity.[32] At the same time, the jester and the dwarf both whisper in Zarathustra's ear (although Zarathustra is wise enough not to believe everything he hears!), while the spirit of gravity is a devil who trips dancers ("On Reading and Writing")—a devil who is easily abolished by disbelief, as Zarathustra counsels the dying tightrope walker who had "long known that the devil would trip me" (Prologue, section 6). And Zarathustra abusively refers to the dwarf as "lamefoot" (*Lahmfuss*) ("On the Vision and the Riddle," section 2), the very same expletive with which the jester had taunted the tightrope walker (Prologue, section 6). But finally, and most significantly, Zarathustra carries both the dead tightrope walker and the dwarf on his shoulders, and both times he unburdens himself of tiresome seriousness with an important insight: he understands that he must not seek the herd-congregation of the old dead god in the Prologue, and he faces the new temporality of the eternal return in Part III, along with the increased difficulty of finding companions to share his insight: "It turned out that he could not find them, unless he created them first" ("On Involuntary Bliss").

The close relation between these two insights—their difference is really a matter of degree—will emerge from a close reading of the passages in *Thus Spoke Zarathustra* where the eternal return is explicitly at issue. Such attention reveals first of all that this strange idea appears indeed to be an attempt to come to terms with the relentless nihilation of temporal passage—even though, as Joan Stambaugh has observed, "Nietzsche never worked out a theory of time."[33] Rather than a theory, eternal return would be a "formula of affirmation," as the passage already cited from *Ecce Homo* suggests: The "it was" of time past, against which the will feels helpless, is "redeemed" for any will strong enough to affirm a life *in its entirety* in order to affirm the present moment; "it was" becomes "thus I willed it."

So perhaps the eternal return is a kind of redeeming categorical imperative for affirmative willing: "Act as though you had to relive your life innumerable times and wish to relive it innumerable times."[34] Or perhaps it is a clever denial of transcendence: If everything happens again in *exactly* the same way, in a profound sense everything happens only once, since distinction between occurrences would in principle be impossible. The attempt to justify the present in terms of some beyond would thereby be short-circuited.[35] Or perhaps the eternal return is the metaphysical aspect of the internal structure of the will to power: Expressed outwardly in a myriad of human practices, the inner essence of the will to power is the desire for eternity implicit in affirmation: "*Doch all Lust will Ewigkeit.*"[36]

Perhaps. But each of these views presupposes that what is claimed by the eternal return is plausible and at least potentially demonstrable, that it should be "taken seriously," as we say[37]—and this is by no means so obviously the case! The willingness to undergo an eternal recurrence of the same events is not a demonstration that the events of our lives actually *do* recur, and without such a demonstration the affirmative gesture is empty.[38] The majority of figures among the first generations of commentators, ignoring Nietzsche's own claims for its centrality, avoided this strange idea altogether—but the scholarly attention that has recently been lavished on it remains bound by the same hermeneutical conventions that forced earlier writers to turn away in dismay. The idea is indeed central. But it is radically subversive, too tough a nut for even the "higher men" to crack. The painful frustration of Nietzsche's solitude, like Zarathustra's final return to his cave, demonstrates no less dramatically than does the subsequent misappropriation of Nietzsche's words by rabid nationalists, fascists, anti-semites and other dangerous madmen that the Wisdom philosophy had traditionally promised to teach us, the Wisdom which Hegel claimed to have achieved, is incommunicable.[39]

This is not to say that there is no wisdom in philosophy, nor that pedagogy is pointless. Indeed, the very opposite turns out to be the case. The wisdom of philosophy is an on-going activity, never concluded in an absolute of finite textual dimensions. The philosopher is a teacher because his wisdom is a way of life which above all values learning and thinking: since these express themselves in speaking and writing, they naturally involve others. Moreover, even if it sounds like a silly ditty in anyone else's repertoire than Zarathustra's, eternal return nevertheless "affirms the return, the rebeginning, and a certain kind of reproduction that preserves whatever comes back."[40] Derrida, whose repertoire is as full of silly ditties as that of any of Nietzsche's progeny, boldly underlines how that duplicitous "doctrine" empowers Zarathustra, the *Lehrer*, "to found new institutions"[41]—even as, like his teacher, Derrida himself protests "I do not teach truth as such" by inviting his readers merely to learn "a certain pleasure in this" from him.[42]

In the last analysis, the philosopher can *only* provide an example: "Do as I do. Thus you also learn from me. Only the doer learns" (*TSZ,*

Part IV, "The Ugliest Man"). And since to rest content with receiving concepts as a gift (*WP*, section 409; *KSA* 11, pp. 486–87) is not what Zarathustra *does*, as a teacher he must finally withdraw his influence from students who have only learned to repeat his words.

What remains for us, then, is to witness what occurs when Zarathustra attempts to communicate his heaviest and hardest thought. From its origins in a passionate desire for redemption from the pessimism and nihilism of metaphysical disillusionment, eternal return receives its first complete formulation in "On the Vision and the Riddle." There it begins to take on the tragic weight of a personal crisis for Zarathustra, the gravity of which again throws into question the very possibility of sharing the burden with others. But Zarathustra finally overcomes the incommunicable depths of night that twice reduce him to silence and deathly despair—with laughter! That his profoundest truth should become, in the mouths of others, a mere "ditty for buffoons and barrel organs" would appear to be a cruel irony for such a devoted teacher. The tragic subjective content of Zarathustra's "vision of the loneliest" is irreverently mocked by its comic objective form, and the prophet of the urgently new is at last overwhelmed by the eternal repetition of his own truths in the litanies of high men and dwarfs, asses, eagles, and serpents—in short, by the empty recapitulation of a motley multitude of disciples intoning a self-parodic absolute. But, to the extent that Zarathustra's real students are Nietzsche's readers, the paradoxical success of his pedagogy—disciples who quote him accurately in defense of their regression to rituals of deification—works the narrative effect of overcoming the self-indulgent sentimentality of romantic pathos with heroic affirmation. Nietzsche had always been drawn to that pre-Socratic vitality that produced tragedies out of courage and strength; at the same time, he lately became aware that the paradigm of tragedy still (or already) involved the decadent desire to justify the world. With Zarathustra, the affirmative spirit of the young philologist who once struggled to recuperate tragedy for an ethos he had in truth already outgrown finally overcomes his own *ressentiment*, the demon of his own anachronism, the corpse of his own dead self—with laughter!

4. Beyond metaphysical solace: Redemption from the spirit of revenge

In section 7 of the belated "Attempt at a Self-Criticism" appended to *The Birth of Tragedy* as a new preface in 1886, Nietzsche writes: "How now? Is your pessimists' book not itself a piece of anti-Hellenism and romanticism, not itself something 'equally intoxicating and befogging,' in any case a narcotic, even a piece of music, *German* music?" The question is severely posed: by 1886, Nietzsche had become suspicious of the traces of romanticism still evident in his own efforts—most conspicuous in that first book from 1872—to redeem the misery and futile finitude of merely human life with some other formula than Christian other-worldliness or Schopenhauerean pessimism. The exchange of art for religion was supposed to rescue metaphysics from nihilism—this, as the young antiquarian Nietzsche had tried to argue, is precisely why Greek drama affects us so profoundly, and why Wagner's music achieves a more authentic Hellenism than can the tedious philological pedantry of academic classicists.

But after the advent of Zarathustra, the search for a "metaphysical solace" (*metaphysiche Trost*) to supplant no longer timely alternatives seems naive. Quoting from his own earlier text, Nietzsche ridicules the quaint urgency of his late romantic quest for an "art of metaphysical comfort":

> "Would it not be *necessary*?"—No, thrice no! O you young romantics: it would *not* be necessary. But it is highly probable that it will *end* that way, that you end that way—namely, "comforted," as it is written . . .—in sum, as romantics end, as *Christians*. (*BT*, Preface, section 7)

The aesthetical ethic proposed in *The Birth of Tragedy* represents, according to Zarathustra, a flight from suffering into Wagnerian indulgence, a metaphysical escapism: "Drunken joy the world once seemed to me" (*TSZ*, Part I, "On the Afterworldly"). The emphasis on embodiment, on passion and frenzy, even the celebration of Dionysus, was rooted in an adolescent soul furious with rebellion and reaction. Even if the impulse to break free of the tradition intervening between antiquity and modernity is fundamentally sound, the last recourse to modernist aestheticism—just as much as the fashionable fetishizing of Greek dramatic heroism—still clung superstitiously to temporality and its bad conscience.[43] "A new will I teach men: to *will* this way which man has walked blindly, and to affirm it, and no longer to sneak away from it like the sick and decaying" (ibid.). As formulas for affirmation of what is *as such*, romanticizing, poetizing, and theologizing are all repudiated as idealizing fantasies in bad faith, born of *ressentiment*, of a spirit of revenge against the suffering of embodiment. That man "*be delivered from revenge*, that is for me the bridge to the highest hope, and a rainbow after long storms" (*TSZ*, Part II, "On the Tarantulas").

And so, the eternal return is first formulated for Zarathustra in terms of a redemption from revenge, although it is no longer merely embodiment that pricks the will. Having learned an affirmative attitude by studying his own strength in solitude, Zarathustra has mastered the future—but since this attitude had to be learned, he remains at the mercy of his own past. The small man and the last man are part of the past of the overman; man must be in order to become overman—and, as Zarathustra will lament in his darkest hour, "the small man recurs eternally!" This is a vexing fact which can lead the will into fits of *ressentiment*, seeking metaphysical solace, so it must be resolved.

> To redeem those who lived in the past and to recreate all 'it was' into a 'thus I willed it'—that alone should I call redemption. . . . Willing liberates; but what is it that puts even the liberator himself in fetters? 'It was'—that is the name of the will's gnashing of teeth and most secret melancholy. Powerless against what has been done, he is an angry spectator of all that is past. The will cannot will backwards. (*TSZ*, Part II, "On Redemption")

After a brief sketch of the sorts of folly that a spirit of revenge is liable to (the moral order of guilt and punishment, for example, is among these "fables of madness"), Zarathustra finally describes the redemption of a retrospective affirmation that implies eternal return—for 'it was' can become 'thus I willed it' only if 'it' will be again.

> I led you away from these fables when I taught you, "The will is a creator." All 'it was' is a fragment, a riddle, a dreadful accident—until the creative will says to it, "But thus I will it; thus shall I will it." (ibid.)

This is no mere reconciliation with the past, no poisonous compromise; "that which is the will to power must will something higher than any reconciliation" (ibid.). Before he falls silent, Zarathustra anticipates his hardest thought by acknowledging the hardest of tasks: willing backwards. But even here, before eternal return is quite explicit, its very invocation paradoxically silences him. Quite suddenly, and marked by a break in the text, Zarathustra cannot go on. Dazed and appalled (*äußerste erschrickt/mit erschrecktem Auge*) at first, evidently at the portent of his own words, Zarathustra soon masters himself with a laugh and, turning to his disciples, he says "It is difficult to live with people because silence is so difficult. Especially for one who is so garrulous."

What he means by this ambiguous remark is clarified by the brief exchange that ends the speech "On Redemption." Throughout, Zarathustra's audience had been composed of his disciples as well as "cripples and beggars" (*Krüppel und Bettler*), one of whom is an inquisitive hunchback. This creature, who originally had proposed that Zarathustra might well heal cripples if he wished to win followers, at last asks him: "But why does Zarathustra speak otherwise to us than to his disciples?" Of course, all that Zarathustra has said was addressed to both his disciples and the cripples—with the exception of his confession that it is hard to live with people "because silence is so difficult." Perhaps it is easier to speak to cripples than to disciples? In any case, it is *possible* also to speak with hunchbacks "in a hunchbacked way" (*"Mit bucklichten darf man schon bucklicht reden!"*); as the hunchback himself rephrases it, "one may well tell pupils tales out of school." The problem is, when it comes to eternal return, Zarathustra's speech is *always* "crooked," as will be that of the attempts of others to guess his thought. "But why does Zarathustra speak otherwise to his pupils than to himself?" the hunchback finally asks. He gets no answer.

5. Zarathustra's account of eternal return: A tale for adventurers only

Part III of *Thus Spoke Zarathustra* presents Zarathustra's struggle to face the thought of eternal return as the "heaviest and hardest burden." Going under to this thought requires a plunge into grim abysses even deeper than those where man dwells—to which Zarathustra had already descended in Part I and where he had loitered throughout Part II. His "going under" will be completed at greater depths, for the heights wax with the depths: "'Whence come the highest mountains?' I once asked. Then I learned that they come out of the sea. . . . From unfathomable depths the highest must rise to its heights" (*TSZ*, Part III, section 1, "The Wanderer"). Although Part III ends with the affirmation of eternity, it begins with heavy foreboding in the "deepest depths" where dwells a "sleeping monster"; and so "soon it happened that he who had laughed wept: from wrath and longing Zarathustra wept bitterly." (ibid.)[44]

What is most striking about the initial rhetoric of Part III is what Heidegger calls its "oppressive" (*Trostlos*) quality: the eternal return which appears in the form of *die grösste Schwergewicht* is anything but a metaphysical solace! Mobilizing metaphors of the deep blue sea and exalted mountain heights, Nietzsche further characterizes the landscape of eternal return in terms of sensuous extremes united in a profound thought: "Peak and abyss—now they are joined together" (ibid.) in an intelligible synthesis of opposites about which Zarathustra is finally preparing to speak directly.[45] Heidegger is an astute reader here when he urges that Nietzsche's use of sensuous imagery in setting the stage for the "revelation" of eternal return is employed deliberately and significantly. "Figures of speech," Heidegger writes, "more directly than other utterances, treat of the thought of eternal return" and, citing Nietzsche's own words from an unpublished note, "The more abstract the truth that one wishes to teach is, the more one must begin by seducing the senses to it."[46] It would seem, then, that in the quest for the faintly Hegelian thought that would span peak and abyss, Nietzsche favors sensuous, metaphorical language to the abstract rigor of the concept. *Vorstellungen* are programatically privileged (once again?) over the supposed rational universality of the *Begriff*. The more "abstract" the truth, the more sensuously concrete the language in which it is to be expressed. What kind of "abstraction" can this be which begins with a sensuous seduction? And to what end does it lead, having thus begun?

Nietzsche's first move, which we have already anticipated, recuperates "tragedy" from the decadent abstraction of late-Greek theorizing, restoring to it the sensuous and passionate immediacy of affirmation. Aristotle's famous claim in the *Poetics* that tragedy accomplishes a "catharsis" of the "depressive" effects of terror and pity is, according to Nietzsche, simply false. "One can refute this theory in the most cold-blooded way," he insists: "tragedy is a *tonic*" (*WP*, section 851; *KSA* 13, pp. 409–10). The tragedy that begins when we think eternal return (*"Incipit tragoedia,"* *GS*, section 342), the tragedy that follows the abolition of both true and apparent worlds and which is played out in *Thus Spoke Zarathustra* ("INCIPIT ZARATHUSTRA," *TI*, "How the 'True World' Finally Became a Fable"), is consistent with that art form which the healthy pre-Socratic Greeks had practiced so successfully as well as with the "active nihilism" which characterizes "the tragic age of Europe" analyzed in unpublished notes from 1887 and 1888 collected at the beginning of *The Will to Power*.[47] Revalued through the affirmative activity of art—"'*the* metaphysical activity' of 'life'"—tragedy appears as "the highest form of affirmation that can ever be achieved" because it heroically affirms the uttermost 'no' of despair and death.[48] "It is the *heroic* spirits who say Yes to themselves in the midst of tragic cruelty: they are hard enough to experience suffering as a *pleasure*" (*WP*, section 852; *KSA* 12, p. 556). Zarathustra's "tragedy" began with his heroic "going under"—the old saint in the forest whom Zarathustra met in the Prologue is not courageous enough for that. And only courage defeats the depressive spirit of gravity: "courage is the best slayer, courage which attacks," courage "which slays even death itself" in affirming eternal return ("On the Vision and the Riddle," section 1).

Having thus re-interpreted tragedy at least since his first published book, Nietzsche's portentous rhetoric at the beginning of Part III sets the stage for what promises to be an important event in the life of Zarathustra. The reader is prepared for a tragedy of great depth—that is to say, for a springboard to great heights. And in fact, in describing his "vision" to the dwarf, the spirit of gravity whom he has made curious with his own grave self-possession, Zarathustra offers the only account of eternal return we will ever get from his lips—an account which plunges him vertiginously into a horrible hallucination, the darkest riddle of his career, an abyss like a nightmare from which it will prove difficult to wake.

When he does recover, Zarathustra will be different; a new and unbridge-able gulf will have isolated him from even the creatures who have tried hardest to understand him, and through the inaccessibility of his silence he will teach a last lesson which none of his disciples have ears to hear.

Having gone down to the sea, embarking from "the blessed isles" on a ship manned by bold and adventuresome sailors, Zarathustra is finally encouraged to relate "the riddle that I *saw*" by stories he hears around him, "For there was much that was strange and dangerous to be heard on this ship."[49] It is significant that Zarathustra finds the courage and motive to break his silence among others who are telling their own tales: in such company he may fairly expect that his strange story will not be misconstrued as a doctrine of truth for others to follow. What counts as truth in such tales is no more than that they are *mine*—and "my" truths, whoever "I" am, are not Zarathustra's. The "divine nature of language," as we have already seen, protects what is most mine with the deceptive screen of universality.

And so, Zarathustra tells of how he had been climbing a stony and bleak mountain path, forcing himself up against a gloominess in which everything oppressed him, until finally his courage challenged the spirit of gravity—"although he sat on me, half dwarf, half mole, lame, mak-ing lame, dripping lead into my ear, leaden thoughts into my brain." Once again, the ear is a problematic organ: too easily seduced by Ger-man music and metaphysics, the passivity of listening runs very great risks. Even Zarathustra is vulnerable to the impressive gravity of that tradition, to the subterranean profundity of the scholarly mole.[50]

But he masters his courage, and challenges the grim dwarf/mole to a duel of gravity suspended over an abyss. "Stop, dwarf," Zarathustra commands. "It is I or you! But I am the stronger of us two: you do not know my abysmal thought. *That* you could not bear!" Zarathustra then describes to the dwarf his vision of the gateway Moment—in fact, a vision within a vision, since Zarathustra is also relating these "thoughts behind his thoughts" to sailors.

> Behold . . . this moment! From this gateway, Moment [Augenblick], a long, eternal lane leads *backward*: behind us lies an eternity. Must not whatever *can* walk have walked on this lane before? Must not what-ever *can* happen have happened, have been done, have passed by before? And if everything has been there before—what do you think, dwarf, of this moment? Must not this gateway too have been there before? And are not all things knotted together so firmly that this moment draws after it *all* that is to come? Therefore—itself too? . . . [M]ust not all of us have been there before? And return and walk in that other lane, out there, before us, in this long dreadful lane—must we not eternally return?

Although the dwarf has offered that Zarathustra's vision means "All that is straight lies," all "truth is crooked; time itself is a circle," he is rebuked for making things too easy on himself (*"mache dir es nicht zu leicht!"*). In other words, since the account of the gateway Moment *could* be characterized briefly in the dwarf's words, Zarathustra's anger is ambiguous. But in any case, the dwarf does not get a second chance, for the scene suddenly changes when Zarathustra's attention is caught by the howling of a dog. "Had I ever heard a dog howl like this?" he asks himself urgently. "My thoughts raced back. Yes, when I was a child, in the most distant childhood: then I heard a dog howl like this."

This ominous reverie breaks the spell cast by dwarf and gateway, leading Zarathustra precipitously into a vision of horror. "Where was the dwarf gone now? And the gateway? And the spider? And all the whispering? Was I dreaming, then? Was I waking up?" Lost in ephemeral nightmares and vertiginous uncertainty, in an epistemological limbo, Zarathustra goes on to tell of the heavily symbolic culminating vision that had taken the place of dwarf and gateway:

> A young shepherd I saw, writhing, gagging, in spasms, his face distorted, and a heavy black snake hung out of his mouth. Had I ever seen so much nausea and pale dread on one face? He seemed to have been asleep when the snake crawled into his throat, and there bit itself fast. My hand tore at the snake, and tore in vain; it did not tear the snake out of his throat. Then it cried out of me [Da schrie es aus mir]: "Bite! Bite its head off! Bite!" Thus it cried out of me—my dread, my hatred, my nausea, my pity, all that is good and wicked in me cried out of me with a single cry.

Zarathustra's cry is effective, and a transformation takes place. Biting off the snake's head "with a good bite" and spewing it far away, the shepherd leaps up as one reborn: "No longer shepherd, no longer *human*—one changed, radiant, *laughing*." Having challenged his audience to guess the riddle of *this* vision, "On the Vision and the Riddle" concludes with a hopeful new ambition: "My longing for this laughter gnaws at me; oh, how do I bear to go on living! And how could I bear to die now!"

Who is the shepherd in Zarathustra's vision? What is the meaning of the riddle? These are questions which need to be asked, surely—just as it was important to ask about the jester (another motley fellow!) and the tightrope walker. But it is beginning to appear that answers such as "all interpreters of characters" might give somehow miss the point. Heidegger, for example, identifies the "thick black snake" as the "counter-image" of Zarathustra's pet, the friend of his eagle, insisting that eternal return always is capable of the antithetical valuations of nihilism and freedom. The thick black snake, then, "represents" nihilism; in "The Convalescent," Zarathustra says "The great disgust with man—*this* choked me and had crawled into my throat" ("disgust with man" is one of the ways Nietzsche describes nihilism in the *Nachlaß*—it is an "active nihilism" because it leads to the urge to go beyond man [*WP*, section 22; *KSA* 12, pp. 350–51]). So Heidegger reasonably asserts "it becomes transparently clear that the young shepherd is Zarathustra himself,"[51] and again "The Convalescent" seems to confirm this reading when Zarathustra describes how "that monster crawled down my throat and suffocated me. But I bit off its head and spewed it out." On the other hand, such suggestions may set us to wondering instead about the heavy-handed symbolism of snakes and shepherds, pausing perhaps at such curiosities as the "Ouroboros," the mythical serpent that eternally regenerates itself by devouring itself. Does the shepherd bite himself free of eternity? But *"alle Lust will Ewigkeit."* Perhaps the shepherd bites himself free of the bite of eternity, the old rancor against time? Or yet again, perhaps it is a battle for power and the power to create that is played out in this allegory; as Eliade warns, "snakes and dragons are nearly everywhere identified with the 'masters of the ground,' with the autochthons against whom the newcomers, the 'conquerors,' those who are to form (i.e., create) the occupied territories, must fight."[52] And Freud—how can one fail to think of Freud when shepherds are swallowing thick black snakes! So, a feeling of futility sets in whenever some particular interpretation of this vertiginously overwrought "vision" is offered. "In short, as the proverb of Zarathustra says, 'What does it matter?'" (*TSZ*, Part IV, "The Drunken Song," section 1).

6. The failure of Zarathustra's disciples: Eternal return as rote repetition

The rest of *Thus Spoke Zarathustra* is about this futility, about the impossibility of interpreting Zarathustra's vision and the falseness of its truest meaning—eternal return—in the mouths of anyone but Zarathustra himself. "The inadequacy of Zarathustra's disciples," Stanley Rosen writes, "is an enduring theme of the book."[53] His profoundest teaching, the central doctrine of Nietzsche's whole philosophy, becomes a "hurdy-gurdy song" and a mere ditty for "buffoons and barrel organs" when anyone, dwarf or disciple, pretends to understand it. Disciples, too, though they have ears to hear, turn out (like the "inverse cripple") to have little else, and in their master's absence they regress at last to deification, devotion, and even plagiarism, worshiping the one among them with the biggest ears and justifying themselves with Zarathustra's own faithfully remembered words.[54]

Although the episode with the dwarf has already raised the question of the intelligible content of eternal return, it is not too difficult to imagine that the dwarf has a bad attitude, or is simply too dense to understand, even though he can repeat the appropriate words. In fact, Zarathustra admonishes the dwarf "it was I that carried you to this *height*" ("On the Vision and the Riddle")—understanding eternal return is attained not by listening, but by climbing. "If you would go high, use your own legs," Zarathustra recommends in Part IV. "Do not let yourself be carried up; do not sit on the backs and heads of others. . . . You creators, you higher men! One is pregnant only with one's own child" ("On the Higher Man," sections 10, 11). Curiously, then, repetition (and thus, originality) is just what eternal return problematizes:[55] is knowledge recollection and repetition—or spontaneous, even if not autonomous, creation? Is it wise, or even really possible, to learn and teach someone else's truths? Is it even possible to believe in one's own—how should one be capable of belief anyway, being so dappled and motley, a montage of other people's beliefs?

Well, a dwarf is a dwarf (although this one is also a mole), but Zarathustra's animals have a more exalted stature. At the Prologue's end the serpent is eulogized as avatar of wisdom, the eagle as winged pride; unlike the dwarf, and unlike even the highest of men, Zarathustra's animals have throughout the text been comfort and good counsel to him. So when, in "The Convalescent," they tell Zarathustra in explicit detail about the meaning of eternal return and, in particular, about its meaning for him—"behold, *you are the teacher of the eternal recurrence*"—it is reasonable to anticipate an enlightened report.

The passage begins with the sudden onset of the illness from which Zarathustra's animals will help him convalesce.[56] Challenging the "sleepy worm" of his "abysmal thought" to wake and meet him halfway, Zarathustra faces eternal return as one would face death itself. The horror of the encounter sends him reeling, however; collapsing "as one dead" for seven days, he finally wakes to find a banquet set out at his feet by his solicitous animals. Their "chatter" cheers him further— "where there is chattering, there the world lies before me like a garden"—because words and sounds are "rainbows and illusive bridges between things which are eternally apart." Like the tales of adventure on board the ship which bore him away from the blessed isles,[57] his animals' words lure Zarathustra out of himself, out of his grim and solitary communion with his abysmal thought: "For me—how should there be any outside-myself? There is no outside. But all sounds make us forget this; how lovely it is that we forget."

Besides offering the retrospective elucidation of the vision of shepherd and snake already noted, Zarathustra himself nevertheless does not add to our knowledge of eternal return when he finally manages to speak.

Instead, he merely re-affirms that the thought is dreadful, especially given the return of "the small man" (but no man is found to be very big), while he chides his animals for having "already made a hurdy-gurdy song [ein Leier-Lied] of this," of being "buffoons and barrel organs [Schalks-Narren und Drehorgeln]" for knowing so well both his pain and the healing comfort of song. It is for such "knowledge," then—like the mechanically produced "music" of the hurdy gurdy—that Zarathustra rebukes his animals (although with a smile), and indeed they prove to be knowledgeable: telling Zarathustra that it is his profound destiny to teach the eternal return, they specify "You teach that there is a great year of becoming, a monster of a great year." The reference to Plato[58]—another instance of "quoting scripture," this time in the very act of quoting Zarathustra—is not accidental, for his animals go on to tell Zarathustra that, like Socrates in the *Phaedo* but without the prop of an immortal soul, he has conquered death. Thinking they know him, his animals lecture like professors, supplying the footnotes that render Zarathustra's most personal thought as just one account among many; thus is the project which began at the end of the Prologue at last completed. "And if you wanted to die now, O Zarathustra," his animals proclaim, "you would speak, without trembling but breathing deeply with happiness, for a great weight and sultriness would be taken from you. . . . Thus *ends* Zarathustra's going under."

And thus begins his going over—at last Zarathustra discovers that it is only pity for the higher men (the last refuge of pedagogy) which has persuaded him of the need for disciples, and in overcoming his pity Zarathustra once again goes over man into solitude. In the final four sections of Part IV, Zarathustra returns to his cave like Moses from Mt. Sinai[59] to find that the higher men have regressed to their old habits of deification and worship; the ugliest man has reawakened the dead god (as the wanderer and his shadow remarks, "in the case of gods death is always a mere prejudice" ["The Ass Festival," section 1]), and he leads the higher men in a litany of praise for the ass:

> He does not speak, except he always says Yea to the world he created: thus he praises his world. It is his cleverness that does not speak: thus he is rarely found to be wrong.
> But the ass brayed: Yeah-Yuh. . . .
> What hidden wisdom is it that he has long ears and only says Yea and never No! Has he not created the world in his own image, namely, as stupid as possible?
> But the ass brayed: Yeah-Yuh. ("The Awakening," section 2)

In his search for "great human beings," Nietzsche/Zarathustra "always found only the *apes* of their ideals" (*TI*, "Maxims and Arrows," section 39)—even when to ape theological ideals is to be an ass. For "God seems relatively most credible to me in this form," replies the conscientious man to Zarathustra's outrage; "God is supposed to be eternal, according to the witness of the most pious: whoever has that much time takes his time" ("The Ass Festival," section 1). And in defense of his blasphemous re-awakening of the dead god, the ugliest man quotes Zarathustra himself: "Whoever loves his God, chastises him" ("The Awakening"—but also the Prologue, section 4); "Not by wrath does one kill, but by laughter" ("The Ass Festival," section 1—but also "On Reading and Writing" in Part I); "'Was *that* life?' I want to say to death. 'Well, then! Once more!'" ("The Drunken Song," section 1—but also "On the Vision and the Riddle," section 1). The revered ass, with his empty and automatic yea-saying, is the center of all this aping of Zarathustra's own teaching. In "On the Spirit of Gravity" (section 2), Zarathustra had said "Always to bray Yeah-Yuh—that only the ass has learned, and whoever is of his spirit."[60] By now, the "secret wisdom" of the ass' long ears has become public knowledge: like the inverse cripple, the receptive patience of scholarship can go too far;[61] "(but what convinces is not necessarily true—it is *merely convincing*. A note for asses)" (*WP*, section 17; *KSA* 12, p. 540). And Zarathustra himself—he too, "from overabundance and wisdom," from the habit of speech that is always already a repetition, "could easily turn . . . into an ass" ("The Ass Festival," section 1)—as, indeed, he began, ridiculed for his pompous sermons by the crowd. The burden of communication always threatens to reduce even the most godless of thinkers to babbling "theo-asininities" (*Götter-Eseleien*): "Can an ass be tragic? To perish under a burden one can neither bear nor throw off? The case of the philosopher" (*TI*, "Maxims and Arrows," section 11).

But although he admits that "All of us know, some even know from experience, which animal has long ears," Nietzsche is quick to add, in an autobiographical boast: "Well then, I dare assert that I have the smallest ears. . . . I am the *anti-ass par excellence* and thus a world-historical monster—" (*EH*, "Why I Write Such Good Books," sect. 2). Accordingly, the high point of Nietzsche/Zarathustra's self-parody, the moment of greatest ironic distance from the pedagogical imperatives of this didactic book of sermons, occurs just after the most precious and personal doctrine of them all is appropriated by the ugliest man. "My friends, what do you think?" he asks the gathered disciples (among whom the reader can count himself, having passed the test of the Prologue). "Do you not want to say to death as I do: Was *that* life? For Zarathustra's sake! Well, then! Once More!"

"For Zarathustra's sake"?! Zarathustra has succeeded, then, in finding, in *creating* the disciples he imagined in the Prologue—companions who "want to follow themselves—wherever I want" (section 9); readers who are like cows (*GM*, Preface, section 8), "herd animals in the realm of knowledge" (*WP*, section 421; *KSA* 11, p. 153). But it is almost *midnight*, not midday, when the ugliest man speaks Zarathustra's words; those "most intrepid, most midnightly men" demand names for unnameable things (*WP*, section 1067; *KSA* 11, p. 611) because, in the darkness, they are but blind ass-moles—they, too, are all ears, their courage is stupidity. And with the blasphemous usurpation of eternal return by the ugliest man, the narrative voice shifts: departing from the complete identity with Zarathustra's narrative, which had been dominant from the beginning,[62] Nietzsche suddenly addresses the reader directly. "And what do you suppose happened then?" A possible conclusion is suggested, but others are also mentioned ("as some of the chroniclers think . . ."; "there are even some who relate . . ."); like the redactor of an ancient manuscript who is uncertain of its veracity, Nietzsche emerges in the text, distinguishing and thus distancing himself from it. And the effect is to reduce *Thus Spoke Zarathustra* to one "chronicle" among many, just the braying of another ass; the preacher/teacher's authority is undermined in a decisive way.

7. Closing the circle: Zarathustra's return to solitude

At the end of Part I, Zarathustra first takes his leave of those "who called themselves his disciples" ("On the Gift-Giving Virtue"), reproving them "One repays a teacher badly if one always remains nothing but a pupil" and commanding them "Now I bid you lose me and find yourselves; and only when you have all denied me will I return to you" (ibid.). But by the end of Part IV, Zarathustra has learned that "Philosophy"—to choose a convenient name—"is hard to learn because it cannot be taught: one must 'know' it from experience—" (*BGE*, "We Scholars," section 213). And so, taking some comfort in the creative imagination evident even in the ass festival, Nietzsche/Zarathustra shares his final epiphany: a remarkable dithyramb that appears in section 12 of "The Drunken Song" after each of its eleven lines is separately, obliquely celebrated in visionary prose.[63]

But there is yet one last passage, an epilogue to close the circle where the Prologue had opened it. Rising with the sun while his disciples, still exhausted from the previous night's festivities, slumber on, Zarathustra finds himself in the presence of adoring doves and a loving lion. Distracted by sweet bliss that makes him weep, a rather ridiculous scene takes place that it is difficult to imagine or describe without embarrassment—until the idyll is broken by the trespass of the higher men, who upon waking have come in search of their master. They startle the lion, whose sudden roar in turn scatters them in panic as

Zarathustra gradually returns to consciousness from out of his reverie. But he finds that he has finally lost patience and pity for these higher men when his memory returns to him: "My suffering and my pity for suffering—what does it matter? Am I concerned with *happiness*? I am concerned with my *work*."

What is Zarathustra's work?

Like Socrates, "the purest thinker in the West," Zarathustra is not a writer—although he is a prodigious talker. Like Socrates, his profoundest thought has prepared him for death—although song, which momentarily entered Socrates' life just before the end, is Zarathustra's salvation. Like Socrates, Zarathustra's final pedagogical gesture is withdrawal. And whereas Socrates takes leave of his disciples in an exemplary heuristic death, Zarathustra returns to himself, to his solitude. No one can follow him there; when we think we have, "we are right only with respect to the way in which we can conceive it." As Karl Jaspers wrote more than fifty years ago, through the transcendence of his own uniqueness, "Nietzsche, as it were, enters an atmosphere that is inaccessible to us; it is as though he left us and sank into a void."[64] From "everyone"—the herd of The Motley Cow in the Prologue—Zarathustra's audience has shrunk to "no one." "What? You search? You would multiply yourself by ten, by a hundred? You seek followers? Seek *zeros*!" (*TI*, "Maxims and Arrows," section 14).

What is Zarathustra's work?

"Ich trachte nach meinem *Werke*!" Zarathustra proclaims—but Nietzsche writes. So it is a matter of "*Werke*," not "*Arbeit*": Zarathustra's "work" is his *oeuvres*. And yet, to reiterate: like Socrates, Zarathustra is not a writer.

"Alle Formen sind *unser* Werk," Nietzsche writes in his notebooks—"*we* express *ourselves* in such a way as we *must* now recognize things" (*KSA* 9, p. 621). Zarathustra's work—*our* work—cannot be reduced to a doctrine or even a genre; it is inherently dynamic, a verb rather than a noun. We are the builders of the scaffolding of concepts described in "On Truth and Lies"; spiders that spin webs of words in which to trap sensations ("nerve impulses")—or better, spinners and unspinners of fabrics of fancy, like Penelope at a loom of eternal return. We are the constituters of value, and therefore of reality, after the death of God. Zarathustra's work—*our* work—is being itself. But this answer is not meant to invoke philosophical ontology, fundamental or not, or indeed any metaphysical commitment whatsoever. Just the opposite: being, as everything that is, cannot be driven into theoretical containment. "No longer joy in certainty but in uncertainty; no longer 'cause and effect,' but the continually creative; no longer will to preservation, but to power; no longer the humble expression 'everything is *merely* subjective,' but 'it is also *our* work [Werk]'—let us be proud of it!" (*WP*, section 1059; *KSA* 11, p. 225).

Like Plato,[65] Nietzsche did "not want to persuade anyone to philosophy: it is inevitable, it is perhaps also desirable, that the philosopher should be a *rare* plant" (*WP*, section 420; *KSA* 11, p. 271). But perhaps this is because "philosophy" must now become still rarer, losing its privilege among other species of "*Werke*" with the loss of the credulity of those who would read it. The Western philosophical project from Plato to Hegel forfeited the majestic company of metaphysics by confusing reality and make-believe as a prodigious child might do; its grave seriousness seems now to be quaintly buffoonish.

So—if Socrates, like Zarathustra, respects the imperative of "living truths" and thus refuses to be pinned down by writing—what of Plato and Nietzsche? Can writing, too, refuse to be pinned down? Can "philosophy" be poured out of a vessel so empty as eternal return: can writing beget talking? "Speaking is a beautiful folly: with that man dances over all things. How lovely is all talking, and all the deception of sounds! With sounds our love dances on many-hued rainbows" ("The Convalescent").

After all, Zarathustra's "*Werke*" is Nietzsche's "*Arbeit*," even as Nietzsche's "*Werke*" is Zarathustra's "truer theology"—a labor of love, a many-hued rainbow: a metafiction.

EPILOGUE

From Metaphysics to Metafictions

Jesus said, "If you bring forth what is within you, what you bring
forth will save you. If you do not bring forth what is within you,
what you do not bring forth will destroy you."
—Gospel of Thomas (Gnostic)

Whoever does not know how to lay his will into things, at least he
lays some *meaning* into them: that means, he has a faith that they
already obey a will.
—Nietzsche, *Twilight of the Idols*

. . . the final belief must be in a fiction . . .
—Wallace Stevens

In the course of these readings it has become increasingly clear that the
development in thinking that succeeds Hegel's apocalyptic finality
emphasizes the constitutive role played by language and narrative in the
formulation of metaphysical claims. But this has become clear in the
course of demonstrating that a concealed turn to or reliance upon mediating narrative structures is already evident in the supposedly passive
observation Hegel calls "phenomenology." The hermeneutic circularity
of dialectic affirms at the outset that the Preface is already at the end;
when naive sense-certainty tries to claim pre-linguistic immediacy as the
ground of truth, we are prepared in advance for the linguistic turn to
mediation, which reinterprets given being as the construct of a certain
narrative about knowledge and its origins. We *know* only mediation: the
particular we mean is rendered universal as soon as we speak it. Yet the
heuristic communicative potential of experience is itself a function of its
expression: the "divine nature of language" negates inscrutable immediacy in order to reconstitute it dialectically. Thus begins the long story of
recovery, of re-cognition, Hegel's idealist *Bildungsroman* in which
"Spirit" is the protagonist.

That Hegel's project is at the same time and above all metaphysical
emerges explicitly from the encounter between selves narrated in the
lordship and bondage dialectic. Since the recursive teleology of the absolute is already evident from the outset—philosophy is always and only
concerned with redescriptions—Hegel is consistent when he denies con-

sciousness direct access to the being of its own self. As *desire*, self-consciousness is a return from otherness that depends on the aspiration of becoming and is dissolved by the satisfaction of being. Consequently, Hegel develops a dramatic scenario in which the insight that will lead to self-consciousness is located in a denial of Life (the merely physical) for the sake of the Spiritual (the evidently *meta*-physical). Such a desire for self-creation is against nature, artificial—a negation for the sake of creation, the negation of the negation of the (natural, immediate) other.[1] Thus, with dialectical double-think, divinity is read in degradation so as to resurrect finitude in the absolute freedom of thought, while at the same time "The subject must make the world its own doing if it is to recognize itself as the only reality."[2] The project of self-knowledge is a project of self-creation, and this in turn is a constitution of the other, from whose reflection consciousness first comes to know its own self.

In effect, the *Phenomenology* begins by denying that the world can speak for itself, proceeds to speak for it by dialectically elaborating the fiction of a world created by Hegelian desire, and concludes by redeeming the ersatz world of Spirit's "shapes" thus created precisely by affirming its artificiality! The end is a return to the beginning, an epilogical reconstruction premised on a deconstruction—but a return "for the first time," as it were. For the beginning itself is impossible, unintelligible; only as mediated by memory, which in turn presupposes historical expression, is meaning possible at all. "By reading the end in the beginning and the beginning in the end," notes Paul Ricoeur,

> we learn also to read time itself backward, as the recapitulating of the initial conditions of a course of action in its terminal consequences. In this way, a plot establishes human action not only within time . . . but within memory. Memory, accordingly, *repeats* the course of events according to an order that is the counterpart of time as "stretching along" between a beginning and an end.[3]

To read events symbolically, posthumously, is to redeem them, to affirm their return—but at the same time, it is to construe them as fictions, to "read the world" as taking determinate form in a teleological narrative. Acknowledging the value of narrativity in the representation of reality leads to a recognition of "the fantasy that *real* events are properly represented when they can be shown to display the formal coherency of a story"; as Hayden White observes of historical "truth," if it "can be given narrative closure, can be shown to have had a *plot* all along" then the "reality" it portrays comes to bear "the odor of the *ideal.*"[4]

Of course, the metaphysical humility of this mediated narrative relation with the world is not what Hegel promotes. Nietzsche, however, will paraphrase such ontology only to deflate it. If we "make of logic a criterion of true being," he writes, then "we are on the way to positing as realities all those hypostases: substance, attribute, object, subject, action, etc.; that is, to conceiving a metaphysical world, that is, a 'real world' (—*this, however, is the apparent world once more*—)" (*WP*, section 516; *KSA* 12, p. 390). Fictional narratives are didactically misleading when they claim too much; what is really at stake in them is smaller and more personal. Metaphysical testaments are heuristic autobiographies possessing at most an exemplary value—and, as William Earle observes, the "proper style of autobiography is narration, not proof or explanation."[5]

A universal element remains, however, in the divine nature of language. As experiments in narrative form, philosophical texts are critically accessible—and a significant number of contemporary thinkers have construed the role of philosophy as that of an articulate reflection on metafictions. In describing Nietzsche's work as an "effort to create an artwork out of himself, a literary character who is a philosopher,"[6] Alexander Nehamas details a particular case of what Alasdair MacIntyre has observed writ large in societies: that "human life has a determinate form, the form of a certain kind of story."[7] MacIntyre also speaks of "characters," but whereas Nietzsche deployed them in order to multiply himself, to describe many perspectives, to complicate his oneness and solace his aloneness, societies deploy "characters" in order to simplify, exemplify. They are, writes MacIntyre, "the moral representatives of their culture . . . because of the way in which moral and metaphysical ideas and theories assume through them an embodied existence in the social world" (p. 28). As he is explicitly concerned with the ways in which "the virtues" have been historically construed, MacIntyre circumscribes his hypothesis, asserting that "generally to adopt a stance on the virtues will be to adopt a stance on the narrative character of human life"; belief in the virtues implies "belief in human life exhibiting a certain narrative order" (p. 144). But, even more generally, MacIntyre further asserts that "the act of utterance becomes intelligible by finding its place in a narrative" (p. 210).

This view is anticipated by critics who have addressed questions regarding the narrative structure of eschatological or apocalyptic texts—a genre which, as we have seen, may be said to include Hegel's *Phenomenology*. Spengler's morphology of historical forms, his prophetic scheme of the return of cultural and historical archetypes, is perhaps most conspicuous among these. "Truth," he writes, is the thinker's incarnation in words, "himself over again: his being expressed in words; the meaning of his personality formed into a doctrine which so far as concerns his life is unalterable, because truth and his life are identical."[8] The *Phe-*

nomenology, M. H. Abrams observes, is just such an incarnation of thought, which furthermore "is deliberately composed not in the mode of philosophic exposition or demonstration, but in the mode of a literary narrative."[9] The important result of such intentions—the final intelligibility of the phenomena narrated—is guaranteed in advance as a consequence of the structure itself. "Everything is relevant if its relevance can be invented," writes Frank Kermode in a book about eschatological teleology; the "merely successive character of events has been exorcised; the synthesizing consciousness has done its work."[10] Thus, "in 'making sense' of the world we still feel a need, harder than ever to satisfy because of an accumulated scepticism, to experience that concordance of beginning, middle, and end which is the essence of our explanatory fictions."[11]

The "accumulated scepticism" to which Kermode refers is an inevitable result of the habit of distinguishing between fiction and reality—a distinction both apparently natural and just as evidently essential to the identity of philosophy as the intellectual, "scientific" discipline it has traditionally taken itself to be. Unlike the inscrutable enormity of "reality," the controlled causality of finite fiction constitutes a self-sufficient totality, a "rigorous scheme of attentions, echoes and affinities" that Borges calls a "teleology of words and episodes": rather than the natural result of endless and uncontrollable processes, the causality of fiction must be "magic, in which—clear and defined—every detail is an omen and a cause."[12] That such is not the case when it comes to plain facts would seem obvious. Nevertheless, it is precisely the unintelligibility of simple immediacy that is overcome through dialectical redescription, through participation in the "magic causality" of non-natural textuality, and for the metaphysical story subsequently narrated Hegel claims a formal adequacy to its content altogether superior to the mere stories told by religions through myths and images.

That the *Phenomenology* concludes with religious *Vorstellungen* in spite of Hegel's explicit claims for the special status of philosophical discourse thus looks in retrospect like an act of accidental prescience.[13] If the pretension of philosophy is to "make sense" of the world—while to do so is to supplant the world with a narrative that is intelligible by virtue of its teleological form—then the task of contemporary philosopher-critics is to provide analyses of that form, and thus to render "literary" what takes itself to be real. From a post-Nietzschean perspective that reads a hermeneutical imperative already in the legacy of Kant's criticism, the fully self-conscious thinker must look for hidden master narratives that secretly establish the rules in our language-games of "truth." This is a meta-critical activity that altogether lacks the ontological arrogance of metaphysics; philosophy becomes just a "conversation" in the cultural history of mankind.[14]

Such "postmodernism," with its "incredulity toward metanarratives,"[15] leaves us with what may feel like an impoverished sense of the vocation of philosophy: how shall it now be possible to ground metafictional unities that are constructed, not discovered or given? But if credulity toward all narrative is abrogated, the result—paradoxically—is to render all reality "virtual." Where hierarchies of metanarratives govern the distinctions between "true" and "false," "right" and "wrong," "reality" and "fiction," adjudicating between these poles of belief, these ontological alternatives, will become impossible in their absence. Frederic Jameson speaks of a "political unconscious" of master narratives "passing underground";[16] it would undoubtedly take some time for thinking to be relieved altogether of traditional metanarrative centerings. Nevertheless, the conditions which would make this possible are already evident in, for instance, the decline in historical consciousness resulting from pragmatic, "polytechnic" approaches to education. A future is imaginable in which a kind of epistemological totalitarianism dictates "reality" to a public which lacks traditions and commitments so totally that it has become a virtual blank slate.

Fortunately, metafictions are not metanarratives; indeed, as Habermas has shown (and as Lyotard's own rhetoric reveals even within his account of the presumably postmodern),[17] incredulity toward faith as such is already characteristic of the Enlightenment. Truthfulness as a method undermined the piety of Truth as a dogma long ago: Nietzsche's account in the third essay of *On the Genealogy of Morals* remains the locus classicus for this demystification. Rather, the liberation from aporetic regress must express itself as *credulity*—but in *fictions*. A riddle, a crisis, an aporia? Again: how are we to believe in what we know we have ourselves invented?

Perhaps belief is just disingenuous, an old habit in bad faith which is neither needed nor even in question except in that pathological discourse of suspicion called philosophy. Like Hegel's "unhappy consciousness," or the "*Ressentiment*" of the Judeo-Christian slave who perverts the values which Nietzsche's Zarathustra will attempt to restore, Sartre describes "bad faith" as a self-conscious deception in which one plays a role of truthfulness; he concedes, moreover, that bad faith "*can* be the normal aspect of life for a very great number of people," that one "*can* live in bad faith."[18] "To believe is to know that one believes, and to know that one believes is no longer to believe";[19] the striving for a sufficient ground of belief is an expression of man's "useless passion to be God." What, then, would be "good faith"? After all, Sartre does confess that even the most self-deluded modern consciousness may experience "awakenings to cynicism and good faith."[20] Is "cynicism" the "truth value" of metafictions? Is irony a postmodern substitute for faith?[21]

It is precisely here that Nietzsche's most apparently disturbing insights into the impossibility of originality prove paradoxically to be capable of great affirmation. Creation is recreation, the manipulation and recombination of available words, ideas, roles. "Whatever lives obeys" (*TSZ*, Part II, "On Self-Overcoming"); the choice is between composing one's own orders, from given possibilities, or submitting to the intelligible expression of the will of another. Either way, in the end the world will be ordered, will be thinkable, "it shall yield and bend for you."

NOTES

PREFACE

1. The style or voice of this first paragraph may already signal to a wary reader the ambitious scope of *Metaphysics to Metafictions*. It is not, for the most part, the strategy of this book to engage in polemics with the latest commentaries; rather, an interpretation of what is perhaps the most fundamental paradigm shift in Western thought is developed here, a change that sees the philosophic aspirations of the ancient Greeks first realized and then abandoned in the precipitous intellectual metamorphosis of absolute idealism into nihilism. If this story is to be told with sufficient narrative power to be compelling, a certain grand gesture will be necessary at first and last, framing the more traditional scholarly discourse carried out in the chapters directly concerned with Hegel and Nietzsche. And yet, "God is in the details"; a really thorough account of that "end of philosophy" associated with the so-called death of Western metaphysics would require far greater erudition than I command, and far more dedication to its elaboration than any one individual could hope to manage.

As a compromise, I have found it convenient to produce here, in these notes, a parallel discourse. Sometimes, a polemical engagement that would have distracted the following out of the threads laid down by Hegel and Nietzsche themselves in the body of the work is explored in the notes instead, in a somewhat more extended fashion than is judged by some to be in good form. Such is the case, for example, in note 23 of Chapter Five, where Alexander Nehamas's recent and important interpretation of Nietzsche is distinguished from the reading developed here (which is nonetheless indebted to it). At other times, the notes attempt to provide the reader with a basic overview of some relatively esoteric context that is linked to—or even provides a link between—the principal antagonists whose struggle is narrated in the text (the twelfth-century abbot Joachim of Fiore is the subject of such a note). Nor have I denied myself an occasional indulgence in the interesting aside. I hope the reader may find observations about, for example, Menippean satire as a literary model for the finale of *Thus Spoke Zarathustra* worthy of remark in their own right, even if such considerations open doors onto other avenues than the one purposefully travelled here.

Of course, inasmuch as the "modern" and the "postmodern" collide somewhere in Nietzsche's turbulent wake, the uncertainty of a fragmented voice that cannot decide if it is to declaim with grand gestures above the line or elaborate with pedantic compulsiveness below it is perhaps to be expected. More, the ironic tension between the two textual selves, redoubled now by being confessed, constitutes a symptom of the instabilities which herald the end.

2. Jürgen Habermas, *Der philosophische Diskurs der Moderne: Zwölf Vorlesungen* (Frankfurt am Main: Suhrkamp Verlag, 1985); *The Philosophical Discourse of Modernity*, trans. Frederick G. Lawrence (Cambridge, Mass.: MIT Press, 1987).

3. Jean-Francois Lyotard, *La Condition postmoderne: rapport sur le savoir* (Paris: Les Editions de Minuit, 1979); *The Postmodern Condition: A Report on Knowledge*, trans. Geoff Bennington and Brian Massumi (Minneapolis: University of Minnesota Press, 1984).

4. Lyotard, *The Postmodern Condition*, p. xxiv; *La Condition postmoderne*, p. 7.

5. *WP*, sects. 13, 43 (*KSA* 12, p. 351; 13, p. 264). References to Nietzsche's published works will cite section number and name whenever possible, the title of the work being an abbreviation of its English equivalent according to the statement on Citation Conventions above. Unpublished fragments which appeared in *The Will to Power* (*WP*) will be cited in both that text and in the *Kritische Studienausgabe* of Nietzsche's works edited by Giorgio Colli and Mazzino Montinari, abbreviated *KSA*. Full bibliographical data may be found in the statement on Citation Conventions above and in the Bibliography below.

6. Habermas, *The Philosophical Discourse of Modernity*, p. 408; *Der philosophische Diskurs der Moderne*, p. 246.

7. *The Philosophical Discourse of Modernity*, p. 408; *Der philosophische Diskurs der Moderne*, p. 247.

8. *The Philosophical Discourse of Modernity*, p. 409; *Der philosophische Diskurs der Moderne*, p. 247.

9. Lyotard, *The Postmodern Condition*, p. xxv; *La Condition postmoderne*, p. 9.

10. See *The Postmodern Condition*, section 12, "Education and Its Legitimation through Performativity," pp. 47–53; *La Condition postmoderne*, pp. 69–78.

11. *The Postmodern Condition*, p. 7; *La Condition postmoderne*, p. 18.

12. *The Postmodern Condition*, p. 18; *La Condition postmoderne*, p. 36.

13. In lecture XI, which elaborates his own position, Habermas recognizes three linguistic components as "equiprimordial" elements in the rationality of communicative practice: the "propositional function" (this is the only relevant element for the subject-centered paradigm), the "illocutionary component" which articulates the dynamics of interpersonal relationships, and linguistic components that reveal the intention of the speaker which make poetic discourse possible. Applauding these additional dimensions of meaning, Habermas concludes: "[t]his concept [of communicative rationality] is richer than that of purposive rationality, which is tailored to the cognitive-instrumental dimension, because it integrates the moral-practical as well as the aesthetic-expressive domains. . . . It brings along with it the connotations of a noncoercive unifying, consensus-building force of a discourse in which the participants overcome their at first subjectively biased views in favor of a rationally motivated agreement" (*The Philosophical Discourse of Modernity*, pp. 314–15; *Der philosophische Diskurs der Moderne*, p. 366).

14. Lyotard, *The Postmodern Condition*, p. 67: *La Condition postmoderne*, p. 108.

15. *The Postmodern Condition*, p. 66; *La Condition postmoderne*, p. 107.

16. Massimo Riva, "1888–1988: Some Remarks on Nihilism and Secularization," *History of European Ideas*, Vol. II (1989), p. 979.

17. Guy Debord, *The Society of the Spectacle*, trans. Donald Nicholson-Smith (New York: Zone Books, 1995), epigraph, p. 11.

18. Ibid., para. 1, p. 12. This view, minus its political urgency, anticipates the postmodernist Jean Baudrillard's notion of "the simulacrum."

19. See ibid, para. 30, p. 23. The proximity to Marxian lines of thought which results from the attempt to interpret the commodity culture politically is quite obvious in this formulation, as are echoes of Georg Simmel's analysis of the proliferation of "objective culture" at the expense of "subjective culture." According to Simmel, technology "entangles us in a web of means" by virtue of its manic productivity of such teleologically sophisticated and effective objects that they become fetishized as ends in themselves. See, for example, "The Crisis of Culture," in P. A. Lawrence, ed., *Georg Simmel: Sociologist and European* (New York: Barnes and Noble Books, 1976); and "The Conflict in Modern Culture," in K. Peter Etzkorn, trans. and ed., *The Conflict in Modern Culture and Other Essays* (New York: Teachers College Press, no date).

20. Ibid., para. 8, p. 14.

21. Ibid., para. 20, p. 18.

22. Ibid., para. 34, p. 24.

23. Ibid., preface, p. 10. In para. 11, Debord insists again that his purpose in describing the spectacle is to identify "whatever forces may hasten its demise."

24. These included publicly posted slogans ("Down With the Spectacular-Commodity Society"); collage installation pieces composed of fragments taken from various print media, advertising images, and a cacophony of other familiar icons of modern life; even simple provocations, such as pelting lecturers with tomatoes or speaking for the student occupation committee which took control of the Sorbonne in May of 1968.

25. Elisabeth Sussman, Introduction to *On the Passage of a Few People through a Rather Brief Moment in Time: The Situationist International, 1957–1972*, ed. Elisabeth Sussman (Cambridge, Mass.: MIT Press/Boston: Institute of Contemporary Art, 1989), p. 13.

26. Greil Marcus, "Guy Debord's *Mémoires*: A Situationist Primer," in ibid., p. 127.

27. Ibid., p. 126.

28. For a wide-ranging consideration of repetition in the light of contemporary culture, see Hillel Schwartz, *The Culture of the Copy: Striking Likenesses, Unreasonable Facsimiles* (New York: Zone Books, 1996).

29. Debord, *The Society of the Spectacle*, para. 33, p. 24.

30. It might seem that Nietzsche's ideas are particularly susceptible to political and social abuse, not immune from it—but in fact, a close look at the lessons of Nazi and other nefarious misappropriations actually supports a reading of Nietzsche identical to the one developed here. See my essay "Unreading

Nietzsche: Nazi Piracy, Pyrrhic Irony, and the Postmodern Turn," *New Nietzsche Studies*, Vol. I (1996).

Situationist rhetoric, on the other hand, can easily become radicalized and even actualized as terrorism. For example, a comparative reading of Debord's text with the notorious polemic "Industrial Society and Its Future"—the so-called Unabomber Manifesto—reveals startling similarities of conception. The Unabomber, too, argues that the consumerism of "the system" alienates human beings from themselves. In his terms, the satisfactions of "the power process," in which significant struggle and effort leads to accomplishment, can no longer be had from the struggle to survive, since in mainstream modern society survival is all but a matter of course. Still needing a project to stimulate the power process and the satisfying sense of one's role in it, modern man turns to "surrogate activities" instead. But the hallmark of surrogate activity is its essential arbitrariness: if the agent had to devote most of his "physical and mental facilities in a varied and interesting way" to the task of survival, he would not feel "seriously deprived" by the abandonment of the surrogate activity he no longer had time for (para. 39). Accordingly, the satisfaction gleaned from surrogate activities misses the mark, is in fact irrelevant, and the system which offers only surrogate activities in satisfaction of the need to participate in the power process must be destroyed no matter what the cost. Thus, with an unnerving inevitability, the Unabomber matter-of-factly declares: "In order to get our message before the public with some chance of making a lasting impression, we've had to kill people" (para. 96).

Of course, the situationists did not go this far! But in many ways these are similar arguments, with the Unabomber's term "surrogate activity" doing the work that the notion of the "spectacle" does for the situationists: both are necessarily alienating; both are substitute, derivative activities that block access to something more "natural"—and both must be subverted.

31. William Gass, "Philosophy and the Form of Fiction," in *Fiction and the Figures of Life* (New York: Alfred A. Knopf, 1970), pp. 24ff.

32. Larry McCaffery, *The Metafictional Muse* (University of Pittsburgh Press, 1982), p. 252.

33. David Lodge, *The Art of Fiction* (New York: Penguin Books, 1992), p. 206.

34. Gass, "Philosophy and the Form of Fiction," p. 25.

35. Gass, "Imaginary Borges and His Books," in *Fiction and the Figures of Life*, p. 126

36. Ibid., p. 127.

37. Hayden White, *Metahistory: The Historical Imagination in Nineteenth-Century Europe* (Baltimore and London: Johns Hopkins University Press, 1973), p. 5.

38. Ibid., p. 7.

39. Hayden White, "The Value of Narrativity in the Representation of Reality," *Critical Inquiry*, Vol. 7, No. 1 (Autumn 1980), p. 24.

40. Ibid. This formulation recalls Baumgarten's aesthetics, in which the artist is conceived as a "good metaphysician" because, having created his own world, he is also in the desirable position of being able to fully understand it.

41. Ibid. Much the same point is made by Paul Ricoeur in his analysis of narrative time: when "a group of protagonists" begins to understand itself and its tradition, he writes, there occurs a "communal act of repetition, which is at the same time a new founding act and a recommencement of what has already been inaugurated, that 'makes history' and that finally makes it possible to write history" ("Narrative Time," *Critical Inquiry*, Vol. 7, No. 1 [Autumn 1980], p. 189).

42. For the distinction between "active" and "passive" nihilism in Nietzsche, see *WP*, sects. 13, 14, 22 (*KSA* 12, pp. 350–53).

43. See sect. 295, entitled "Brief Habits," in *GS*: "I always believe that here is something that will give me lasting satisfaction—brief habits, too, have this faith of passion, this faith in eternity—."

44. Harold Bloom, *The Anxiety of Influence* (Oxford University Press, 1973), p. 80.

45. Lodge, *The Art of Fiction*, p. 207.

46. Borges explains the theory of this act of creative will in strikingly similar fashion. "The fact is that every writer creates his precursors," he reflects, having observed Kafkaesque elements in texts from Zeno's paradoxes to Lord Dunsany. "His work modifies our conception of the past, as it will modify the future." ("Kafka and His Precursors," in *Labyrinths*, ed. Donald A. Yates and James E. Irby [New York: New Directions, 1962], p. 201.)

47. Richard Rorty, *Contingency, Irony, and Solidarity* (Cambridge: Cambridge University Press, 1989), p. 29. Rorty explicitly links this part of his discussion with Bloom's notion of "giving birth to oneself" in *The Anxiety of Influence*. Such views constitute elements in a constellation with a wide reach; they may also be associated with Alexander Nehamas's influential interpretation of Nietzsche's corpus (the word is telling here) as an attempt to live the life of a literarily conceived character who happens to be a philosopher (*Nietzsche: Life as Literature* [Cambridge, Mass.: Harvard University Press, 1985]).

48. Friedrich Albert Lange, *Geschichte des Materialismus und Kritik seiner Bedeutung in der Gegenwart* (Iserlohn: Verlag von J. Baedeker, 1873); *The History of Materialism and Criticism of Its Present Importance*, trans. Ernest Chester Thomas, 3d ed. (New York: Humanities Press, 1950).

49. Hans Vaihinger, *Die Philosophie des Als Ob. System der theoretischen, praktischen und religiösen Fiktionen der Menschheit auf Grund eines idealistischen Positivismus* (Leipzig: Felix Meiner Verlag, 1911); *The Philosophy of 'As if': A System of the Theoretical, Practical and Religious Fictions of Mankind*, trans. C. K. Ogden, 2d ed. (London: Routledge & Kegen Paul, 1935).

50. Bertrand Russell, "Introduction: Materialism Past and Present," in Lange, *The History of Materialism*," p. ix.

51. Ibid., p. xvii. The relevance of Lange's work to contemporary debates in the philosophy of mind regarding the ontology of "consciousness" as the subjective correlate of objective "brain states" (Chalmers, Crick, Dennett, Edelman, Penrose, Searle, et al.) is anticipated by Russell, who notes that even physics is no longer materialistic in the traditional sense insofar as it no longer regards matter as permanent substance deterministically governed by laws. George Stack neatly summarizes the historical chiasmus:

> While today we have philosophers in Australia, England and the United States appealing to data in physiology to support reductive materialism, in the latter part of the nineteenth century we find many physiologists, physicists and natural scientists admitting that the discoveries in their fields, although tending towards materialism, do not provide justification for a strict materialistic account of human experience. Physiological theories may show the dependence of mind on physiological changes in the brain, they say, but they do not *explain* the origin, derivation or activity of human consciousness. (*Lange and Nietzsche* [Berlin and New York: Walter de Gruyter, 1983], p. 91)

Russell's attention notwithstanding, the general neglect of Lange's insightful and scholarly contribution to discussions of the mind-body problem, or the dialectic of *Geist* and *Natur*, extends to this recent "analytic" literature.

52. Robert B. Pippin examines this genealogy with great subtlety and at considerable length in order to reveal what is of essential philosophical importance in Hegel's thought, whatever one makes of the perplexing ambiguity of his metaphysical claims. Summarizing the argument of his book, Pippin writes: "Simply put, I propose to take Hegel at his word when he tells us, in an early work, that it was the argument of Kant's Transcendental Deduction that first came close to and made possible the speculative identity theory he ultimately created, and, in a later work, that his own theory of the Notion, and indeed the relation between the Notion and reality, or the basic position of his entire philosophy, should be understood as a direct variation on a crucial Kantian theme, the 'transcendental unity of apperception'" (*Hegel's Idealism* [Cambridge: Cambridge University Press, 1989], p. 6).

53. Lange, *History of Materialism*, pp. 336–37; *Geschichte des Materialismus*, p. 540.

54. Lange, *History of Materialism*, p. 337; *Geschichte des Materialismus*, p. 541.

55. Lange, *History of Materialism*, p. 338; *Geschichte des Materialismus*, p. 541.

56. Lange, *History of Materialism*, p. 340; *Geschichte des Materialismus*, p. 543.

57. Lange, *History of Materialism*, p. 346; *Geschichte des Materialismus*, p. 548.

58. Lange, *History of Materialism*, p. 342; *Geschichte des Materialismus*, p. 545.

59. Lange, *History of Materialism*, p. 360; *Geschichte des Materialismus*, p. 561.

60. Lange, *The History of Materialism*, p. 341; *Geschichte des Materialismus*, p. 544.

61. Vaihinger, *The Philosophy of 'As if,'* p. 342; *Die Philosophie des Als Ob*, pp. 772–73.

62. *The Philosophy of 'As if,'* p. 343; *Die Philosophie des Als Ob*, p. 773. Jörg Salaquarda has also examined the relationship between Lange and Nietzsche in two important articles ("Nietzsche und Lange," *Nietzsche-Studien*,

Vol. 7 [1978] and "Der Standpunkt des Ideals bei Lange und Nietzsche," *Studi Tedeschi*, Vol. XXII, no. 1 [1979]); the first of these takes note of a small library of books (by Anders, Bernoulli, Del-Negro, Dickopp, Hocks, and Mittasch) which similarly acknowledge the connection.

More recently, George J. Stack has explored Nietzsche's indebtedness to Lange in the definitive book on the subject (*Lange and Nietzsche*, op. cit.) and in several essays. With dramatic understatement, he affirms at the outset of his major study:

> Although there is no reason to assume that all of the patterns in Nietzsche's philosophical tapestry are woven after the manner of Lange [!], it is astonishing, I believe, to see how many threads are borrowed from a man whose thought is assumed to have had little impact on later thinkers. . . . Despite the fact that Nietzsche rarely mentions Lange in his *Nachlaß* (usually critically) or in his letters, and not at all in the published writings, does not mitigate the enormous influence that Lange had on his thinking [*sic*]. There is justification in Hans Vaihinger's remark that "Nietzsche must definitely be set down as a disciple and successor of Lange." (*Lange and Nietzsche*, pp. 6, 15; citing Vaihinger, *The Philosophy of 'As-if,'* p. 341).

This global claim is borne out by many particular arguments and observations. Among them, Stack maintains that "What Lange insinuated in Nietzsche's mind was the idea that categories such as unity, substance, being, object, cause, etc., were basically convenient hypothetical notions that have practical value but no ontological reference" ("Kant, Lange, and Nietzsche: Critique of Knowledge," in *Nietzsche and Modern German Thought*, ed. Keith Ansell-Pearson [London and New York: Routledge, 1991], p. 38) and that "The outcome of 'On Truth and Lying' owes a great deal to Lange's skeptical interpretation of Kant's agnosticism" (ibid., p. 34). Summarizing his findings, Stack writes:

> What is often overlooked by those who refer to the influence of Lange on Nietzsche is that he was profoundly impressed by the two major aspects of Lange's philosophy: the conception of the world of appearances as a representation determined by "our organization" (and the consequent agnosticism that follows from this) *and* the appeal to "figurative" or "poetic" ideals that carry us beyond the realm of empirical actuality. (*Lange and Nietzsche*, p. 12)

63. Vaihinger, *The Philosophy of 'As if,'* "Autobiographical: The Origin of the Philosophy of 'As if'," p. xxvii.

64. Ibid., p. xxxvi.

65. *The Philosophy of 'As if,'* p. 341; *Die Philosophie des Als Ob*, p. 771. Vaihinger may admit to being "a disciple of F. A. Lange," but his indebtedness to Nietzsche is at least as profound. Having earlier written a brief book on Nietzsche (*Nietzsche als Philosoph* [Berlin: Reuther und Richard, 1902]), the decisive final chapter of *The Philosophy of 'As if,'* entitled "Nietzsche and His Doctrine of Conscious Illusion," assigns to Nietzsche's thought a role parallel to that served by "The Standpoint of the Ideal" in Lange. That is to say, Vaihinger's

transformation of Kant is accomplished through an interpretive appropriation of Nietzsche's "perspectivism": "These fictions," he admits, "Nietzsche calls perspectives" (*The Philosophy of 'As if,'* p. 355; *Die Philosophie des Als Ob,* p. 783).

66. *The Philosophy of 'As if,'* p. xxvii.
67. Ibid.
68. Ibid., p. xlvii.
69. *History of Materialism,* p. 342; *Geschichte des Materialismus,* p. 545.
70. *The Philosophy of 'As if,'* p. 336–37; *Die Philosophie des Als Ob,* p. 765–66.

INTRODUCTION

1. Quoted in Martin Heidegger, *Nietzsche,* Vol. II: *The Eternal Return of the Same,* trans. David Farrell Krell (San Francisco: Harper and Row, 1984), p. 38; *Nietzsche,* Erster Band (Pfullingen: Verlag Günther Neske, 1961), p. 290. Heidegger cites the *Grossoktavausgabe* of Nietzsche's works (Leipzig, 1905 ff.), Vol. XI, p. 159.

2. Alexandre Kojève, *Introduction to the Reading of Hegel,* ed. Allan Bloom and trans. James H. Nichols, Jr. (New York: Basic Books, 1969), p. 88; *Introduction à la lecture de Hegel,* assembled and published by Raymond Queneau (Paris: Gallimard, 1947), p. 282.

3. References to the *Phenomenology* are cited within parentheses in the text. Full bibliographical data may be found in the statement on Citation Conventions above and in the Bibliography below.

Robert Pippin is impatient with this too-familiar style of apocalyptic Hegelian hagiography. Although he terms it "the textbook version of Hegel's position," Pippin takes his own point of departure from such "ambiguity and confusion" as is "especially obvious in those commentators who treat Hegel as an idiosyncratic Christian, romantic metaphysician, a 'world-soul,' or a 'cosmic spirit' theologian (some of the German literature refers to Hegel's 'onto-theological metaphysics')" (*Hegel's Idealism,* pp. 3–4). Sweeping proclamations about Hegel's supposed prophetic ambitions, Pippin implies, are responsible for "a puzzling irony": although Hegel's influence and importance are beyond any doubt "extraordinary," still "it is widely believed that no one really knows what he was talking about" (ibid.).

In place of such an anachronistic and otherwise compromised approach, but not wishing to deny that "Absolute Idealism" is the key to understanding Hegel, Pippin hopes instead that the interpretive aporia might be "solved if it could be shown that Hegel's speculative position, basically his theory of the Absolute Idea, his claim that such an Idea alone is 'what truly is,' could be interpreted and defended in a way that is not committed to a philosophically problematic theological metaphysics" (ibid., p. 5). In order to accomplish this, Pippin argues persuasively for interpreting Hegel as a post-Kantian whose consistent idealism finds a way, via Fichte, to transform Kant's theory of concepts so as to dispense with the troubling empirical remainder of "intuition," and thus the commitment to "things-in-themselves," in Kant's account of the transcendental unity of apperception.

But acknowledging the validity of situating Hegel's claims in this fashion does not commit one to repudiating all other interpretations, including the obvious ones. Moreover, if Hegel's importance is linked to his influence, as Pippin suggests that it is, then the very freshness of Pippin's own approach suggests that its value will not lie in an appreciation of influence. The present study looks less backward to the roots of Hegel's idealism in Kant than forward to resonances audible today. And in the service of this influence, theology lends a crucially important weight of authority, religion its medium of dissemination; the intellectual event wrought by the *Phenomenology* was in fact contextualized culturally by the invocation of (even if ultimately in order to trump) familiar tropes of the divine. Pippin himself cannot help noting this, if only negatively: "Kant and Fichte reenact a Christian, religious tragedy of human finitude," he writes; "they insist on a fundamental, eternal difference between the human and divine perspectives, and ascribe to the latter the only genuine, absolute knowledge of things in themselves" (ibid., pp. 92–93). Thus, Hegel's *assumption* of the divine perspective must also profoundly "enact" a Christian allegory, even if it be of a Gnostic temper, as we will see in some detail in Chapter Four below.

4. References in parentheses to Nietzsche's published works will cite section number and name whenever possible, the title of the work being an abbreviation of its English equivalent according to the statement on Citation Conventions above. References to unpublished fragments will be cited in the *Kritische Studienausgabe* of Nietzsche's works edited by Giorgio Colli and Mazzino Montinari, abbreviated *KSA*. Unpublished fragments which appeared in *The Will to Power* (*WP*) will be cited in both that text and in *KSA*. Full bibliographical data may be found in the statement on Citation Conventions above and in the Bibliography below.

5. Friedrich Nietzsche, "On Truth and Lies in a Nonmoral Sense," in *Philosophy and Truth: Selections from Nietzsche's Notebooks of the Early 1870s*, ed. and trans. Daniel Breazeale (New Jersey: Humanities Press, 1979), p. 61; "Über Wahrheit und Lüge im aussermoralischen Sinne," *KSA* 1, p. 875.

6. See, for example: *UM* I, sections 6, 12 and II, section 8; *D*, Preface, section 3 and section 193; *GS*, sections 99, 357; *BGE*, sections 204, 211, 252; *CW*, section 10; *TI*, "What the Germans lack," section 4; *EH* III, "The Birth of Tragedy," section 1, "The Case of Wagner," section 3 and IV, section 8; *WP*, sections 1.3, 95, 382, 410, 412; 415, 416, 422 (*KSA* 12, p. 126; 440–43; 523–25; 143–44; 259; 162–63; 113; *KSA* 11, pp. 530–31 respectively). Nietzsche's view, in fact, is largely derivative and, at least before 1876, it is principally derived from Schopenhauer, whose violent animus against Hegel is notorious. In any case, such stray remarks as these (and most of them are glancing and insubstantial besides) are not sufficient to justify the claim made by Gilles Deleuze that one has failed to understand Nietzsche altogether unless Hegel is identified as the implicit enemy against whom Nietzsche's anti-dialectical polemics are directed (*Nietzsche and Philosophy*, trans. Hugh Tomlinson [New York: Columbia University Press, 1983]; *Nietzsche et la philosophie* [Presses Universitaires de France, 1962], passim). Indeed, in *GS*, section 357 (one of the

most sustained and considered of any of these passages), Hegel is first praised for having "introduced the decisive concept of 'development' into science," thereby preparing Europe for Darwinism—and then criticized for having delayed the "triumph of atheism . . . with his grandiose attempt to persuade us of the divinity of existence"! Both of these opinions are pithy but incidental: "aphoristic."

In contrast with Deleuze's position, Stephen Houlgate's squares more easily with the textual evidence: "Nietzsche, as far as I can tell, did not study Hegel's texts in any depth and relied mainly on secondary sources for his interpretation and his evaluation of Hegel's thought. Furthermore, his understanding of Hegel's philosophy was in my view superficial and largely misconceived" (*Hegel, Nietzsche and the Criticism of Metaphysics* [Cambridge: Cambridge University Press, 1986], p. 24). Houlgate's analysis, on the other hand, presumes that Nietzsche's "interpretation and . . . evaluation of Hegel's thought" is meant to be taken at face value, as if it were a scholarly commentary. This approach fails even to acknowledge the extreme exegetical and hermeneutic peculiarity of Nietzsche's "philosophy" from *The Birth of Tragedy* on. It is a fundamental methodological premise of the present study that a prosaic "comparison and contrast" approach to the juxtaposition of Hegel and Nietzsche, however valuable it may be as a scholarly foundation (and Houlgate succeeds admirably in this), will likely fail to be attentive to the larger intellectual and cultural resonances that are of greatest interest and moment here.

7. Daniel Breazeale, "The Hegel-Nietzsche Problem," *Nietzsche-Studien*, Vol. 4 (1975), p. 149. In the introductory first chapter of Houlgate's *Hegel, Nietzsche and the Critique of Metaphysics* (ibid.), a scholarly map of "The Hegel-Nietzsche debate" shows three main hermeneutic territories defended by "(a) those commentators who clearly take Nietzsche's side against Hegel, (b) those who are primarily interested in pointing out certain similarities between the two philosophers, but who also may lean more towards one than the other, and (c) those who use Hegelian arguments to criticize Nietzsche" (p. 4). Houlgate's own position on this map develops a "parallel, stressed by Daniel Breazeale, between the two philosophers as 'critics of is/ought, this world/other world dualism'" (p. 16, citing Breazeale, p. 151) in order to reveal Hegel's critique of conceptual oppositions (the belief in which, Houlgate claims, "is identified by both these philosophers as 'metaphysical'"; p. 22) as more "profound" than Nietzsche's. This view accordingly locates Houlgate's study "in the third category of commentators" (ibid.) identified above.

8. In his book on Hegel, Kaufmann insists that Hegel's "System" consists of "hundreds of short aphorisms . . . what is systematic is merely the arrangement," while in his book on Nietzsche he describes both philosophers as "dialectical monists," "Spirit" and "will to power" having as much in common as have Nietzsche's use of *sublimieren* and the meaning of *aufheben* in Hegel (*Hegel: A Reinterpretation* [Notre Dame, Ind.: University of Notre Dame Press, 1978] p. 293; see also *Nietzsche: Philosopher, Psychologist, Antichrist*, 4th ed. [Princeton, N.J.: Princeton University Press, 1974] pp. 235ff.). For a catalogue of literature that elaborates the "*rapprochement* thesis," see the Bibliography below.

9. Fredric Jameson, Preface to Jean-François Lyotard, *The Postmodern Condition: A Report on Knowledge*, trans. Geoff Bennington and Brian Massumi (Minneapolis: University of Minnesota Press, 1984), p. xix. Charles Taylor, while noting that "a renewed interest [in Hegel] continues unabated to this day," concurs that nonetheless "his actual synthesis is quite dead . . . no one holds the Hegelian ontology" (*Hegel* [Cambridge: Cambridge University Press, 1975], p. 538). Finally, that interest in Hegel remains very active in spite of the unfashionable apparent nature of his metaphysical absolutism, provokes John McCumber to wonder whether this impression itself is correct: "When the beetle is squashed, we cease to stomp. . . . If Hegel is well and truly dead, why does his corpus still twitch so tantalizingly?" (*The Company of Words: Hegel, Language, and Systematic Philosophy* [Evanston, Ill.: Northwestern University Press, 1993], p. 2).

10. J. N. Findlay, *Hegel: A Re-examination* (London: George Allen & Unwin, 1956), p. 148. According special importance to the *Phenomenology* has a long and distinguished history of advocacy; it is, after all, one of only two books Hegel actually wrote during his career (the other being the *Science of Logic*), as Robert Pippin points out (see *Hegel's Idealism*, p. 13).

11. Karl Löwith, *Meaning in History* (Chicago: University of Chicago Press, 1949), p. 150.

12. Marxist and Existentialist commentators—whose joint rediscovery of Hegel's phenomenological descriptions of "an unhappy religious and historical consciousness reminiscent of themes in Kierkegaard or Feuerbach" constituted a "genuine revelation for an entire generation" (Jean Hyppolite, *Studies on Marx and Hegel*, trans. John O'Neill [New York: Basic Books, 1969], p. vi)—symptomatically fail to come to terms with that *telos*. Marxists, determined to read Hegel as an inspired historian, either ignore the absolute (Lukács) or else take its metaphysical finality so seriously that they are led into absurd speculations about "post-historical animals of the species *Homo Sapiens*" (Kojève). Existentialists, on the other hand, in emphasizing Hegel's pithy account of struggle, fear and domination, openly admit that they "prefer what Hegel calls 'unhappy consciousness' to what he calls 'spirit'" (Hyppolite), such that "Human reality is therefore by nature consciousness with no possibility of surpassing its unhappy state" (Sartre). For a critical discussion of Lukács, see Chapter Two, Part I, section 1; of Kojève, Hyppolite, and Sartre, see Chapter Three, Part II, section 1.

13. Friedrich Nietzsche, "On Truth and Lies," Breazeale, trans., op. cit. p. 86; *KSA* 1, p. 884.

14. This term, which names the literary genre exemplified by Goethe's *Wilhelm Meisters Lehrjahre* and Hölderlin's *Hyperion*, was perhaps first applied to Hegel's *Phenomenology* by Josiah Royce (see *Lectures on Modern Idealism* [New Haven, Conn.: Yale University Press, 1919]). Subsequent Hegelian commentaries which affirm the parallel include: H. S. Harris, *Hegel's Development: Night Thoughts (Jena 1801–1806)* (Oxford: Clarendon Press, 1983), pp. 222–23; Walter Kaufmann, *Hegel: A Reinterpretation*, p. 158; Cyril O'Regan, *The Heterodox Hegel* (Albany: State University of New York Press, 1994), pp. 49–57; Mark C. Taylor, *Journeys to Selfhood: Hegel and Kierkegaard* (Berkeley: University of California Press, 1980), pp. 77ff. The *Bildungsroman* is a genre in

which, as M. H. Abrams describes it, "the course of human *Bildung* [development or education], in the individual as in the race, is a fall from the paradisal unity of being into division and conflict between the self and the outer world, which turns out to have been a necessary departure on the way back to a higher reunion with alienated nature" (*Natural Supernaturalism* [New York: W. W. Norton, 1971], p. 237). Cyril O'Regan sketches how this structure is recognizable in the *Phenomenology*: "Hegel's account of the movement toward full self-recognition, and appropriation by detour through ever richer and more adequate perspectives and comportments toward reality, is nothing less than a metalevel discursive translation of *Bildungsroman*" (*The Heterodox Hegel*, p. 51).

15. Letter to Jacob Burkhardt, dated January 6, 1889 (but postmarked Turin, January 5).

16. *UM*, "On the Uses and Disadvantages of History for Life," section 6.

CHAPTER ONE. LANGUAGE AND TRUTH: THE *AUFHEBUNG* OF IMMEDIACY

1. G. W. F. Hegel, "Aphorismen aus der Jenenser Zeit," No. 45, in *Dokumente zu Hegels Entwicklung*, ed. Johannes Hoffmeister (Stuttgart: Fr. Frommanns Verlag, 1936), p. 363.

2. In the *Phenomenology*, Hegel rarely provides really careful critiques of actual historical positions; rather, traditional attitudes are characterized in very general ways to serve as foils for his own "synthetic" alternative. This is true, for example, in his treatment of "Stoicism" and "Skepticism" (see Chapter Three, Part I, section 7). This is another aspect of Hegel's special strategy in the *Phenomenology*: as a "conceptual history of Spirit," the structure of this text more closely resembles that of a novel (specifically, a *Bildungsroman*) than it does a "history of philosophy." More detailed accounts of traditional views can be found in the *Lectures on the History of Philosophy*, to which we shall occasionally have recourse.

3. A peculiarity of English allows this formulation to be somewhat neater in Miller's translation than in Hegel's original German, which reads: "Wir haben uns ebenso *unmittelbar* oder *aufnehmend* zu verhalten, also nicht an ihm, wie es sich darbietet, zu verändern und von dem Auffassen das Begreifen abzuhalten."

4. These traditions are not named as such by Hegel, and this part of the dialectic is not treated historically, but the methodological paradigms associated with the historical traditions named in their most essential forms are here rigorously interrogated and found to be wanting.

5. Parallels between Hegel's and Husserl's phenomenological methods are strong in this first chapter. The claim that simple immediacy is an abstraction is akin to Husserl's principle that consciousness is always intentional, always consciousness-*of* and hence relational or mediated, while in paragraph 94 Hegel rejects the idea that objectivity can be examined in-itself: we have only to "consider the way in which it is present in sense-certainty."

6. Friedrich Nietzsche, "On Truth and Lies in a Nonmoral Sense," trans. by Daniel Breazeale, in *Philosophy and Truth* (New York: Humanities Press, 1979), p. 83; "Über Wahrheit und Lüge im aussermoralischen Sinne," in *Sämtliche Werke*, Kritische Studienausgabe, Vol. I, ed. by Giorgio Colli and Mazzino Montinari (Berlin: Walter de Gruyter, 1980), p. 879.

7. Breazeale, p. 86; Colli and Montinari, p. 884.

8. Curiously—and tellingly—Hegel's own terminological formalism gets tangled in this attempt. Rejecting the pure being that we mean as inaccessible to expression in the sense-certainty dialectic, Hegel calls this principle the "divine nature" of language (para. 110; p. 89)—an odd choice of words in the long run, since the divine language of religious *Vorstellungen* is precisely what conceptual, philosophical expression overcomes. Are we to suppose, then, that Hegel's tongue is in his cheek the whole while that he narrates the divine comedy of Spirit's phenomenology? Yet the final chapter, which articulates a non-alienating, post-metaphorical absolute, itself concludes with a host of images drawn from Christian theology! See Chapter Four, section 2 below.

9. The resonance with Husserl's phenomenology noted earlier is perhaps stronger in this phrase than anywhere else in the *Phenomenology*.

10. See below, pp. 23f.

11. "Mystery" in *Encyclopedia Britannica*, 14th ed. (1944), Vol. 16, p. 45.

12. Robert Gordon Wasson, Albert Hoffmann and Carl A. P. Ruck, *The Road to Eleusis*, (New York: Harcourt, Brace, Jovanovich, 1978). Indeed, as this book also urges, the well-documented custom of diluting wine and drinking it in measured quantities does not square with the sometimes raucous results, given the primitive vinifying methods of the time, which could produce a wine of only a relatively low alcohol content. Ruck suggests that this "secret" ingredient was not completely exclusive, and that wealthy Athenians indulged in specially treated wines with their guests (p. 37).

13. "O Ceres, die du in Eleusis throntest! / Begeistrung trunken fühlt' ich jetzt." G. W. F. Hegel, "Eleusis," in *Dokumente zu Hegels Entwicklung*, ed. Johannes Hoffmeister (Stuttgart: Fr. Frommanns Verlag, 1936), p. 381. The poem describes the mystical uniting of sense (*Sinn*) and intuition (*Anschaung*)— "what mine I called vanished, / I gave myself to the immeasurable, / I am in it, am all, am only it [was mein ich nannte schwindet, / ich gebe mich dem unermeßlichen dahin, / ich bin in ihm, bin alles, bin nur es]"—only at last to lament, in a manner that anticipates Heidegger, the departure of the gods:

> But your temples are silenced, O Goddess!
> Fled is the Gods' circle back to Olympus
> from the blessed alters,
> fled from the desecrated grave of humanity
> the innocent genius which conjured you here!—
> [Doch deine Hallen sind verstummt, o Göttin!
> Geflohen ist der Götter Kreis zurück in den Olymp
> von den geheiligten Altären,
> geflohn von der entweihten Menscheit Grab
> der Unschuld Genius, der her sie zauberte!—]

The poem, it is relevant to note, is dedicated to Hölderlin and dates from the same year as the "Earliest System Programme of German Idealism" (see below, Chapter Four, section 3).

For a brief account of the various and not always harmonious textual sources for this poem, see H. S. Harris, *Hegel's Development: Towards the Sunlight, 1770–1801* (Oxford: Clarendon Press, 1972), n.1, p. 245.

14. See Chapter Four.

15. For a discussion of the constitutive relation between the essential productive ambiguity of Hegel's language and the reader's necessarily active participation in the production of meaning, see my essay "The Ontological Status of Style in Hegel's *Phenomenology*," *Idealistic Studies*, Vol. XIII, No. 1 (January 1983).

16. "The reality of the being of external things as '*Thises*' [*diesen*] or sense things [*sinnlichen*] has absolute truth for consciousness" (para. 109; p. 87).

17. As Jean Hyppolite writes, the entire phenomenological development "has 'at the beginning its own end as its goal.' In this sense, we shall have to compare absolute knowledge—the last chapter of the *Phenomenology*—with sensuous certainty—the first chapter." *Genesis and Structure of Hegel's Phenomenology of Spirit*, trans. Samuel Cherniak and John Heckman (Evanston, Ill.: Northwestern University Press, 1974), p. 81.

18. G. F. W. Hegel, *Science of Logic*, trans. A. V. Miller (London: George Allen and Unwin, 1969), p. 80; *Wissenschaft der Logik*, Erster Band: Die Objektiv Logik (1812–1813), ed. Friedrich Hagemann and Walter Jaeschke, in *Gesammelte Werke*, Vol. 11 (Hamburg: Felix Meiner Verlag, 1978), p. 47.

19. J. Loewenberg, "The Comedy of Immediacy in Hegel's 'Phenomenology'" in *Mind*, Vol. XLIV (1935), p. 28.

20. Taylor, *Hegel*, p. 142.

21. G. W. F. Hegel, *Logic*, Part I of the *Encyclopedia of the Philosophical Sciences*, trans. William Wallace (Oxford: The Clarendon Press, 1975), section 66; *Enzyklopädie der Philosophischen Wissenschaften im Grundrisse* (1830), ed. F. Nicolin and O. Pöggeler (Hamburg: Felix Meiner Verlag, 1969). Subsequent references to Hegel's section numbers appear within parentheses in the text. English renderings are substantially my own, although in some cases I have followed William Wallace's rather free but very readable translation.

22. See the Conclusion (Part VII) of Hyppolite's *Genesis and Structure*.

23. Ibid., p. 82.

24. Hyppolite: "The beginning of the *Logic* corresponds to that of the *Phenomenology*" (p. 87, n.9). It is also to be noted that, at the time of the first edition of the *Wissenschaft der Logik*, Hegel thought of the *Phenomenology* as a necessary part of the "System": "Logic . . . forms the first sequel to the *Phenomenology of Spirit* in an expanded arrangement of the System" (Preface to first edition of 1812, p. 29).

25. I have chosen to render Hegel's *Begriff* with the English "Notion" for several reasons. First, it is the usage already familiar in the work of Hegel's two best and most prolific translators, William Wallace and A. V. Miller. Second, the *Oxford English Dictionary* offers a definition of "notion" as a "general concept," implying a broader scope than is surveyed by "concept," and this nuance is appropriate to Hegel's meaning. Finally, although rather quaint in contemporary English, the word "notion" is very much more at home in nineteenth-century usage.

26. Yet another iteration of these arguments occurs, very briefly indeed, in passages near the end of the *Encyclopedia* (sections 418 and 419 of the *Philosophy of Spirit*), which summarize the progress of dialectic in the *Phenomenology*. The telling there does not differ in substance from the otherwise very much more fully developed accounts in the *Phenomenology* and the *Logic*.

27. Martin J. de Nys, "'Sense-Certainty' and Universality: Hegel's Entrance into the *Phenomenology*" in *International Philosophical Quarterly*, Vol. 18, No. 4 (December, 1978), p. 455.

28. Robert Solomon, *In the Spirit of Hegel* (Oxford University Press, 1983, p. 329, n. 16.

29. Loewenberg, p. 31.

30. Ludwig Feuerbach, *Principles of the Philosophy of the Future*, trans. M. H. Vogel (Indianapolis, Ind.: Bobbs-Merril, 1966), p. 43. Subsequent references appear within parentheses in the text.

31. Karl Löwith, "Mediation and Immediacy in Hegel, Marx and Feuerbach," trans. K. R. Dove, in *New Studies in Hegel's Philosophy*, ed. Warren E. Steinkraus (New York: Holt, Rinehart and Winston, 1971), p. 136.

32. Karl Löwith, "Hegel und die Sprache," in *Neue Rundschau*, No. 76 (1965), p. 286. Translations are my own.

33. Löwith in Steinkraus, p. 132.

34. Ibid.

35. Loewenberg, p. 24. Subsequent references appear within parentheses in the text.

36. Solomon, *In the Spirit of Hegel*, p. 338. Subsequent references appear within parentheses in the text.

37. Löwith in Steinkraus, p. 137; quoted by De Nys, p. 451.

38. Charles Taylor, "The Opening Arguments of the *Phenomenology*," in *Hegel: A Collection of Critical Essays*, ed. Alasdair MacIntyre (Notre Dame, Ind.: University of Notre Dame Press, 1976), p. 163. Subsequent references appear within parentheses in the text.

39. Derrida writes in his next paragraph: "The movements of deconstruction . . . are not possible and effective, nor can they take accurate aim, except by inhabiting those structures [Nietzsche's, Heidegger's—and Hegel's]. Inhabiting them *in a certain way*, because one always inhabits, and all the more when one does not expect it [quand on ne s'en doute pas]." Jacques Derrida, *Of Grammatology*, trans. Gyatri Chakravorty Spivak (Baltimore: John Hopkins University Press, 1974), p. 24; *De la grammatologie* (Paris: Les Editions de Minuit, 1967), p. 39.

40. *Grammatology*, pp. 23–24; *Grammatologie*, p. 38.

41. De Nys, p. 457.

CHAPTER TWO. SELF AND OTHER: THE MASTERY OF MEDIATION

1. Charles Taylor, *Hegel*, p. 104.

2. Klaus Hartmann, "Hegel: A Non-Ontological View," in Alasdair MacIntyre, ed., *Hegel: A Collection of Critical Essays* (Notre Dame, Ind.: University of Notre Dame Press, 1976), pp. 101–24.

3. Paul Ricoeur, lecture on "Lordship and Bondage" delivered at the University of Chicago on October 26, 1978.

4. Solomon, *In the Spirit of Hegel*, p. 219.

5. Ibid., p. 220. Solomon cites Theodore Haering and Otto Pöggeler; the latter argues that Chapter VI, "Spirit," does not even belong in the *Phenomenology* at all! See "Zur Deutung der *Phänomenologie des Geistes*" in *Hegel-Studien*, Vol. 1 (1961), pp. 255–91. Subsequent references to Solomon appear within parentheses in the text.

6. Georg Lukács, *The Young Hegel*, trans. by Rodney Livingstone (Cambridge, Mass.: MIT Press, 1976), p. 471. Subsequent references appear within parentheses in the text.

7. Solomon, for example, notes that "Hegel himself confuses the issue in his terminology, since he is perhaps too quick to use the term 'self-consciousness' when it is not at all clear that there is as yet any such thing" (*In the Spirit of Hegel*, p. 30). And indeed, just *when* self-consciousness properly so-called can be said to have appeared is important to know, for if it comes only with recognition ("Hegel does not say that we [as self-consciousness] want to be recognized; he says we cannot be self-consciousness *unless* we are recognized"; ibid., p. 438), then it appears only at the end of history and therefore cannot be said to be the agent of history. On the other hand, if self-consciousness has been with us since the return from objectivity in the sense-certainty dialectic ("Self-consciousness does not entirely begin in chapter 4; the 'I' has been with us since sense-certainty" [ibid., p. 432]), then it is bewildering that Hegel should regard lordship and bondage as the key moment in the larger chapter called "Self-Consciousness" whereas sense-certainty initiates the chapter on "Consciousness." In fact, this confusion is (again) mostly Solomon's; Hegel is ambivalent, but finally self-consciousness in-and-for-itself is *desire*, not recognition, and desire properly so-called—human desire—is always desire for another self-consciousness, not for a mere thing. Self-consciousness, therefore, is the unsatisfied desire for recognition; only absolute Spirit achieves that satisfaction.

8. J. N. Findlay, "Analysis" of para. 167 in *Phenomenology of Spirit*, p. 518.

9. Hyppolite, *Genesis and Structure*, p. 159.

10. Paul Ricoeur, lecture on "Lordship and Bondage" delivered at the University of Chicago on October 26, 1978.

11. Solomon, *In the Spirit of Hegel*, p. 397. Subsequent references appear within parentheses in the text.

12. Philosophers will recall the tale Aristophanes tells in Plato's *Symposium*, according to which we all seek a sexual companion in order to regain a state of primal completeness in which human beings had two faces, four arms and legs—and two sets of genitals. It was the *hubris* of this original race, presuming to advance against the gods, that led Zeus to split them down the middle into the desperate, desiring half-creatures that we are (*Symposium*, 189–93). The final inadequacy of love on Hegel's account is consistent with the parodic tone of "Aristophanes'" suggestion. Freud, in *Beyond the Pleasure Principle*, cites this passage, adding that "what is essentially the same theory is already to be found in the Unpanishads" (*Beyond the Pleasure Principle*, trans. and ed.

James Strachey [New York: W. W. Norton, 1961], p. 52). Specifically, the story appears in the *Brihadaranyaka-Upanishad*, the most ancient of these early (ca. 800 B.C.) Hindu texts, but this version may in turn derive from Babylonian origins that are even older.

13. Hyppolite, *Genesis and Structure*, p. 160.

14. Lukács, *The Young Hegel*, p. 476.

15. Throughout the *Phenomenology*, Hegel contrasts the term *Wessen*, which can mean either "essence" or "being," and is often translated as "essential being," with *Sein*, which means only "being" and which implies a category of existence that is at once more immediate and less "self-conscious." To make this distinction clear, I have rendered *Sein* as "mere being" where context requires it, giving the German in square brackets. Martin Heidegger's protracted inquiry into the history of the *mis*understanding of *Sein* can hardly go unremarked here. However, his observations and contentions are peripheral to Hegel's focus on the essence of self-consciousness in this chapter.

16. The bondsman does not form the object according to his *own* idea, as some commentators have mistakenly asserted. It is the lord who tells him what to make. Thus, although "a manufactured object incarnates an idea," it is still the case that "the Slave who *works* for the Master represses his *instincts* in relation to an *idea*, a *concept*" that does not originate in his own consciousness (Kojève, *Introduction to the Reading of Hegel*, p. 51).

17. The peculiar grammar of the word "subject" in English lends a convenient emphasis to these formulations. The word designates the doer of an action and, almost contrariwise, someone under the power or authority of another. Thus, here we find that the subjectivity or autonomous selfhood of the lord derives from the subjectivity of his bondsman, that is, his "subject." The lord's "subject" is the dialectical locus of his own subjectivity.

18. Stanley Rosen writes "the master-slave relation . . . is an excellent illustration of the dialectic of the inverted world. As dependent upon the slave, the master's consciousness is slavish or inessential, and precisely as dominant or essential. As that upon which the master depends, the slave comes to recognize his own independence, and precisely as dependent. Each is the opposite of himself; each is implicitly the other" (*G. W. F. Hegel* [New Haven, Conn.: Yale University Press, 1974], p. 162).

This protean "power of the negative" is much more than a mere analytical tool: it threatens the ontological integrity of otherness as such, which is "always already" within the assimilative scope of an omnivorous dialectic. The Absolute can never be far for a *Kraft* that makes day of night, mastery of slavery. It is this pretended power that Marx will resist with the "flesh and blood" of socio-political materialism and that Nietzsche will deflate with subtle irony. But these battles must wait for Hegel to assemble his Army of the Absolute on the field of the final chapter!

19. Heidegger will make a similar distinction, although he assigns terminological priority to *Angst*.

20. This last clause—"den es hat die Furcht des Todes, des absoluten Herrn, empfunden"—which crucially anticipates the morphologically analogous role of religion in Hegel's phenomenological account, appears in the Hoffmeister edition, but not in Miller's translation.

21. G. W. F. Hegel, *Early Theological Writings*, trans. T. M. Knox, with intro. and fragments trans. Richard Kroner (New York: Harper and Torchbooks, 1961), pp. 67–181.

22. Ibid., pp. 302–308. Subsequent references appear within parentheses in the text.

23. Solomon, *In the Spirit of Hegel*, p. 59.

24. Consider, for example, Herbert Marcuse's *Eros and Civilization*, Norman O. Brown's *Life Against Death*, Paul Ricoeur's *Freud and Philosophy*—and let us not forget Sartre's definitive engagement with both Hegel and Freud in *Being and Nothingness*. This is just to cite the most conspicuous cases. It is not, however, my intention here to launch into a thorough exploration of the Freudian connection. Rather, I wish only to survey quickly the variety of possible approaches to reading "Lordship and Bondage" in order to establish a context for the subsequent selection.

25. Solomon, *In the Spirit of Hegel*, p. 449.

26. J. M. E. McTaggart, *Studies in Hegelian Cosmology* (Cambridge: Cambridge University Press, 1918), p. 262.

27. In his brilliant editor's introduction to *The Portable Greek Reader* (New York: Viking Press/Penguin Books, 1977), W. H. Auden notes how both of the two principal erotic paradigms in Western literature—Tristan and Isolde and Don Juan—are fundamentally foreign to Greek cultural consciousness for reasons analogous to those that make erotic love insufficient for Hegel as a resolution of the lordship and bondage dialectic. "The Tristan-Isolde myth is unGreek," Auden writes, "because no Greek could conceive of attributing absolute value to another individual," while "The Don Juan myth is unGreek, as Kierkegaard has pointed out, not because he sleeps with a number of women, but because he keeps a list of them" (p. 28). For Hegel, the exclusivity of romantic love precisely as such fails to satisfy the desire of emerging Spirit: to the extent that Tristan and Isolde (or Romeo and Juliette, etc.) love one another to the exclusion of the rest of the world, which is allied against them, their love denies social and political reality, the intersubjective context essential for Spirit's historical self-unfolding. Such a love is thus other-worldly, a love incompatible with the Real, and consequently it can only end in the death, rather than the satisfaction, of the lovers' desire. As for Don Juan, love motivated by the desire for recognition of the other is simply supplanted by "an arithmetical reason . . . Don Juan is in torment because, however great the number of his seductions, it still remains a finite number and he cannot rest until he has counted up to infinity" (ibid.).

28. G. W. F. Hegel, *Lectures on the Philosophy of Religion*, trans. E. B. Speirs, B. D. and J. Burdon Sanderson (London: Routledge and Kegan Paul, 1968), Vol. III, p. 106.

29. Hyppolite, *Genesis and Structure*, p. 146.

30. Rosen, *G. W. F. Hegel*, p. 155.

31. Of these, it is fair, and perhaps even customary, to single out Kojève as the richest. Rosen casually calls him "The standard commentary on the master-slave dialectic" (*G. W. F. Hegel*, p. 155, n. 2), and indeed, Kojève's influence on Hegel scholarship, particularly in France, is partly responsible for the importance of lordship and bondage in general discussion. Of course, on this Kojève

follows Marx's lead. But Marx's critique of Hegel's retreat from the battlefield into abstraction will be considered in Chapter Three, when we turn to the absolute directly. For now, Kojève's hegemony need not unduly predetermine our reading of "lordship and bondage"; the consequences of his sometimes rather ludicrous literalism in treating of Hegel's world-historical ambitions will, like the Marxian attack it tries to face, be central to the project of understanding the Hegelian absolute proper to the next chapter.

The passages most relevant to lordship and bondage occur in Kojève's summary of the *Phenomenology* and in the long first chapter entitled "In Place of an Introduction." This text, by interspersing abundant commentary in a translation of Hegel's "deduction of Desire," mitigates substantially the excessive density of the argumentation about which Solomon (*In the Spirit of Hegel*, p. 396 and passim), along with many other commentators, complain so much. Because we have already looked closely at these passages, a general review of Kojève would be superfluous here.

32. Herbert Marcuse, *Reason and Revolution* (Boston: Beacon Press, 1960), p. 116.

33. Emil Fackenheim, *The Religious Dimension in Hegel's Thought* (Chicago: University of Chicago Press, 1967), p. 41.

34. Taylor, *Hegel*, p. 152. Further support for this reading can be found in Findlay, *Hegel: A Re-examination*, p. 98; in Taylor, p. 154; and in Fackenheim, *The Religious Dimension in Hegel's Thought*, p. 42.

35. Marcuse, *Reason and Revolution*, p. 95.

36. Findlay, *Hegel: A Re-examination*, p. 96.

37. Taylor, *Hegel*, p. 150.

38. See, for example: Kojève, *Introduction to the Reading of Hegel*, pp. 13 and 46; Hyppolite, *Genesis and Structure*, p. 162; Rosen, *G.W.F. Hegel*, p. 172; and Lukács, *The Young Hegel*, p. 476.

39. Fackenheim, *The Religious Dimension in Hegel's Thought*, p. 39. Subsequent references appear within parentheses in the text.

40. Kojève, *Introduction to the Reading of Hegel*, p. 26.

CHAPTER THREE. ABSOLUTE KNOWING: THE END OF PHILOSOPHY

1. "The negation of the object is thus its preservation as a mode of my consciousness" (Rosen, *G. W. F. Hegel*, p. 156).

2. Taylor, *Hegel*, p. 206.

3. Hyppolite, *Genesis and Structure*, p. 195.

4. The reference Hegel made earlier to the Eleusinian Mysteries (para. 109; p. 87) is fleeting and undeveloped (see the commentary in Chapter One, Part I, section 3 above), while the critiques of object- and subject-centered philosophical starting points are not explicitly historical (see Chapter One, Part I, section 2).

5. G. W. F. Hegel, *Lectures on the History of Philosophy*, Vol. II, trans. E. S. Haldane and Frances H. Simpson, M.A. (New York: Humanities Press,

1974), p. 234; *Vorlesungen über die Geschichte der Philosophie*, Vol. II, in *Sämtliche Werke*, Vol. XVIII, ed. Hermann Glockner (Stuttgart: Fr. Frommans Verlag, 1928), p. 425. English renderings are substantially my own. Subsequent references appear within parentheses in the text.

6. Dialectic first appears to consciousness as something "*dem es preisgegeben ist*" (para. 204; p. 156). Later, Hegel describes how the unhappy consciousness "surrenders" (*preisgibt*) its material form in aspiration for the Unchangeable (paras. 219f; pp. 154f.). The usage is consistent, and affords an early insight into the tragic flaw of Stoic and Skeptic "thought."

7. These are sub-divided into ten "earlier Tropes," which are deployed against ordinary consciousness generally, and five "later Tropes," which proceed against philosophical reflection.

8. See Chapter Two, Part I, section 4, p. 51 above.

9. Erich Heller exploits the same pun when he describes the unhappy consciousness as "the affliction of self-consciousness, the grown man's shame and embarrassment at being his naked separate self" (*The Disinherited Mind* [New York: Harcourt Brace Jovanovich, 1975], p. 322).

10. See Chapter One, Part I, section 1 above.

11. There are, of course, several concentrically enclosed dialectics of the historical development of religion. Perhaps the largest circle is sketched in Chapter VII of the *Phenomenology*, where the primitive worship of natural objects holds place as the dialectical first moment. Hegel interprets the Egyptian Sphinx as a transitional entity: the struggle of consciousness to recognize itself and rise above the primitive animism of animal forms is expressed in a creature that is half human, and who *speaks*—albeit still only in riddles. The heroic gods of Hellenism do manifest the Spirit as human subject, but excessively: like the unhappy consciousness, with which the Greek "*Kunstreligion*" is associated, such an emphasis on the self ultimately kills the gods. It is the night in which "Substance was betrayed and made itself into Subject" (para. 703; p. 492). This image, used in the description of the internal contradiction to be dialectically exploited by Spirit in moving beyond the Greek religious consciousness, is in fact taken from the story of Gethsemane, a Christian *Vorstellung*—another concentric circle.

12. That embodiment is the site of corruption and that corruption is the dialectical seed of resurrection is demonstrated in a startling way via Hegel by the ingenious Slavoj Zizek (*The Sublime Object of Ideology* [London: Verso, 1989]). Taking as his Hegelian cue the infamous passage that concludes discussions of phrenology—the passage that remarks what "Nature naively expresses when it combines the organ of its highest fulfillment, the organ of generation, with the organ or urination" (para. 346; p. 254)—and linking this passage to Augustine's "theory of the phallus," Zizek advances the dialectic with "a certain well-known vulgar joke." For Augustine, sexuality is not the sin for which man is punished, but rather the *punishment itself*: "This excessive, non-functional, constitutively perverse character of human sexuality represents God's punishment for man's pride and his want of power" (p. 222). The phallus turns out to be "the point at which man's own body takes revenge on him for his false pride" (p. 223) by stubbornly acting as if on its own, beyond the control of the will. But then, this preliminary moment of material self-alienation is dialectically overcome by means of

the promised "vulgar joke": the phallus is the lightest thing in the world because it can be "elevated by mere thought" (ibid.)! In Augustine, the will is vanquished by the flesh and man is humbled thereby; but equally plausible is the "vulgar" insight that the phallus materially manifests the power of thought.

13. Hegel writes that his consciousness "casts upon the middle term [Mitte] or minister [Diener] its own freedom of decision, and herewith the responsibility for its own action" (para. 228; p. 169)

14. It is curious that Hegel has so little to say about Gnosticism and Cabala, "mystical" doctrines centered on mind as the immanent locus of absolute transcendence. But echoes of the eternally recurring millennial doctrine of the twelfth-century abbot Joachim of Fiore are strong in Hegel's trinitarian and teleological world history: comprehension of present and past finally implies the heresy of knowing the future. For an interpretation of these influences or resonances in the context of questions regarding attempts to make Hegel's claims strictly historical and literally factual, see Chapter Four below.

15. It is accordingly tempting to divide the *Phenomenology* into two simple parts with unhappy consciousness as the watershed: Taylor insists that the first part is concerned with individual consciousness, while the second pursues the analysis of "spirit as a supra-personal subject" (*Hegel*, p. 167).

16. In general, as Paul Ricoeur reminds us, "*Vorstellung*" for Hegel "covers not only stories and symbols—images, if you will—but also such highly refined conceptualized expressions as Trinity, Creation, Fall, Incarnation, and Salvation, not only in religious but also in theological discourse" ("The Status of *Vorstellung* in Hegel's Philosophy of Religion," in *Meaning, Truth, and God*, ed. Leroy S. Rouner [Notre Dame and London: University of Notre Dame Press, 1982], p. 70).

17. "Picture thought" is Miller's interesting barbarism for Hegel's *Vorstellung*. A highly unconventional rendering with obvious shortcomings, Miller's suggestion nevertheless vividly captures the image-oriented resonance on which Hegel relies in order to contrast *Vorstellungen* with *Begriffen*. Ricoeur points out that Hegel's use of *Vorstellung*—opposed to *Begriff* rather than, as in Kant, to *Ding as Sich*—"should not be translated as 'idea,' but as 'figurative thinking'" (ibid.). And yet, there is also an implicit critique of Kant embedded in the choice of vocabulary here: the image before the mind's eye, the *Vorstellung* that is structured by the forms of intuition and the pure concepts of the understanding, is for Hegel not the substance and limit of our knowledge but rather a *Gleichnis* (like *alles Vergängliche*): something to be interpreted, something to be transcended through knowing interpretation.

18. Hyppolite, *Genesis and Structure*, p. 573. Ricoeur observes further that *Vorstellungen* and abstraction are linked in both places (lecture on "Absolute Knowing" delivered at the University of Chicago on February 8, 1979).

19. Solomon, *In the Spirit of Hegel*, p. 635.

20. Taylor, *Hegel*, p. 538.

21. "Diotima's ladder" in Plato's *Symposium* is one of the principal sources for this image (although the cave allegory in the *Republic*, the progression of knowing through four distinct phases leading toward "knowledge of the fifth" in the *Seventh Letter*, and the counsel of philosophy concerning the separation of soul and body in the *Phaedo* are other more or less immediate

instances). But Christian mystical theology, neo-Platonist and otherwise, abounds in texts that declare themselves spiritual ladders of enlightenment. See, for example, Johannes Klimakos, *The Holy Ladder of Perfection*, trans. Fr. Robert (London, 1958); Walter Hilton, *The Scale of Perfection*, ed. Evelyn Underhill (London, 1923).

22. "Given the nature of Skepticism, one cannot ask for any system of propositions . . . ," *Lectures*, Vol. II, p. 345; *Vorlesungen über die Geschichte der Philosophie*, Vol. II, in: *Werke in zwanzig Bänden*, Vol. 19, ed. Eva Moldenhauer and Karl Marcus Michel (Frankfurt am Main: Suhrkamp Verlag, 1971), p. 374. See also, *Lectures*, p. 367; *Vorlesungen*, p. 397. The clause quoted in this note does not appear in the edition of Hegel's *Vorlesungen* cited earlier; there are altogether nine versions of these lectures, and—like Beethoven, Bruckner, and Mahler—Hegel died while at work on the tenth. Haldane and Simson's very uneven translation was made from the second edition of 1840.

23. Hyppolite writes that, whereas Stoicism is the Truth of the slave's consciousness, asceticism (i.e., "religious Stoicism") is the Truth of the unhappy consciousness (*Genesis and Structure*, p. 212).

24. Hyppolite writes that this passage rehearses the history of philosophy "in one page" (*Genesis and Structure*, p. 573), although it is longer than a single page even in his own French translation.

25. Herbert Marcuse, *Eros and Civilization* (New York: Vintage Books, 1962), p. 106.

26. Kojève, *Introduction to the Reading of Hegel*: Nichols, pp. 87–88; Queneau, p. 282. Subsequent references appear within parentheses in the text, "Nichols" referring to the English, and "Queneau" to the original French. I have occasionally modified Nichols's reliable and frequently ingenious translation, and I have inserted important or problematic French terms in square brackets when this seemed advisable. French terms in brackets are italicized only when, in Kojève's text, they are italicized.

27. Karl Marx, "Economic and Philosophical Manuscripts" of 1844, in *Karl Marx: Selected Writings*, ed. David McLellan (Oxford: Oxford University Press, 1977), p. 99.

28. Kojève will make this explicit, arguing that discourse is already an historical phenomenon that as such cannot survive the end of History.

29. A version of this claim (which Sartre suggests) is urged persuasively by Marx.

30. Hyppolite, *Genesis and Structure*, p. 190. Subsequent references appear within parentheses in the text.

31. Indeed, Sartre concurs; in *Being and Nothingness* (trans. by Hazel Barnes [New York: Philosophical Library, 1956], p. 90; *L'être et le néant* [Paris: Gallimard, 1943], p. 129) he writes

> The being of human reality is suffering because it rises [surgit] in being as perpetually haunted by a totality which it is without being able to be it, precisely because it could not attain the in-itself without losing itself as for-itself. Human reality is therefore by nature consciousness with no possibility of surpassing its unhappy state.

The impossibility of really uniting with the other is, Sartre insists, a fundamental given of human reality, and so the Hegelian fantasy of absolute knowing indulges the "delicious consciousness of failure" in a project of metaphysical masochism (*Being and Nothingness*, p. 379; *L'être et le néant*, p. 428–29).

32. The "true dog," "killed" by the *Aufhebung* of dialectic, was Kojève's victim once before, and not in a footnote but in the body of the text (Nichols, p. 140; Queneau, pp. 272–72).

33. Footnotes like these seem to bear out, even demand, the extra attention accorded to the "marginal" by Derrida. So far as I am aware, however, Derrida has not written on this remarkable sequence of marginalia in Kojève. Instead, Francis Fukuyama has done so, initially in an essay that enjoyed a brief cult status in America during the Bush administration when it heralded the fall of the Berlin Wall and the break-up of the Soviet Union as markers of the advent of eternal democracy. See: "The End of History?," *The National Interest* (Summer 1989) and *The End of History and the Last Man* (New York: Free Press, 1992).

34. Marx in McLellan, p. 99. Subsequent references appear within parentheses in the text.

35. "An objective being has an objective effect and it would not have an objective effect if its being did not include an objective element. It only creates and posits objects because it is posited by objects, because it is by origin natural" (ibid., p. 103).

36. *Phenomenology*, para. 63; *Phänomenologie*, para. 52. See the discussion above, Chapter Three, Part I, section 4.

CHAPTER FOUR. ANTICIPATORY REPETITION: HETERODOX SPIRITUALITY AND HEGEL'S PHILOSOPHICAL ESCHATOLOGY

1. In his classic of literary criticism *Natural Supernaturalism* (New York: W. W. Norton, 1971), M. H. Abrams goes so far as to suggest that Marx's interpretation of history as proceeding in three socio-political dispensations that conclude, through violent revolution, in the secular paradise of communism is a synthesis of Hegel's historical dialectic with biblical apocalypse. See pp. 313–16.

2. Curiously, the very last words of the *Phenomenology* are not Hegel's—although they are not quite Schiller's either, being rather an "adaptation" (or misquotation). It is also interesting to note in anticipation that Schiller's "*drittes Reich*" alludes to the "third dispensation" prophesied by Joachim of Fiore; the concluding lines of the *Phenomenology* are a palimpsest of clues. See Wilkinson and Willoughby's note in their edition of Schiller's *On the Aesthetic Education of Man* (Oxford: Oxford University Press, 1967), p. 296, and Abrams, p. 351.

3. Paul Ricoeur, lecture on "Absolute Knowing" delivered at the University of Chicago on February 8, 1979.

4. Fackenheim, *The Religious Dimension in Hegel's Thought*, p. 164. This point is driven home with considerable vigor: "The testimony of speculative thought will be possible only because the testimony of Christian faith is already actual" (p. 190). Furthermore, "speculative thought . . . does not expose

religious representation as a mere human projection and illusion as it reflects on it. Careless readers have always mistaken it for such a reflection, and they have therefore viewed Hegel as a demythologizing enemy of religious faith" (p. 155). In this context we should also recall the end of the *Lectures on the Philosophy of Religion* cited earlier.

5. Hyppolite, *Genesis and Structure*, p. 191. Regarding Hegel's ambivalence about Christianity, see p. 193.

6. Findlay, *Hegel: A Re-examination*, p. 140.

7. In 1910, William Bousset warned that "It is a mistake to regard the Gnostics and Gnosticism as an intellectual tendency chiefly concerned with philosophical speculation, the reconciliation of religion with philosophy and theology" ("Gnosticism," in *Encyclopaedia Britannica*, 11th ed. [1910–11], Vol. 12, p. 153). While this may be good advice with which many scholars would still agree, the radical Gnostic denial of materiality nevertheless implies a rigorously intellectualist ontology. In this, Gnosticism "anticipated eighteenth-century aesthetics and nineteenth-century philosophical idealists" as it was characterized principally by a "speculative, philosophical mood" among early Christians which found sympathy with Hellenistic intellectualism (see Harold O. J. Brown, *Heresies* [Garden City, N.Y.: Doubleday, 1984], pp. 55ff.). In effect, the historical reality of Christ was of less interest to Gnostics like Saturninus and Basilides than were the *idea* of an unseen God (Cf. John 1:18) and the *images* of angels, archangels, and divine principalities (Cf. Eph. 1:21, 6:12). The dramatic discovery in 1945 of a nearly complete Gnostic library in Nag Hamadi, Egypt, also forces a re-evaluation of earlier views, and goes some distance toward vindicating Hegel's claim that Gnostic "Aeons" were synthetic Notions (*Lectures on the History of Philosophy*, Vol. II, pp. 394ff.). The nihilistic consequences of the Gnostic *dues absconditus* are also relevant to the Hegelian usurpation of religious transcendence and its Nietzschean legacy; see the Epilogue "Gnosticism, Existentialism, and Nihilism" in Hans Jonas, *The Gnostic Religion* (Boston: Beacon Press, 1958), pp. 320–40.

It should be noted by way of qualification of this usage, however, that *gnosis* or knowledge does not by itself constitute a generic criterion of apocalypse, nor does Joachim of Fiore, with whose thought we will be primarily concerned here, represent a straightforward extension of Gnosticism. However, a principled distinction between Gnostic apocalypse and Judeo-Christian apocalyptic, of which Joachimite apocalyptic is an exemplary meta-version, can be affirmed without compromising the argument made below to the effect that Hegel's vacillation between the demands of *Vorstellung* and *Begriff* recalls Joachim. I agree with Cyril O'Regan concerning this analytic (although not necessarily historical) distinction, and I am in debt to him for helping me to clarify the intertextual dynamics that touch on it.

In light of these remarks and in anticipation of the scholarly evidence that follows, I acknowledge that I will be applying the term "Gnostic" to Hegelian eschatology with some contextual latitude and with an admittedly tendentious agenda: by linking the intellectualist implications of the word's Greek etymology with certain heterodox Christian theologies that bear a family resemblance, I hope to show how Hegel's success in usurping divine transcendence by linguistic means is the key to understanding both the "nihilism" associated with Nietzsche's proclamation that "God is dead" and the cultural strategies (variously labeled "post-nihilist," "post-historical," "post-modern") developed, and still developing, in response to this "apocalypse."

8. O'Regan, *The Heterodox Hegel*, Chap. 6, section 6.2, "The Genre of Hegelian Apocalypse," pp. 298–310.

9. See Thomas J. J. Altizer, "History as Apocalypse," in *Deconstruction and Theology* (New York: Crossroads, 1982), passim; O'Regan, *The Heterodox Hegel*, pp. 298ff.; Eric Voegelin, *From Enlightenment to Revolution*, ed. John H. Hallowel (Durham, N.C.: Duke University Press, 1975), pp. 240–302 and *Science, Politics and Gnosticism* (Washington, D.C.: Regnery Gateway, 1968), passim.

10. O'Regan, *The Heterodox Hegel*, p. 302. These features are enumerated on p. 301, their Hegelian corollaries on pp. 302–303.

11. Ibid., p. 310.

12. See Ibid., pp. 303–307 and p. 368.

13. Ibid., p. 310 and p. 267.

14. O'Regan identifies seven Joachimite elements recapitulated in Hegel, concluding that "for Joachim, revelation is (was) not once and for all, but continuous, progressive, and eschatologically perfect and universal—features that are stunningly replicated in the Hegelian account" (ibid., p. 279). Specific to the *Phenomenology*, O'Regan finds that Hegel's exposition of three kinds of religious relation in the chapter on unhappy consciousness "suggests Joachim's historical schema" (p. 271).

15. "Hegel's schematization in *PS* [the *Phenomenology*]," O'Regan notes, tends "to recall the Joachimite developmental movement from Father to Spirit through son by unfolding a pattern of relation between the human and the divine that connotes an increasing validation of the finite" (*The Heterodox Hegel*, p. 272).

16. Quoted from Joachim's *Liber Concordie Novi ac Veteris Testamenti* (Venice, 1519) by Jürgen Moltmann in *Trinity and the Kingdom: The Doctrine of God*, trans. Margaret Kohl (New York: Harper and Row, 1981), pp. 204–205.

17. In a letter dated 8 June 1188, Pope Clement III alluded to two of Joachim's works, and encouraged him to continue them. Subsequently, Joachim was aided financially by the Emperor Frederick II and ecclesiastically by popes Celestine III and Innocent III in establishing the monastery of San Giovanni in Fiore. Finally, Pope Honorious III formally recognized Joachim as orthodox in a bull of 1220.

However, the appropriation of his millennial prophesies by Franciscan Spirituals and other more marginal mendicant sects led ultimately to papal condemnation of Joachim's ideas. Already in 1215, Joachim's tract against Peter Lombard was censured by the fourth Lateran Council, and in 1254 a book appeared in Paris by the Franciscan Spiritual Gerardo de Borgo San Donnino that provoked Pope Alexander IV, through a council held at Arles in 1260, to condemn Joachim's writings and his supporters. The heterodox Italian movements of the thirteenth and fourteenth centuries—the Dolcinists, the Fraticelli, and other sects—were also decisively influenced by Joachim. So was Roger Bacon, while Dante placed Joachim in Paradise (*Paradiso* XII, 14041).

18. Karl Löwith, *From Hegel to Nietzsche* (London: Constable, 1965), pp. 32, 41.

19. Hans Blumenberg has offered the most sustained and perhaps also the most incisive alternative account in two major books (*Die Legitimität der Neuzeit* [Suhrkamp, 1966] and *Arbeit am Mythos* [Suhrkamp, 1979]) and many essays. The first of these books is concerned to show, at great length and with considerable subtlety, that the secularization hypothesis advanced principally by Löwith is not necessary to explain the modern idea of progress.

Bernard Yack (*The Longing for Total Revolution* [Berkeley: University of California Press, 1992]) provides another perspective on the Rise and Fall of Western Metaphysics that substantially skirts the ontotheological dimension by reading eighteenth- and nineteenth-century European intellectual history as late Enlightenment dissatisfaction and discontent assuaged by Hegelian idealism following upon Schiller's secular *Kunstreligion*. But crediting Hegel for "taming the longing" of his time only begs the question of the nature of that longing. Moreover, Yack's most challenging claims are built upon foundations laid by Blumenberg.

20. See Marjorie Reeves, *Joachim of Fiore and the Prophetic Future* (London: SPCK, 1976), chapter 6, "Joachim and Protestantism," pp. 136ff. and O'Regan, *The Heterodox Hegel*, pp. 263–64.

21. See Michael Murray, *Modern Philosophy of History: Its Origin and Destination* (The Hague: Martinus Nijhoff, 1970), pp. 90–91. Murray cites two passages in Hegel that acknowledge Lessing's importance on this point (*The Philosophy of Right*, section 343, and *Reason in History* [*Die Vernunft in der Geschichte*, 1955, p. 150]). Murray also briefly describes "the attraction of the young Hegel to Lessing" in the context of Hegel's review of Schiller's *Letters on the Aesthetic Education of Man*—in which Hegel tellingly refers to the text using Lessing's term *Menschengeschlechts* in place of Schiller's *Menschen*—and in connection with Schelling's 1795 characterization of Hegel as "*Vertrauten Lessings.*"

22. O'Regan, *The Heterodox Hegel*, pp. 275, 263.

23. Murray, *Modern Philosophy of History*, pp. 94, 99. Moreover, he goes on, "The ambivalent unity of the speculative way of knowing (transcendental) and the speculated upon (transcendent) . . . begins in Joachim a development that comes to an end in Hegel" (p. 112).

24. In the *Odyssey*, for example, Agamemnon tells Odysseus in the underworld of how his evil end had inverted for him what would otherwise have been a great life, thereby demonstrating the extent to which the meaning of mortal events depends on ends, on final causes, which need to work themselves out in time. According to what Aristotle would later call *peripeteia*, Agamemnon's fortunes— won through deception of a noble enemy and the cruel sacrifices of his daughter and of the Greeks who died in vain while Achilles refused to fight (a refusal provoked by Agamemnon's gratuitous despotism)—these ill-begotten fortunes are all consumed and negated by the domestic treachery that ends and defines his life. See also the *Nicomachaen Ethics*, 1100a (end of Book I, Chapter 9).

For Hegel, as Kojève observes, the structure of historical temporality is similarly governed by its outcome and engendered by future-oriented Desire, which is action in terms of what does not yet exist. The phenomenologist reads the past from this implicitly future perspective in order to comprehend the present. See chapter 5, "A Note on Eternity, Time and the Concept" in Kojève, *Introduction to the Reading of Hegel*, pp. 100ff.

25. Paul Daniel Alphandéry, "Joachim of Floris" in *Encyclopaedia Britannica*, 11th ed. (1910–11), vol. 15, p. 418.

26. Karl Löwith, *Meaning in History*, p. 152.

27. Norman Cohn, *In Pursuit of the Millennium* (New York: Oxford University Press, 1970), p. 109.

28. Besides the establishing of historical grounds of influence, linking Hegel with Joachim and Joachimite ideas noted earlier, a broad spectrum of research into the intellectual affinity between these two German dialecticians draws them together even more closely. Cohn, for example, observes that "it is unmistakably the Joachite phantasy of the three ages that reappeared in, for instance, the theories of historical evolution expounded by the German Idealist philosophers Lessing, Schelling, Fichte and to some extent Hegel" (ibid., p. 109); Charles Taylor notes that "Hegel discerns three levels of theology, which he identifies with the Joachimite messianic language, later taken up by Böhme, of the realms respectively of father, son and holy ghost" (*Hegel*, p. 211); Erich Heller describes how Hegel's "secular messianism" redeems the unhappiness of embodied consciousness (*The Disinherited Mind*, p. 322); and Richard Kroner more generally argues that there "passed through the epoch something of the breath of the eschatological hopes of the era of emergent Christianity" (*Von Kant bis Hegel*, Vol. I [Tübingen: Mohr, 1924], p. 1).

29. Löwith, *Meaning in History*, p. 55. Subsequent references appear within parentheses in the text.

30. Frank Kermode observes this singular paradox, relieved of its transcendent pretension, in a book about eschatological narrative: "All plots have something in common with prophesy, for they must appear to educe from the prime matter of the situation the forms of a future" (*The Sense of an Ending: Studies in the Theory of Fiction* [Oxford: Oxford University Press, 1966], p. 83).

31. Löwith, *Meaning in History*, p. 159.

32. Kermode, *The Sense of an Ending*, p. 28.

33. Saint Augustine, *The City of God*, Book XII, Chapter 14, trans. Marcus Dods, D.D. (New York: Modern Library, 1950), p. 394.

34. Uncertainty about the status of those parentheses will be a central concern of post-Hegelian thought, as it is the profound aporia that drives Nietzsche's pen. Indeed, the post-modernity of Nietzsche consists (at least) in this, that after (Hegel's) repetition, the (im)possibility of "originality" becomes a problematic imperative generative of irony.

35. Murray, *Modern Philosophy of History*, p. 67.

36. Ibid., p. 111.

37. "Sacraments are rather signs which point toward reality (*signum, designatio, similtude*). The reality signified here is no transcendent *res* but a future historical actuality." Ibid., p. 109. See also Ernst Benz, *Ecclesia Spiritualis*,

Kirchenidee und Geschichtstheologie der franziskanischen Reformation (1934), pp. 17–18.

38. O'Regan, *The Heterodox Hegel*, p. 267. See Bernard McGinn, *The Calabrian Abbot: Joachim of Fiore in the History of Western Thought* (New York: Macmillan, 1985) pp. 123–60, for exegesis of "anagogic-futural."

39. Recall, for example, the description of logic as the thought of God before the creation of the world. Among the very many ways in which an exegesis of this correlation might be carried further, attention to the closing arguments of the *Encyclopedia* linking religious and philosophical "syllogisms" and to the theological commentary on philosophical categories carried on in the *Zusatzen* of that same text would be worthwhile. (In the *Zusatz* for section 161 of the *Encyclopedia Logic*, for instance, Hegel remarks that the "movement of the notion" in which "the other . . . it sets up is in reality not an other" is also expressed in the Christian teaching whereby the Son mediates between God and world such that these others do not remain alienated.) For a good summary exegesis of Hegel's view of the "correlation of trinitarian and logical development" as an "apologetic justification of the determinate, or self-determining, nature of God," see O'Regan, *The Heterodox Hegel*, sect. 2.1 of chapter 2, "Hegelian Logic as Logica Divina," pp. 86–107 (the passages quoted in this note and in the main text above appear on p. 89).

40. O'Regan adopts the term "swerve" from Harold Bloom's literary critical theory of "the anxiety of influence" to signal the deviation from traditional ontotheology in Hegel's text that is the subject of *The Heterodox Hegel*. See Harold Bloom, *The Anxiety of Influence: A Theory of Poetry* (London, Oxford, and New York: Oxford University Press, 1973).

41. O'Regan, *The Heterodox Hegel*, pp. 127 and 128.

42. G. W. F. Hegel, *Lectures on the Philosophy of Religion*, vol. 3 (1821 manuscript), ed. Peter Hodgson, trans. R. F. Brown, P. C. Hodgson, and J. M. Steward (Berkeley: University of California Press, 1985), p. 86; *Vorlesungen über die Philosophie der Religion*, Vol. 3, ed. Walter Jaeschke (Hamburg: Felix Meiner Verlag, 1987), pp. 23–24.

43. See above, Chapter Two, Part I, section 4.

44. O'Regan, *The Heterodox Hegel*, p. 96.

45. Ibid., p. 332.

46. O'Regan affirms that "it is appropriate to think of the concept as grounding the very categories it presupposes. Similarly with the relation of concept to representation, what is presupposed genetically is, from a truly structural point of view, constituted by that which presupposition made possible." Ibid., p. 359.

47. Ibid., p. 340.

48. Ibid., p. 341.

49. All three of these "operators" are introduced on p. 340 of O'Regan's book. Discussion of their functioning follows on pp. 341–57.

50. Ibid., p. 341.

51. See above, Chapter One, Part I, section 1. See also Tom Rockmore, *Hegel's Circular Epistemology* (Bloomington: Indiana University Press, 1986), passim.

52. O'Regan, *The Heterodox Hegel*, p. 355.

53. Ibid., p. 357.

54. Saint Augustine, *The City of God*, trans. Marcus Dods (Chicago: Encyclopaedia Britannica, 1952), pp. 353–54.

55. O'Regan, *The Heterodox Hegel*, p. 169. The immediately preceding sentence seems to implicate Augustine in this dismissal as well: "First among equals is Hegel's explicit critique of the punctiliarity of biblical representation and also, though less explicitly, of any theological representation, either directly normed by biblical narrative optics (Luther) or normed by it in the last instance (Augustine)."

56. Saint Thomas Aquinas, *The Summa Theologica*, trans. Fathers of the English Dominican Province, Rev. Daniel J. Sullivan (Chicago: Encyclopaedia Britannica, 1952), p. 154.

57. That ontotheology should be the *shared* site of *discontinuity* and *rupture* is a significantly ambivalent claim. Recent debates concerning the crisis of "modernity" and the advent of "postmodernity" center on this very ambivalence: the "incredulity toward metanarratives" which has resulted from the bankruptcy of absolute idealism is supposed by some to herald the death of metaphysics. And yet, eternally returning like a phoenix from this nihilistic void, others insist that the intelligibility of the crisis is itself evidence of the perdurance of traditional foundations ("reason," "communicative action," etc.), even if in the mode of self-critique. What is lost—credulity, not metanarratives—is purely theoretical, not practical; the "crisis of legitimation" may be over-rated. But the status (the perdurance) of the theoretical discourse of philosophy is thereby called into question. These matters will occupy us in the concluding chapter of the present study.

58. O'Regan, *The Heterodox Hegel*, p. 363.

59. Ibid., p. 128.

60. To repeat the characterization offered above, where his own attempt to meet this demand is exposited and evaluated, "Hegel's metaphysical apotheosis is neither more nor less than a formal innovation, a matter of style." See Chapter Three, Part I, section 4.

61. Murray, *Modern Philosophy of History*, p. 109.

62. Ibid., p. 111.

63. "*Manifestatio*, then, elucidation or clarification, is what I would call the first controlling principle of Early and High Scholasticism. But in order to put this principle into operation on the highest possible plane—elucidation of faith by reason—it had to be applied to reason itself: if faith had to be 'manifested' through a system of thought complete and self-sufficient within its own limits yet setting itself apart from the realm of revelation, it became necessary to 'manifest' the completeness, self-sufficiency, and limitedness of the system of thought. And this could be done only by a scheme of literary presentation that would elucidate the very processes of reasoning to the reader's imagination just as reasoning was supposed to elucidate the very nature of faith to his intellect. . . . Small wonder, then, that a mentality which deemed it necessary to make faith 'clearer' by an appeal to reason and to make reason 'clearer' by an appeal to imagination, also felt bound to make imagination 'clearer' by an appeal to the

senses. Indirectly, this preoccupation affected even philosophical and theological literature in that the intellectual articulation of the subject matter implies the acoustic articulation of speech by recurrent phrases, and the visual articulation of the written page by rubrics, numbers, and paragraphs." Erwin Panofsky, *Gothic Architecture and Scholasticism* (New York: Meridian Books, 1957), pp. 30–31 and 38–39.

64. Joachim's *Liber Figurarum* exists in three complete or nearly complete manuscripts (Oxford, Corpus Christi College, 255 A; Reggio Emilia, Episcopal Seminary; Dresden, Sächs. Landesbibl., A 121), as well as in various fragments held by the Vatican, the Biblioteque Nationale in Paris, and in Milan. A facsimile edition with commentary and bibliographies is more easily accessible; see: *Il Libro delle Figure dell'Abate Gioachino da Fiore*, ed. Leone Tondelli, Marjorie Reeves, and Beatrice Hirsch-Reich (Turin: Società Editrice Internazionale, 1953), in two volumes.

65. *Il Libro delle Figure*, Vol. II, Tavola XI a and XI b.

66. The spelling is discussed in the *Exposito in Apocalypsim* of Joachim (Venice, 1527), *Introductorius*, pp. 36–38. See also McGinn, *The Calabrian Abbot*, pp. 179ff. and Reeves, *Joachim of Fiore and the Prophetic Future*, pp. 6ff.

67. Murray comments that this figure "suggests that revelation unfolds like the letters of a word which can be subsequently interpreted in the literal or spiritual sense" (p. 107). However, the Tetragrammaton is *not* a word, although it is composed of letters; it cannot be spoken, and can be read only as a signifier of that which transcends language as such.

68. G. W. F. Hegel, "Eleusis," in *Dokumente zu Hegels Entwicklung*, ed. Johannes Hoffmeister (Stuttgart: Fr. Frommanns Verlag, 1936), p. 381. See above, Chapter One, Part I, section 3.

69. "Between philosophical concept and representation, it could be said, there is a special kind of dialectical shuttle" (O'Regan, *The Heterodox Hegel*, p. 362).

70. Ibid., p. 363.

71. Ibid., p. 365.

72. The authorship of the "System-Program" is unclear; it may have been written by Schelling or Schelling and Hölderlin together and sent to Hegel, who then copied it out! For a discussion of questions of authority regarding this text, see H. S. Harris, *Hegel's Development: Toward the Sunlight, 1770–1801*, op. cit. Harris' translation of the entire fragment appears on pp. 510–12. As the very existence of this translation implies, Harris believes the author to be Hegel. However, in his "Prelude and Coda" he admits "when I wrote the main body of the text, I did not even suspect, still less believe as I do now, that Hegel was the author of the 'earliest system-programme of German idealism'" (p. xxv).

73. The relevant passage reads:

We must have a new mythology, but this mythology must be in the service of Ideas, it must be a mythology of *Reason*.

Until we express the Ideas aesthetically, i.e. mythologically, they have no interest for the *people*, and conversely until mythology is rational the philosopher must be ashamed of it. Thus in the end enlightened and unenlightened must clasp hands, mythology must become philosophical in order to make the people rational, and philosophy must become mythological in order to make the philosophers sensible [sinnlich]. Then reigns eternal unity among us. (ibid., pp. 511–12; G. W. F. Hegel, "Erstes Systemprogramm des Deutschen Idealismus" in *Dokumente zur Hegels Entwicklung*, p. 221)

This early, romantic side of Hegel also impressed F. A. Lange, whose *History of Materialism* was subsequently to impress Nietzsche. In spite of a "materialist" bias against speculative thought in general ("Our doctrine of the invalidity of all metaphysic as opposed to strict empiricism"), and against Hegel in particular ("His whole system moves within the circle of our thoughts and fancies as to things, to which high-sounding names are given, without our ever getting to understand what validity can be attached to phenomena and to the notions collected from them"), Lange nevertheless concedes that Hegel's "Poetry of concepts [Poesie der Begriffe] has a high value for science. . . . The ideas which the philosopher of this stamp produces are more than dead rubrics for the results of inquiry" (Lange, *The History of Materialism*, Vol. II, p. 239; *Geschichte des Materialismus und Kritik*, p. 281).

74. The same, of course, is true of logic (which cannot, therefore, be a substitution for narrative in the genre of philosophy). Neither reason's *Begriffen* nor religion's *Vorstellungen* are "myths" by themselves; they tell no story, they are mere cognitive functions or media, not yet a content or message. It is tempting to suggest, as O'Regan does, that philosophy "saves metaphoric-narrative discourse by assimilating it, while at the same time supplying the reflective argumentative warrants that metaphoric-narrative is incapable of supplying" (O'Regan, *The Heterodox Hegel*, p. 363); however, philosophical concepts can at best succeed only in repeating the familiar transcendental theme in another key.

75. Habermas, *The Philosophical Discourse of Modernity*, p. 32.

76. Murray, *Modern Philosophy of History*, p. 112.

77. Ibid.

78. Friedrich Nietzsche, *Human, All Too Human*, §20, trans. R. J. Hollingdale (Cambridge: Cambridge University Press, 1986), pp. 22–23.

CHAPTER FIVE. ETERNAL RETURN: RE-TELLING THE END

1. Taylor, *Hegel*, p. 538.

2. Fredric Jameson, Preface to Lyotard, *The Postmodern Condition*, p. xix.

Earlier in this study, Kojève's literalist interpretation of Hegelian eschatology was described as "fundamentalist"—and Francis Fukuyama, an applied Kojèvean (see *The End of History and the Last Man* [New York: Free Press, 1992], which develops the speculations of short-lived renown inaugurated in the earlier essay "The End of History?" [*The National Interest*, Summer 1989, pp. 3–18]) could be so classed as well. There is a sub-genre of apocalyptic literature announced in this repetition: Western history displays a sequence of declarations of a new world followed by rationalizations of the real one. The "Velvet Revolution" and the fall of the Berlin Wall (which, for Fukuyama, constitute the precipitating occasion for his Hegelian fundamentalist prophetic reverie) equally constitute "revelations that, however, do not take place"—the operative topos of which, as Borges notes, is "the *aesthetic* fact." Centuries of repetition of precisely that which is to happen only once finally transform ontotheological pretensions into aesthetic experiments: again metaphysics into metafictions.

3. Solomon, *In the Spirit of Hegel*, p. 635.

4. J. M. E. McTaggart, *Studies in Hegelian Cosmology*, 2d ed. (Cambridge: Cambridge University Press, 1918), p. 196. Subsequent references appear within parentheses in the text.

5. John McCumber considers the same possibility when he argues that "we are defined by our *mis*understandings of Hegel" insofar as we take Hegel to be a "metaphysician" or an "idealist" or indeed any other of the familiar species of perspectives on his thought. Such labels result, McCumber provocatively suggests, from the mistaken belief that Hegel's texts actually make claims about reality. Rather, "At the limit—which is precisely where I will place it—it [Hegel's philosophy] would assert nothing, resolve nothing, lay no claim on reality" (*The Company of Words: Hegel, Language, and Systematic Philosophy* [Evanston, Ill.: Northwestern University Press, 1993], p. 2).

6. Daniel Breazeale writes "the overman is to be understood as the dialectical *Aufhebung* of the Christianized master" ("The Hegel-Nietzsche Problem," *Nietzsche-Studien*, Vol. 4 [1975], p. 152). See also Jean Granier, *Le problem de la Vérité dans la philosophie de Nietzsche* (Paris: Edition du seuil, 1966), p. 47.

7. George Bernard Shaw, "Nietzsche in English," in *Nietzsche: A Collection of Critical Essays*, ed. Robert C. Solomon (Notre Dame, Ind.: University of Notre Dame Press, 1980), p. 374.

8. GM, Preface, section 8. That such artful readers are compared to cows ("*Wiederkäuen*," as the English "rumination," can even mean "to chew the cud") is hardly irrelevant. But we will return to this.

9. For an extraordinarily detailed account of Nietzsche's only serious "love affair" (such as it was), reconstructed from letters, journal entries, Ms. Salomé's subsequent account in fiction, and other sources, see Rudolph Binion, *Frau Lou* (Princeton, N.J.: Princeton University Press, 1968), especially Part Two (pp. 35–171).

10. In a footnote to section 307, Walter Kaufmann writes "It might be interesting to compare this section with Hegel's *Phenomenology of Spirit*." But when Kaufmann attempts such comparisons, the results are facile. In his book on Nietzsche, Kaufmann discusses his own suggestion that "Hegel might have subscribed to the assertion that philosophic systems are educational methods of the spirit," but he fails to qualify this "significant area of agreement" with the recognition that, for Hegel, spiritual education has a definite and final goal which retrospectively determines each provisional *Gestalt* (*Nietzsche*, 4th ed. [Princeton, N.J.: Princeton University Press, 1968], p. 81; see also pp. 78–85).

Such "shapes" do not manifest the randomness of "brief habits." And in his book on Hegel (*Hegel: A Reinterpretation*, p. 293), Kaufmann insists that Hegel's style is aphoristic merely because, apparently as in Nietzsche's works, the *Encyclopedia* is composed of relatively brief numbered sections! This equation elides the whole question of what constitutes aphoristic writing. In fact, Hegel did try his hand at this most demanding form with only meagre success. See for example the *Jaener Schriften* (1801–1807) in Vol. 2 of Hegel's *Werke* (Frankfurt am Main: Suhrkamp, 1970), pp. 540–67.

11. Quoted in Martin Heidegger, *Nietzsche* Vol. II: *The Eternal Recurrence of the Same*, trans. by David Farrell Krell (San Francsico: Harper and Row, 1984), p. 38; *Nietzsche* Erster Band (Pfullingen: Verlag Günther Neske, 1961), p. 290.

12. "The significance of German philosophy (Hegel): to evolve a pantheism through which evil, error, and suffering are not felt as arguments against divinity" (*WP*, section 416; *KSA* 12, p. 113).

13. *Post-Analytic Philosophy*, ed. John Rajchman and Cornell West (New York: Columbia University Press, 1985), p. 259.

14. Maurice Blanchot, "The Limits of Experience: Nihilism," in *The New Nietzsche*, ed. David B. Allison (New York: Delta Books, 1977), p. 121.

15. *KSA* 1, p. 878; trans. Walter Kaufmann in *The Portable Nietzsche* (New York: Viking, 1968), p. 47; trans. Daniel Breazeale in *Philosophy and Truth* (New York: Humanities Press, 1979), p. 81. This often-quoted passage is reiterated in *Thus Spoke Zarathustra* in such a way as to underline the connection between this "perspectivist" critique of objectivity and Nietzsche's related rejection of autonomous subjectivity: "But thought is one thing, the deed is another, and the image of the deed still another: the wheel of causality does not roll between them" ("On the Pale Criminal"). We will return presently to the significance of Nietzsche's critique of the subject.

16. Paul de Man, *Allegories of Reading* (New Haven, Conn.: Yale University Press, 1979), p. 91. The structure of evasion identified here, so characteristic of de Man's "deconstructive" thought, may also inform (as many commentators have suggested) attempts to confront "the de Man affair."

17. These words seem to have made an impression on Nietzsche; they are sketched, without explanation or indeed any accompaniment, in his notebooks from the fall of 1881, where an entire entry reads: "aus diesem Kelche *schäumt* Unendlichkeit" (*KSA* 9, p. 606).

18. The religious color of Nietzsche's prophetic rhetoric, especially in *Thus Spoke Zarathustra,* is too obvious to require any special demonstration, although a great deal could be said about his skillful manipulation of biblical and pre-biblical images. In *The Gay Science*, for example, Nietzsche deliberately recalls Matthew 13:10–16, in a passage that explains to his disciples why he speaks in parables: "All the more subtle laws of any style have their origin at this point: they at the same time keep away, create a distance, forbid 'entrance,' understanding . . . while they open the ears of those whose ears are related to ours" (section 381). And Zarathustra is in many respects a Christ figure, a fisherman who, however, has caught only a corpse (Cf. Matthew 4:19). As George McFadden observes,

Thus Spoke Zarathustra consists of four books, like the four canonical Gospels . . . in them the parallel to the earthly life of Jesus is rounded off. After a period of obscurity Zarathustra enters upon his public life, preaches to the people, travels away from his chosen town to the countryside, attracts twelve disciples (of whom one is "loved"), performs works of power, rebukes a great city, goes away into the desert, is tempted, returns, upbraids the lukewarm, the hypocritical, and the pharisaical, is transfigured before his disciples, holds a final festival supper with them, which he commends them to observe in his memory as a ceremony of mystical communion in the (earthly) good, and finally leaves them to go off into a new phase, where he is to find companions more akin to himself. ("Nietzschean Values in Comic Writing," in *Boundary 2*, Spring/Fall 1981, p. 344)

Although this passage verges on over-reading, the point could not be clearer. But we should not on that account forget what Nietzsche himself points out in *Ecce Homo* ("Why I Am a Destiny"): that the historical Zoroaster was the author of the distinction between good and evil, which it is Zarathustra's task to overcome. Indeed, according to Mary Boyce, "Zoroaster was the first to teach the doctrines of an individual judgment, Heaven and Hell, the future resurrection of the body, the general Last Judgment, and life everlasting for the reunited soul and body" (*Zoroastrians: Their Religious Beliefs and Practices* [London: Routledge and Kegan Paul, 1979], p. 19). Thus, Zoroastrian elements prefigure doctrines that would later be developed in Christianity, Gnosticism, Islam, and even Judaism, Hinduism, and Buddhism! The fact that Nietzsche's Zarathustra retreats to the isolation of his cave at the age of thirty is accordingly a complex reference: it implies an inversion of the career of Jesus, who began preaching at thirty, but it also evokes the historical Zoroaster, whose moral-cosmological revelation came to him at the same age. (In the speech "On the Thousand and One Goals," references to Zoroastrianism are perhaps more plentiful than elsewhere in *Thus Spoke Zarathustra*.)

19. Breazeale, trans., p. 84; *KSA* 1, p. 881. Kaufmann's partial translation of "On Truth and Lies" breaks off just before reaching this passage.

20. Breazeale, pp. 86–87; *KSA* 1, p. 884.

21. De Man, *Allegories of Reading*, p. 91.

22. Cf. Zarathustra's first speech, "On the Three Metamorphoses."

23. *Nietzsche: Life as Literature*, p. 3. Nehamas is by no means the only reader of Nietzsche to have made this suggestion. To choose two conspicuous examples from opposite ends of the chronological spectrum of commentators, in 1935 Karl Jaspers wrote "throughout the whole of Nietzsche's philosophy, *all reality is itself only interpretation*—a kind of exegetical construction" (*Nietzsche*, trans. Charles F. Wallraff and Frederick J. Schmitz [South Bend, Ind.: Regnery/Gateway, 1979], p. 144), and more recently Bernd Magnus has insisted that, for Nietzsche, "knowledge is like a reconstructed text; the world is like the lost original" (*Nietzsche's Existential Imperative* [Bloomington: Indiana University Press, 1978], p. 182). Both of these views are ultimately indebted to Hans Vaihinger's *Die Philosophie Als-Ob* (*The Philosophy of 'As if'*), especially its

final chapter "Nietzsche and His Doctrine of Conscious Illusion." In a discussion of what he calls "the will to illusion," Vaihinger emphasizes two of Nietzsche's "significant aphorisms" that could stand as epigraphs to Nehamas' argument:

> "Not to measure the world by our personal feelings but *as if* it were a play and we were part of the play." This pregnant thought, which comes from the later Stoics, is also found [in another passage]: "To regard our manner of living and acting as part in a play, including therein our maxims and principles." (cited on p. 356, n.2)

Moreover, as Vaihinger demonstrates, the idea of necessary fictions should be traced back one step further to F. A. Lange's *Die Geschichte des Materialismus* (2 vols., Iserlohn and Leipzig, 1866); Nietzsche was among the many readers who were enthusiastic about Lange's claim that human knowledge is impossible except as erected on a basis of heuristic fictions. (See the Preface above for a discussion of Lange and Vaihinger, both in connection with Nietzsche and with the methodological notion of metafiction.) Precursors notwithstanding, Nehamas has explored the consequences of Nietzsche's interpretation and development of this idea with a particularly useful clarity.

Arguing from Nietzsche's repudiation of the substantial subject (see Part II, section 1 of the present chapter), and from an ontology of will to power which holds that "a thing is the sum of its effects," Nehamas insists that, for Nietzsche, the world itself is structured like language: "We can say that Nietzsche looks at the world as if it were a vast collection of what can only, at least in retrospect, be construed as signs; and once again, it appears to be no accident that he likes to think of the world as a text" (p. 82). An irreducible multiplicity of perspectives is mobilized in the generation of the (fictional) unity of a coherent "character," and thus "Nietzsche's effort to create an artwork out of himself, a literary character who is a philosopher, is then also his effort to offer a positive view without falling back into the dogmatic tradition he so distrusted" (p. 8). Accordingly, the eternal return is accounted for as an affirmation of Nietzsche's "logical claim" about the interconnectedness of all life- (character-)constituting events. Since the world is, like language, "a whole without which no part can exist, and not a conglomerate of independent units" (p. 92), a well-lived life is like a well-wrought text in which each event has its place and necessity; to change anything would be to change everything. Nehamas thus proposes that eternal return is to be interpreted as the assertion of the conditional "If my life were to recur, then it could only recur in identical fashion" (p. 153), since Nietzsche "assimilates the ideal person to an ideal literary character and the ideal life to an ideal story" (p. 165) in which "no detail is inconsequential, nothing is out of place, capricious, haphazard, or accidental" (p. 163). Nietzsche's *äesthetisches Verhalten*, Nehamas concludes, demands a hermeneutical ethic: "Like an artwork, the world requires reading and interpretation, 'good philology,' in order to be mastered, understood, and made livable" (p. 91).

As tempting as this interpretation is, it works the curious effect of re-inscribing Nietzsche's *äesthetisches Verhalten* as just another idealism following the old metaphysical habit of attempting to "justify" the world. Moreover, if Nehamas is right, then will to power and eternal return imply regarding the world as a closed totality in which each individual is rigidly determined, a totality which is ideally constituted when it can be accounted for aesthetically. This in turn presupposes an objectivity of the text which speaks of "ideal" characters, lives, and stories without any of the irony and circumspection Nietzsche would no doubt have employed had he himself advanced the position being attributed to him. And the conception of ideal literary works transparently coherent and perfectly unified, such that "characters cannot be related to one another in different ways without themselves changing in the process" (p. 90), not only fails to describe the variousness, the experimental profusion of Nietzsche's literary masks, but it also misrepresents a very large number of successful literary "stories" which do not aim for any such unity. Consider Samuel Beckett, whose novel *The Unnamable* constitutes an instance of what David Lodge identifies as Roland Barthes's notion of "zero degree writing": "literature is vanquished, the problematics of mankind is uncovered and presented without elaboration, the writer becomes irretrievably honest" (David Lodge, *The Art of Fiction* [New York: Penguin Books, 1992], p. 221; the passage quoted may be found in Roland Barthes, *Writing Degree Zero and Elements of Semiology*, trans. Annette Lavers and Colin Smith [Boston: Beacon Press, 1967], p. 78). Far from a Proustian aesthetic self-justification, such writing deliberately attempts to defeat the aesthetic element in order to allow an "irretrievably honest" self to speak. And indeed, the dominance in the twentieth century of literary narratives which are completely inconsistent with Nehamas's "ideal" is in part an historical consequence of Nietzsche's influence. As Frank Kermode writes, "If we think first of modern fictions, it can hardly be by accident that ever since Nietzsche generalized and developed the Kantian insights, literature has increasingly asserted its right to an arbitrary and private choice of fictional norms" (*The Sense of an Ending*, p. 36). Heeding Nietzsche's frequent warnings (e.g., *GM* I, section 13; *TI*, "'Reason' in Philosophy," section 5), we should not be fooled by grammar into reifying linguistic fictions.

Having said this, it remains biographically intriguing to take the claim that Nietzsche regarded life as like literature very seriously. The conviction that the world can be "read" by a "good philologist," besides falling provocatively into a neo-Platonic tradition that stretches from St. Bonaventure's doctrine of "exemplarism" to Swedenborg and beyond into literary modernism, evidences a classic form of paranoid schizophrenia (an extraordinary fictional treatment of which can be found in Vladimir Nabokov's 1958 short story "Signs and Symbols"). "The notion that sequences of real events possess the formal attributes of the stories we tell about imaginary events," Hayden White soberly reminds us, "could only have its origin in wishes, daydreams, reveries" ("The Value of Narrativity in the Representation of Reality," *Critical Inquiry*, Vol. 7, No. 1 [Autumn 1980], p. 27).

24. It is provocative to consider a startling line from the most famous of Nietzsche's "mad letters" in this context: "What is disagreeable and offends my modesty is that at bottom I am every name in history" (letter to Jacob Burkhardt, dated 6 January 1889, but postmarked 5 January). Penned just after Nietzsche's collapse in Turin on January 3, those words perhaps convey the real poignancy that this paradox of originality had for him.

25. In fact, Socrates admits to a lack of knowledge—but this confession is itself a kind of *self*-knowledge. Further, since the one thing Socrates explicitly professes to be a knower of, namely eros, intimately involves others, we may suspect that the master-slave topos has its origins in Socratic self-consciousness. Characteristically, Nietzsche's appropriation of this image appears to invert its epistemological import—until we see that self-knowledge, too, is being called in question.

26. There is a recurrent "nostalgia" in Nietzsche that on occasion he himself found problematic (most wittily and bitterly in the belated Preface to *BT*—see Part II, section 4 of the present chapter) and that is related to, or criticized by, Nietzsche's ultimate rejection of all "metaphysical palliatives" (*metaphysiche Trösterei*). The irony of a passage that proposes some activity, usually "aesthetic," as comfort for a soul troubled by the vicissitudes of life is sometimes self-referential (as is the case here, in the Preface to *GM*—which was written after the advent of Zarathustra). At other times (as with the belated Preface to *BT*), the irony is subsequently imposed. In any event, Nietzsche realizes that there is something suspicious about *any* attempt to "justify" life. Strictly speaking, creative activity ought to be as straightforward and spontaneous as the behavior of healthy animals: a situation very curiously analogous to the description of "post-historical animals of the species *homo sapiens*" that Kojève offers in his attempt to envisage the historical consequences of a realized Hegelian absolute. See Chapter Three, Part II, section 1.

27. Unlike many of Nietzsche's works, the Preface to *On the Genealogy of Morals* is contemporaneous with the main text. Accordingly, the two passages here follow upon one another quite directly. But there are many other places where Nietzsche offers a critique of the notion of a self or subject; see, for example: *The Gay Science*, sections 345 and 347; *Beyond Good and Evil*, sections 16–17, 19, 21, and 54; *Twilight of the Idols*, "'Reason ' in Philosophy" section 5, and "The Four Great Errors" section 6 ("The Error of Free Will"); *The Will to Power*, section 484 (*KSA* 12, p. 549).

28. This image of exclusivity resonates with another already noted that will ultimately prove to be still more significant; the biblical image, borrowed from Matthew, of select disciples whose "ears are related to ours" (Matthew 13:10–16; *GS*, section 381). Once again, it is important to eye the quotation of scripture by Nietzsche with suspicion: the "inverse cripple" is all ears (*TSZ*, Part II, "On redemption") and, in effect, so is the ass who—but wait!

The few "ears" of corn—the "higher men"—that Zarathustra plans to pluck in the Preface are *Ähren* in German, not quite *Ohren*, but the resonance would not have been lost on Nietzsche. (Just so it won't be lost on the reader, Zarathustra literalizes the vowel play immediately by reiterating that he seeks "whoever still has ears for the unheard-of.") As was the case with the first paragraph of the *Phenomenology* (see above, Chapter One, Part I, section 1), translation can sometimes be *revealing*.

29. The first of these metaphors (rope, bridge, abyss) is Zoroastrian: the historical Zarathustra employed the very same images in the *Gothas* (Cf. Boyce, p. 27). And it may also be noted that Zarathustra admonishes "the wisest" among the multitude for being a "a mere conflict and cross between plant and

ghost [Gespenst]" (section 3), emphasizing the "synthetic" *Aufhebung* that would neither be soulless (a plant) nor bodiless (a ghost): "But do I bid you become ghosts or plants? Behold, I teach you the overman" (section 3).

30. Kaufmann, *Nietzsche*, p. 307.

31. Although a famous passage in *Ecce Homo* fetishistically identifies the time and place at which the idea of eternal return first occurred to Nietzsche—in August of 1881, "6000 feet beyond man and time" by a "powerful pyramidal rock" not far from the boarding house in Sils-Maria where Nietzsche spent many productive summers (*EH*, "*Thus Spoke Zarathustra*," section 1), there are several earlier passages in his work that formulate or anticipate the idea (see, for example, "On Truth and Lies" [Breazeale trans., p. 87; *KSA* 1, p. 884], and section 2 of the second of the *Untimely Meditations*). Before the dwarf talks with Zarathustra about eternal return, the idea is explicitly formulated in *The Gay Science* (sections 285 and 341, the latter being nearly identical with part of "On the Vision and the Riddle"), and it is anticipated in Part I of *Thus Spoke Zarathustra* itself ("On the Afterworldly"). Finally, Nietzsche concedes historical precedents. In *Ecce Homo* he acknowledges that "this doctrine of Zarathustra *might* in the end have been taught already by Heraclitus," or, in any event, by the Stoics ("*The Birth of Tragedy*," section 3), and in the *Nachlaß* he admits "I have found this idea in earlier thinkers" (*WP*, section 1066; *KSA* 13, p. 375). Thus, interpretations (e.g., Heidegger and Magnus) that insist on the suddenness and sui generis character of eternal return have been misled by Nietzsche's rhetoric.

It is startling—but symptomatic—that Nietzsche's account of his fateful stroll by the Silvaplana See in August of 1881 has been taken so seriously by so many. A pyramidal rock, supposedly at this sacred site, has been fitted with a commemorative plaque (as if the casual tourist might thereby be inspired to share Nietzsche's "vision"), postcards of the rock are readily available at the Nietzsche-Haus in Sils, and so on. But Kaufmann, although he notes most of the earlier passages just cited (*Nietzsche*, pp. 316f), also participates in this charade by insisting in a footnote to his translation of Nietzsche's *Ecce Homo* account that "clearly, the rock is not the one . . . on which a tablet . . . has been fastened," indicating instead where a "photograph of the right rock" may be found (*Ecce Homo*, Kaufmann trans., p. 295). In this context it is amusing to note what Nietzsche said to a friend upon learning that the house in Nice where Parts III and IV of *Thus Spoke Zarathustra* were written had been destroyed by an earthquake: "This has the advantage for posterity of leaving them one fewer pilgrimage cite to visit" (quoted in Curt Paul Janz, *Friedrich Nietzsche Biographie*, Vol. II [Munich: Carl Hauser Verlag, 1978], p. 514).

32. Zarathustra describes the eternal return as "*die grösste Schwergewicht*," his "heaviest and hardest burden"; *Schwerkraft* means "gravity."

33. Joan Stambaugh, *Nietzsche's Thought of Eternal Return* (Baltimore: Johns Hopkins University Press, 1972), p. 6.

34. Pierre Klossowski, "Nietzsche's Experience of the Eternal Return" in *The New Nietzsche*, ed. David B. Allison (New York: Delta Books, 1977), p. 108. Georg Simmel notes this parallel as well:

Thus, one of Kant's basic themes is transported into a new dimension by Nietzsche. . . . Kant places action into the dimension of infinite repetition in the one-along-side-the-other of society, whereas Nietzsche has action repeat itself in the infinite one-after-the-other of the same person. . . . Both multiplications of action serve the same goal of getting beyond the accidentality that colors representation in their only-now and only-here. (*Schopenhauer and Nietzsche*, trans. by Helmut Loiskandl, Deena Weinstein, and Michael Weinstein [Urbana and Chicago: University of Illinois Press, 1991], pp. 171–72.)

Simmel goes on to point out that "Fichte's development of the Kantian formula already comes close to the transposition into formal time that is accomplished in the doctrine of eternal recurrence" (ibid., p. 172).

35. A version of this view has been advanced by Karsten Harries.

36. Martin Heidegger has developed this interpretation in great detail. He is, however, prefigured by Simmel, who writes:

On the metaphysical level, . . . [t]hrough the thought of recurrence Nietzsche has brought together into a strange union two fundamental and opposed themes of the soul: the need for the finite, for concrete limits, for definite forms in everything given, and the need to lose oneself in the limitless. . . . "Acumen of meditation: the eternal return of everything is the closest approach of the world of becoming to the world of being." Here is the justification for my interpretation of the doctrine of recurrence as a synthesis of the need for finitude and the need for infinity on the highest metaphysical level. (*Schopenhauer and Nietzsche*, pp. 175–76)

The passage from Nietzsche that Simmel quotes (without specific attribution) is section 617 from *The Will to Power* (KSA 12, p. 312): "*Daß Alles wiederkehrt*, is die extremste *Annäherung einer Welt des Werdens an die des Seins: Gipfel der Betrachtung.*"

In light of Simmel's anticipation of Heidegger's interpretation, it is curious to note here in passing that Heidegger also makes important use of this same passage—but that Heidegger's selective elision of Nietzsche's qualification "closest approximation," in the words of David Farrell Krell, "brings his interpretation discomfitingly close to that of Alfred Baeumler" (see Krell's "Analysis" in Martin Heidegger, *Nietzsche*, Vol. II, trans. David Farrell Krell [San Francisco: Harper and Row, 1984], n.2, p. 257). Krell goes on to write that, as a result of the elision, "eternal recurrence ceases to be the "*closest approximation*" of a world of Becoming to one of Being, and is reduced to a metaphysical conception pure and simple" (ibid.). Thus, in 1907 the Jew Simmel constructs a "metaphysical" interpretation of eternal return (in which "the infinity of becoming integrates the finitude of being: the need for boundlessness and measureless transcendence quenches its thirst in the river of becoming" [*Schopenhauer and Nietzsche*, p. 177]) around the (complete) quotation of the same *Nachlaß* fragment which will later, in manipulated form, inspire the Nazi Baeumler (in 1931) and Heidegger (in 1937) to misleadingly construe Nietzsche's idea as the metaphysical "attempt to cancel the image of eternal Becoming and to substitute for it an image of eternal Being" (Alfred Baeumler, *Nietzsche der Philosoph und Politiker* [Leipzig: P. Reclam, 1931], p. 80).

37. It could be argued that the "imperative for affirmative willing" view can be formulated in such a way that the plausibility of eternal return is neither necessary nor even desirable: eternal return would not be some great truth that Zarathustra has realized, but rather an untruth or myth that has been invented to serve the purpose of affirming the will to power. For such a construal, it would no more be necessary to prove the validity of eternal return than to establish the factual veracity of the elements of Christian faith: both are merely possible views of the world, Zarathustra's having the advantage of affirming the will to power. However, this amendment neglects to think through Nietzsche's own admonition regarding the "categorical imperative" (*Twilight of the Idols*, "How the 'True World' Finally Became a Fable," section 4): as a fiction (which is as such known not to be true), such a pure hypothetical would be "Consequently, not consoling, redeeming, or obligating: how could something unknown obligate us?"

Simmel's formulation of the "imperative for affirmative willing" interpretation reveals this confusion with a certain pungency. On the one hand, he affirms that "If the doctrine of eternal recurrence had only the importance . . . of showing tangibly the infinite responsibility of individuals for what they do, then we would not have to broach the question of objective truth. . . . [R]eality can add nothing to the importance of eternal recurrence as a regulative idea of ethics" (*Schopenhauer and Nietzsche*, pp. 172–73). This statement implies that other interpretations of eternal return, and in particular the metaphysical interpretation, *would* require a presumption of the doctrine's "objective truth," a suspicion that is confirmed by Simmel's observation that "insofar as Nietzsche does not stop at that point and insists instead on the reality of eternal recurrence, we cannot be silent about the difficulties of his thesis" (ibid., p. 172). However, notwithstanding the supposed irreality consistent with construing eternal return as a "regulative idea," Simmel also affirms that, on this interpretation, "A momentary action . . . takes on a formidable weight and can no longer be brushed aside *when one knows that it will be infinitely repeated*" (ibid., pp. 170–71; emphasis added).

38. I agree with Berndt Magnus who, dividing mainstream opinion about eternal return into "cosmological" and "normative" camps, concludes that both are "too closely tied to the truth-value of the doctrine of eternal recurrence. The cosmological version argues that Nietzsche thought recurrence is true. The normative version argues that Nietzsche asks us to behave as if it is true" (*Nietzsche's Existential Imperative* [Bloomington: Indiana University Press, 1978], p. 142). Magnus reaches this conclusion only after "careful attention to the language of Nietzsche's allege 'proof' of recurrence," which shows that "there can be no unambiguous empirical argument for recurrence in Nietzsche's works at all, and that he himself was aware of this fact" (ibid., p. 74). I will not recapitulate here the careful textual attention Magnus provides in support of his rejection of mainstream interpretations.

The "scientific" veracity of Nietzsche's "arguments" (which are to be found exclusively in the *Nachlaß*) has been "refuted" by commentators as various as Georg Simmel (*Schopenhauer and Nietzsche*, n.1, pp. 172–73), Arthur Danto (*Nietzsche as Philosopher* [New York: Columbia University Press, 1965], pp. 195–213) and Jorge Luis Borges who, in "The Doctrine of Cycles," explains how Cantor's theory of trans-finite numbers is incompatible with construing Nietzsche's claims as "true." And of course, critiques of the viability of eternal return in pre-Nietzschean contexts go back well before Simmel: besides the arguments of traditional Christian theologians like Augustine already noted in section 2 of Chapter Four above, Nicole Oresme's fourteenth-century treatise *On the Commensurability or Incommensurability of the Celestial Motions* provides a mathematical argument that is "the archetype of the example used by Simmel" (Robin Small, "Incommensurability and Recurrence: from Oresme to Simmel," *Journal of the History of Ideas*, Vol. 52, No. 1 [Jan.–March 1991], p. 122).

It is reasonable then to conclude, with Ivan Soll, that "The presentation of the eternal return in the published works without any substantive argumentation for its truth indicates that it was not primarily the doctrine's truth or theoretical content that concerned Nietzsche" ("Reflections on Recurrence," in Robert Solomon, ed., *Nietzsche: A Collection of Critical Essays* [Garden City, N.Y.: Doubleday, 1973], p. 323). Even Heidegger recognizes this: "the first thing that strikes us is the absence of 'proofs' derived from the natural sciences . . . what we must guard against is our own tendency to extract the import of these statements as though they were formulas of physics" (Heidegger, *Nietzsche* Vol. II, trans. Krell, p. 144; *Nietzsche* Erster Band, p. 405). Unfortunately, Heidegger fails to maintain his guard when it comes to formulas of metaphysics.

But finally, only pedantic readers could really be tempted to take Nietzsche's paltry and unpublished "proofs" seriously in the first place! It is symptomatic of Kaufmann's prosaic devotion that he supposes Nietzsche's plan to live together with Lou Salomé and Paul Rée at a university, hatched in the heat of romance and friendship during the important summer of 1882, "was probably inspired in part by the desire to see if the eternal recurrence of the same events could be proved scientifically" (*Nietzsche*, p. 53)!

39. For a demonstration of the self-defeating hermeneutic consequences of presuming that fascist (mis)appropriations of Nietzsche can be easily disowned, see my essay "Unreading Nietzsche: Nazi Piracy, Pyrrhic Irony, and the Postmodern Turn," *New Nietzsche Studies*, Vol. 1:1/2 (1996).

40. Jacques Derrida, *The Ear of the Other*, trans. Peggy Kamuf, ed. Christie McDonald (Lincoln: University of Nebraska Press, 1988), p. 20.

41. Ibid.

42. Ibid., p. 4.

43. That *The Birth of Tragedy* was hiding Zarathustra "under the scholar's hood, under the gravity and ill-humor of the German, even under the bad manners of the Wagnerian" (section 3) is a persistent theme in the belated Preface. Thus, a continuity is palpable between the "entirely reckless and amoral artistgod . . . who can find salvation only in illusion [Scheine]" (section 5) and the laughter of Zarathustra, with which (citing *TSZ*, Part IV) the belated Preface concludes. Qualifying his self-criticism, Nietzsche writes "you can call this whole artists' metaphysics arbitrary, idle, fantastic; what matters is that it

betrays a spirit [einen Geist] who will one day fight at any risk whatever the *moral* interpretation and significance of existence" (section 5).

44. It is not without reasons that Lawrence Lampert, in his book *Nietzsche's Teaching: An Interpretation of Thus Spoke Zarathustra* (New Haven, Conn.: Yale University Press, 1986), urges that "Part III is the climax and culmination of *Thus Spoke Zarathustra*, the part for the sake of which the two previous parts exist" (p. 155). However, Lampert's relegation of Part IV to the status of an addendum or afterthought, intended in any case for limited distribution, only reveals that he has missed the point of the very "action" he regards as decisive. "The climactic event that brings Zarathustra's course to its close and completes his entry into Nietzsche's philosophy," Lampert writes, "is his 'redemption' through willing eternal return" (p. 156). But this is an empty claim unless some clear content can be given to this "redemption"; Zarathustra's "course" may have been run when he learns to accept eternal return as a redemption from the spirit of revenge, but he is not finished teaching until he has communicated this accomplishment—the perils of which, the necessary failure of which it is the task of Part IV to explore. Neglecting Part IV is thus symptomatic of Lampert's heavy-handed interpretation of "Nietzsche's teaching" that substitutes pat formulas in quasi-Heideggerian terms for Nietzsche's ambiguities. (Although Lampert manifestly owes a great deal to Heidegger, the debt is largely terminological: Heidegger is far more attentive to the irreducible "mystery" in Nietzsche's writing.)

Anke Bennholdt-Thomsen similarly makes light of Part IV in an interpretation of *Thus Spoke Zarathustra* guided by the text's dramatic structure: she argues that the action is complete with the close of Part III, and that Part IV serves a role analogous to that of a satyr play (*Nietzsches "Also sprach Zarathustra" als literarisches Phaenomen* [Frankfurt: Athenaeum, 1974], pp. 196, 205, 210–11). In fact, as Kathleen Higgins notes, "Until recently, the Nietzsche literature in English, had given remarkably little attention to *Zarathustra's* strange ending" (*Nietzsche's Zarathustra* [Philadelphia: Temple University Press, 1987], n. 39, p. 277). The shift in interpretive attitudes with regard to the importance of Part IV in some ways runs parallel to the fate of eternal return in the reception of Nietzsche's work: recent focus on both leads away from the doctrinaire and often politicized interpretations of the last two generations and toward a liberating realization of Nietzsche's rhetorical effects.

45. Zarathustra has invoked this quasi-dialectical negativity at the heart of affirmation before. In Part I, he had already noted that "it is with man as it is with the tree. The more he aspires to the height and light, the more strongly do his roots strive earthward, downward, into the dark, the deep—into evil" ("On the Tree on the Mountainside").

46. Heidegger, *Nietzsche* Vol. II, trans. Krell, pp. 35–36; *Nietzsche* Erster Band, pp. 288–89. The "note" Heidegger quotes also appears as section 128 of "Epigrams and Interludes" in *Beyond Good and Evil*. See also F. D. Luke, "Nietzsche and the Imagery of Height," in *Nietzsche: Imagery and Thought*, ed. Malcolm Pasley (Berkeley: University of California Press, 1978), pp. 104–22.

47. In sections 12B, 14, 22, and 37 (*KSA* 13, pp. 48–49; 12, p. 353; pp. 350–51; and pp. 396–97, respectively), Nietzsche distinguishes between

"active" and "passive" nihilisms. The former, as a destruction of old values, but not necessarily of value as such, and certainly not of the universe itself, heralds a new age.

48. Cf. Heidegger, *Nietzsche* Vol. II, trans. Krell, p. 29; *Nietzsche* Erster Band, p. 279.

49. Until otherwise noted, all of the passages now to be cited are from *Thus Spoke Zarathustra*, Part III, "On the Vision and the Riddle."

50. In a curious article on the figure of the mole in Kant, Hegel, and Nietzsche, David Farrell Krell points out that "the mole (*talpa europaea*) can survive up to 2,000 meters of altitude, i.e., those 6,000 feet beyond man and time which measure the remoteness of the birthplace of eternal return" ("The Mole: Philosophic Burrowing in Kant, Hegel and Nietzsche," in *Boundary 2*, Spring/Fall 1981, pp. 178–79).

51. Heidegger, *Nietzsche* Vol. II, trans. Krell, p. 180; *Nietzsche* Erster Band, p. 443.

52. Mircea Eliade, *The Myth of Eternal Return* (Princeton, N.J.: Princeton University Press, 1967), p. 40.

53. Stanley Rosen, *The Limits of Analysis* (New York: Basic Books, 1980), p. 205.

54. For a discussion of plagiarism in/and Nietzsche, its curious relations with forgery and eternal return, see my essay "Same As It Ever Was: Plagiarism, Forgery, and the Meaning of Eternal Return," *Journal of Nietzsche Studies*, Vol. 6 (Autumn 1993).

55. As Harold Bloom writes, "the central problem for the latecomer necessarily is *repetition*, for repetition dialectically raised to re-creation is the ephebe's road of excess, leading away from the horror of finding himself to be only a copy or a replica." *The Anxiety of Influence* (Oxford: Oxford University Press, 1973), 80.

56. That Heidegger's interpretation "comes to a head in section 8, 'The Convalescent'" ("Analysis" in David Farrell Krell's translation of *Nietzsche* Vol. II, p. 246) is perhaps due to the grim importance of something like *Angst* in the passage. To Heidegger, Zarathustra has become a "hero" for taking on the eternal return as the "heaviest burden." Quoting Nietzsche, Heidegger urges that heroism is "going out to meet one's supreme suffering and supreme hope alike"—and that "everything in the hero's sphere turns to tragedy" (*Nietzsche* Vol. II, Krell trans., p. 60; *Nietzsche* Erster Band, p. 316). Thus, when the heaviest burden is taken on, "*Incipit tragoedia*": the task of *Thus Spoke Zarathustra*, Heidegger says, is to create poetically the figure who will think eternal return. But more: *Thus Spoke Zarathustra* inaugurates the "tragic age" (*WP*, section 37; *KSA* 12, pp. 396–97), an age which "realizes that 'life itself,' being as a whole, conditions 'pain,' 'destruction' and all agony; and that none of these things constitutes an 'objection to this life'" (Krell, p. 61; Heidegger, pp. 316–17, citing *WP*, section 1052). The attitude of tragedy, the early Greek "strong pessimism," is courageous at the abyss, it is an attitude of struggle rather than resignation.

57. The Isles of the Blest, or Fortunate Isles in Greek mythology, were a group of islands supposed to exist near the edge of the Western Ocean, inhab-

ited by men whom the gods had made immortal. They are associated with the islands of the Phaeacians in Homer (*Odyssey*, Bk. VII); it is at the court of the Phaeacians, before King Alkinoos, that Odysseus recounts many of the most extraordinary tales that make up the *Odyssey*—the "play within the play," as it were. This imbedded narrativity is significant in its own right for reading Zarathustra's tale in "On the Vision and the Riddle," implying as it does a second remove of fictionality.

58. *Timaeus*, 39d; *Politicus*, 269c ff. The specific language Zarathustra's animals employ in this passage recalls the fragment (1067) which concludes *WP* (*KSA* 11, pp. 610–11): "This world: a monster of energy . . . eternally changing, eternally flooding back, with tremendous years of recurrence."

The doctrine of a periodic cosmic renewal was also popular among neo-Pythagoreans (see Eliade, *The Myth of Eternal Return*, pp. 129ff.) while, mixing scriptures, the Hellenized Christian Origen argued that God must repeatedly re-create the world in the course of eternity. The created world must be finite, Origen urged in *On First Principles* and his commentary on *Matthew*, because it is part of the definition of God that he knows all things about the world he created. As Aristotle had shown (*Metaphysics* 2.2, 994b22; 3.4, 999a27; *An. Post.* 1.24, 86a6; *Phys.* 1.4, 187b7; 3.6, 207a26; *Rhet.* 3.8, 1408b28; 3.9, 1409b31), it is logically impossible for infinity to be comprehended; therefore, if the world is knowable even by God it must be finite, having both a beginning and an end. Of course, since God himself is not finite, his concern for the world is unending, and it is inconceivable that he could be idle, it follows that the world must have been created again and again. These repetitions, Origen maintained, cannot be identical, as an eternal return of the same would leave no room for free will (see Richard Sorabji, *Time, Creation and the Continuum* [London: Duckworth, 1983], 186). Thus, in particular, the crucifixion did not occur in earlier worlds—a caveat that is consistent with Augustine's refutation of cyclical theories of time: "For once Christ died for our sins; and, rising from the dead, he dieth no more . . . the wicked walk in a circle" (Saint Augustine, *The City of God*, Book XII, Chapter 14, trans. Marcus Dods, D.D. [New York: Modern Library, 1950], 394). Nevertheless, Origen's reasoning led him ultimately to deny the eternity of punishment in hell, a position clearly inconsistent with Christian orthodoxy, and his demonstration of the finitude of creation was itself "taken by Theophilus of Alexandria and by Justinian to be an argument against ascribing unlimited power to God and therefore additional evidence of his blasphemy" (Henry Chadwick, *Early Christian Thought and the Classical Tradition* [New York: Oxford University Press, 1966], p. 118).

Exponents of transmigration were able to turn this line of argument against Christians in so decisive a way that, by the time of the emperor Julian, eternal return had "become a regular part of the anti-Christian arsenal" (Chadwick, 118). In an argument probably taken from Porphyry's commentary on the *Timaeus*, the repetition of creation Origen had defended was shown to imply the eternal return of the same. Origen, following Aristotle, had already affirmed that the world cannot be infinite, since infinity cannot be comprehended; it follows that the changes that distinguish one world from another cannot be infinite either, for the same reason. Thus, with an eternity in which to manipulate a finite number of permutations, God would seem to be condemned to the sisyphian task of repeating himself endlessly!

It is curious that this formula resembles so closely the only "proof" Nietzsche ever sketched for eternal return. In a well-known *Nachlaß* fragment (*WP*, section 1066; *KSA* 13, p. 376), Nietzsche writes: "If the world may be thought of as a certain definite quantity of force and as a certain definite number of centers of force . . . it follows that, in the great dice game of existence, it must pass through a calculable number of combinations. In infinite time, every possible combination would at some time or another be realized; more: it would be realized an infinite number of times." That Origen's argument might have been the origin of Nietzsche's is suggested by Edgar Steiger's recollection of having observed Nietzsche's keen interest in a discourse on Origen's theory delivered by the Basel philosopher Karl Steffensen in October of 1877 (see *Conversations with Nietzsche*, ed. Sander L. Gilman, trans. David J. Parent [New York: Oxford University Press, 1987], 95–97).

59. In "On the Gift-Giving Virtue" at the end of Part I—a crucial passage in which Zarathustra sermonizes on the importance of losing him as a teacher in order to find oneself—the "many who called themselves his disciples" present their master with "a staff with a golden handle on which a serpent coiled around the sun," thereby opening the comparison between Zarathustra and the biblical character of Moses. In Exodus 4:3, Moses throws his staff on the ground and it becomes a serpent—a miracle he will later make use of to confound Pharaoh and his court.

60. Kaufmann ingeniously renders the German "I-A," the conventional representation of an ass' braying, as "Yeah-Yuh"; "I-A" when spoken sounds like a drawled "ja," meaning "yes."

The absurd acclaim the ass receives from the higher men, who take his braying for heroic affirmation, is similarly interpreted by Kathleen Marie Higgins and Tracy Strong. For Higgins, "it indicates the higher men's absorption of Zarathustra's doctrine without genuine spiritual comprehension" (*Nietzsche's Zarathustra* [Philadelphia: Temple University Press, 1987], p. 218). And Strong notices the irony here as well. The litany of the higher men in praise of the ass constitutes for him the "realization that *not just any* affirmation will do": the higher men "are incapable of an affirmation that is also a negation and can only repeat the Yea-Yuh (I-A, *Ja*) of the ass who brays acceptance at everything" (*Friedrich Nietzsche and the Politics of Transfiguration*, expanded ed. [Berkeley, Los Angeles, London: University of California Press, 1988], p. 257).

The interspecial pun linking the ass' braying to some human word for affirmation suggests that "The Ass Festival" and other passages in Part IV are instances of the literary genre known as Menippean satire. Kathleen Higgins has cogently sketched this connection in Chapter 7 of her *Nietzsche's Zarathustra* (op. cit.; see also "*Zarathustra* Is a Comic Book," *Philosophy and Literature*, Vol. 16, No. 1 [April 1992]); the genre as such is discussed by Northrop Frye (*Anatomy of Criticism* [Princeton, N.J.: Princeton University Press, 1957], pp. 308–12) and Mikhail Bakhtin (*Problems of Dostoevsky's Poetics*, ed. and trans. Caryl Emerson [Minneapolis: University of Minnesota Press, 1984], pp. 106–22), among many others. Frye goes so far as to imply (perhaps archly?) that

Menippean satire is somehow the form of his own text: insofar as Burton's *Anatomy of Melancholy* is "the greatest Menippean satire in English before Swift," and given that Burton uses the term "Anatomy" (very much as Frye himself does) to mean "a dissection or analysis," Frye concludes that "We may as well adopt it [Anatomy] as a convenient name to replace the cumbersome and in modern times rather misleading 'Menippean satire'" (pp. 311–12).

However that may be, Nietzsche's familiarity with the genre in its classical exemplars (Lucian, Petronius, Apuleius, et al.) grounds irresistible intertextual comparisons. Besides anticipating Nietzsche's play on "I-A" (Apuleius' "Golden Ass" protests an unjust accusation with "Non-non" and attempts to reveal a complex erotic deception with "He-whore! He-whore!"), the parodying of Zarathustra's words and ideas during the "Ass Festival" constitutes a version of the stock Menippean caricature of the *philosophus gloriosus*.

Significantly, satire is, by its very rhetorical structure, formally self-referential: the style *must* intrude in order to qualify the usual expectation of epistemic seriousness and fidelity to the empirically possible. A more extreme version of this effect reaches the comic when satire marks its own literal falsehood by reporting a borrowed story as if it were autobiographical. When he has heard the story before, the reader experiences the peculiar thrill of knowing that he is being lied to by a clever con artist; it is as if "plagiarist" were now added to the already ridiculous persona of the ass-fool. Thus, Apuleius transforms his precursors Lucius of Patra and Lucian of Samosata—the only transformation that literally takes place here. But not everyone will get the joke: even Saint Augustine seems undecided whether Apuleius "invented" or "reported" his misfortunes, apparently unaware that the plot of *The Golden Ass* was derived. With the help of repetition, Apuleius makes an ass of Augustine! Nor is Zarathustra any less obviously "being called an ass in a certain sense" in Nietzsche's text (Higgins, *Nietzsche's Zarathustra*, p. 226). But who is it that makes an ass of Nietzsche?

Finally, it might also be noted here that the "ass festival" has many colorful cultural manifestations—that is, instances in folk history which are not strictly literary. Such would include both burlesque and quasi-religious festivals like the celebrations at Beauvais and Sens, as well as secular "*fêtes des fous*" traceable to the pagan Saturnalia of ancient Rome—but also such bizarre cognate phenomena as the Tibetan "Jalno" and his annual mock-disputation with the "King of the Years" (see Sir James George Frazer, *The Golden Bough* [New York: Macmillan, 1951], pp. 662–65).

61. The inverse cripple is a particularly vivid example of what in German is called a *Fachidiot*: a specialist whose rigorously narrow training has made him incapable of anything but one thing. As Nietzsche had written in *The Gay Science* (section 366):

> Almost always the books of scholars are somehow oppressive, oppressed; the "specialist" emerges somewhere—his zeal, his seriousness, his fury, his overestimation of the nook in which he sits and spins, his hunched back; every specialist has his hunched back. A scholarly book always mirrors a soul that has become crooked; every craft

makes crooked. . . . Grown into their nook, crumpled beyond recognition, unfree, deprived of their balance, emaciated and angular all over except for one place where they are downright rotund.

62. Higgins is also attentive to this philologist's rhetorical swerve:

Part IV is told in a narrative voice that is unprecedentedly strong; it makes ironic asides about the story being told and makes comments that suggest it speaks from a perspective that is temporally removed from the events is describes. . . . [T]he presence of the distinct narrating voice . . . does lend Part IV a sense of closure that had been absent since the Prologue (*Nietzsche's Zarathustra*, pp. 204, 210).

Significantly, this stylistic device—what the sociologist Erving Goffman calls "breaking frame"—is characteristic of the literary technique of "metafiction" found among a large enough group of writers to merit some critical attention (see the discussion in the Preface, above). David Lodge, taking the story "Lost in the Funhouse" by John Barth as exemplary of the sub-genre, comments on a passage that comments on itself, the narrator evidently having found the story's main character yearning for freedom and fulfillment in an altogether too hackneyed fashion:

The authorial voice abruptly intervenes to comment that Ambrose's situation is either too familiar or too deviant to be worth describing, which is as if a movie actor were to turn to the camera suddenly and say, "This is a lousy script." In the manner of *Tristram Shandy*, the voice of a carping critic is heard, attacking the whole project. . . . The author seems to be suddenly losing faith in his own story, and cannot even summon up the energy to finish the sentence in which he confesses that it is too long and rambling. (*The Art of Fiction* [New York: Penguin Books, 1992], p. 209)

As a literary technique, "metafiction" thus conveys a sense of impatience and even impertinence with respect to the entire gamut of available (that is, traditional) narrative vehicles—an attitude of "passive nihilism" in Nietzsche's sense, which must be transcended in order for "literature" to go on. But as a device for disarming metaphysical pretensions, as here in *TSZ* Part IV, the metafictional impetus is not *self*-defeating; on the contrary, Nietzsche's ironic dismissal of the edifying gravity his reader will expect in this climactic passage is instead liberating and self-*creating*.

63. "The Drunken Song" thus illustrates, in miniature, the method described in the Preface to *On the Genealogy of Morals*: "an aphorism is prefixed to this essay, the essay itself is a commentary on it" (section 8). By a gradual gathering of poetic forces in each of the prose sections that anticipate it, "the song whose name is 'Once More' and whose meaning is 'into all eternity'" (section 12) concludes Zarathustra's speeches with a stylistic tour de force.

64. Karl Jaspers, *Nietzsche*, trans. Charles F. Wallraff and Frederick J. Schmitz (South Bend, Ind.: Regnery/Gateway, 1979), p. 365.

65. See *Letter VII*, 340e–342a, from which the motto quotation for this chapter was taken.

EPILOGUE

1. "True metaphysics," writes Michael Murray, "needs to press beyond (meta) and the activity of pressing beyond is called by Hegel conception" (*Modern Philosophy of History*, n.3, p. 62).

2. Marcuse, *Reason and Revolution*, p. 95.

3. Paul Ricoeur, "Narrative Time," *Critical Inquiry*, Vol. 7, No. 1 (Autumn 1980), p. 180.

4. Hayden White, "The Value of Narrativity in the Representation of Reality," *Critical Inquiry*, Vol. 7, No. 1 (Autumn 1980), p. 24.

5. William Earle, "Ontological Autobiography," in *Phenomenology in America*, ed. J. M. Edie (Chicago: Quadrangle Books, 1967), p. 77. Without developing his position as an interpretation of Nietzsche (to do so would lead to a view much like Nehamas's), Earle goes on to suggest that "if ontology aims at what is ontologically richest, and therefore at what Being has become, it would reverse this traditional aspiration toward the universal" (p. 78). This suggestion is further elaborated in Earle's early book *The Autobiographical Consciousness* (Chicago: Quadrangle Books, 1972).

6. Nehamas, *Nietzsche: Life as Literature*, p. 8.

7. Alasdair MacIntyre, *After Virtue: A Study in Moral Theory* (Notre Dame, Ind.: University of Notre Dame Press, 1984), p. 124. Subsequent references appear within parentheses in the text.

8. Oswald Spengler, *The Decline of the West*, trans. Charles Francis Atkinson (New York: Alfred A. Knopf, 1932 [one-volume edition]), p. xiii. Spengler explicitly names Goethe and Nietzsche as his primary influences, but Hegel's presence is also palpable.

9. Abrams, *Natural Supernaturalism*, pp. 227–28.

10. Kermode, *The Sense of an Ending*, p. 56.

11. Ibid., pp. 35–36.

12. Jorge Luis Borges, "Narrative Art and Magic," in *Borges: A reader*, ed. Emir Rodriguez Monegal and Alastair Reid (New York: E. P. Dutton, 1981), p. 38.

13. As Michael Murray notes, Heidegger's response to Hegel hinges on this regression:

> Assuredly Heidegger does not allow Hegel to escape the limitation of the metaphysical standpoint; quite the contrary, Heidegger argues that Hegel absolutizes the metaphysical articulation of things. So Heidegger must assimilate Hegel to the representational model. The case must be made that conceptual thinking itself implicitly falls under the representational heading; indeed if Heidegger's reading is to retain its force, it must be the supreme instance of it. (Murray, *Modern Philosophy of History*, p. 59.)

This insight suggests that Heidegger's "post-metaphysical" thought may provide another way than the metafictional approach described here to respond to the uncertain imperatives after the end of philosophy. Eschewing the very word "philosophy," Heidegger calls his own practice simply "thinking," and proclaims a commitment to the engaged, involved perspective of doing rather than knowing, the non-theoretical attitude of "average everydayness" transcended only by the "authenticity" of "resolutely" facing up to death as one's "ownmost possibility," the ultimate ground of radical individuality. That such a turn away from metaphysical speculation arises out of an assessment of the legacy left by Hegel and Nietzsche substantially similar to the one offered here is perhaps indicated by a tellingly anticipatory formulation of Vaihinger's: "We do not understand the world when we are pondering over its problems, but when we are doing the world's work" (Vaihinger, *The Philosophy of 'As-if,'* p. xlv). And in fact, Murray goes on to explicitly situate Heidegger's thought in the context of the "dissolution" of Hegel's:

> Heidegger's thinking of Being attempts to cultivate the thought-provoking in this time of need. In the aftermath of modern philosophy the thinker can only search for the meaning of Being. Modern philosophy of history has found its culmination in Hegel; what follows is no further consummation but a dissolution of metaphysical energies, a flying apart at the center." (p. 128)

It may be still further remarked that in *Being and Time*, the ground of an authentic commitment, which must be expressed not merely in an abstract "resolution to be resolved" but in specific choices and concrete action, is to be found in repetition! Even though the inherited past is not as such authoritative—one must choose from among the available roles of what Heidegger calls the "they-self," authenticity being nothing more than an "existential modification of the they-self"—nevertheless, as Karsten Harries puts it in an essay about Heidegger's unfortunate political engagement, "Authentic action is repetition . . . as a response which does not forsake the present for the past" ("Heidegger as Political Thinker," in *Heidegger and Modern Philosophy*, ed. Michael Murray [New Haven, Conn.: Yale University Press, 1978], p. 311).

The complex question of Heidegger's "postmodernity," however, as well as the related matter of the status as "last metaphysician" that Heidegger assigns to Nietzsche, exceed the scope of this study. Moreover, the tone of crisis in Heidegger, the nostalgia for "the gods" that have withdrawn from man, and the mysticism of "essential thinking" articulated in what Habermas derisively terms a "propositionally contentless speech about Being" (*The Philosophical Discourse of Modernity*, p. 140), share little in common with either Zarathustra's laughter or the anti-didactic irony of metafictions.

14. This humble view of philosophy has been advanced by Richard Rorty in concluding his *Philosophy and the Mirror of Nature* (Princeton, N.J.: Princeton University Press, 1979): "If we see knowing not as having an essence, to be described by scientists or philosophers, but rather as a right, by current standards, to believe, then we are well on the way to seeing *conversation* as the ultimate context within which knowledge is to be understood" (p. 389). This conception of philosophy receives remarkably similar statement in MacIntyre's *After Virtue*, where it is held that "conversation, understood widely enough, is the form of human interactions in general" (p. 211); MacIntyre urges that he is "presenting conversations in particular then and human actions in general as enacted narratives" (ibid.).

15. Lyotard, *The Postmodern Condition*, p. xxiv; *La Condition postmoderne*, p. 7.

16. Forward to Lyotard, *The Postmodern Condition*, p. xii.

17. As Daniel Herwitz writes, "It is precisely at the point where Lyotard inherits without criticism the mentality of the avant-garde (and, one must add, of Hegel) that he falters in an excellent analysis. . . . This claim to impose by theoretical fiat an essential shape onto the complexities of current times, making current times into an 'age' in the manner of Hegel, is a modernist coup of theory. . . . Lyotard's is, in this respect, a modernist analysis of postmodernism." (*Making Theory/Constructing Art: On the Authority of the Avant-Garde* [Chicago: University of Chicago Press, 1993], pp. 280–81.)

18. Sartre, *Being and Nothingness*, p. 50; *L'être et le néant*, p. 85.

19. *Being and Nothingness*, p. 69; *L'être et le néant*, p. 106.

20. Ibid.

21. "In Irony," writes Hayden White,

figurative language folds back upon itself and brings its own potentialities for distorting perception under question. This is why characterizations of the world cast in the Ironic mode are often regarded as intrinsically sophisticated and realistic. They appear to signal the ascent of thought in a given area of inquiry to a level of self-consciousness on which a genuinely 'enlightened'—that is to say, self-critical—conceptualization of the world and its processes has become possible. (White, *Metahistory*, p. 37)

BIBLIOGRAPHY

HEGEL—PRIMARY WORKS

Hegel, G. W. F. *Werke*, 20 vols., ed. Eva Moldenhauer and Karl Markus Michel. Frankfurt am Main: Suhrkamp Verlag, 1970–71.

———. *Phänomenologie des Geistes*, ed. Johannes Hofmeister. Hamburg: Felix Meiner Verlag, 1952.

———. *Phenomenology of Spirit*, trans. A. V. Miller. Oxford: Clarendon Press, 1977.

———. *The Phenomenology of Mind*, trans. J. B. Baillie. New York: Harper Torchbooks, 1967.

———. *The Berlin Phenomenology*, ed. and trans. M. J. Petry. Dordrecht: D. Reidel, 1981.

———. *Wissenschaft der Logik*, ed. Friedrich Hagemann and Walter Jaeschke, in *Gesammelte Werke*, Vol. 11. Hamburg: Felix Meiner Verlag, 1978.

———. *Science of Logic*, trans. A. V. Miller. London: George Allen & Unwin, 1969.

———. *Dokumente zu Hegels Entwicklung*, ed. Johannes Hoffmeister. Stuttgart: Fr. Frommanns Verlag, 1936.

———. *Enzyklopädie der Philosophischen Wissenschaften im Grundrisse* (1830), ed. Friedhelm Nicolin and Otto Pöggeler. Hamburg: Felix Meiner Verlag, 1969.

———. *Encyclopedia of the Philosophical Sciences*. Part I, *Logic*, trans. William Wallace; Part II, *Philosophy of Nature*, trans. A. V. Miller; Part III, *Philosophy of Spirit*, trans. William Wallace and A. V. Miller. Oxford: Clarendon Press, 1975, 1970, 1971.

———. *Philosophy of Right*, trans. T. M. Knox. London: Oxford University Press, 1967.

———. *Vorlesungen über die Geschichte der Philosophie*, in *Sämtliche Werke*, ed. Hermann Glockner, Vols. 17–19. Stuttgart: Fr. Frommanns Verlag, 1928.

———. *Lectures on the History of Philosophy*, trans. E. S. Haldane and Frances H. Simson. 3 vols. New York: Humanities Press, 1974.

———. *Reason in History*, trans. Robert S. Hartman. Indianapolis and New York: Bobbs-Merrill, 1953.

———. *The Philosophy of History*, trans. J. Sibree. New York: Dover, 1956.

———. *On Christianity: Early Theological Writings*, trans. T. M. Knox and Richard Kroner. New York: Harper Torchbooks, 1961.

———. *Faith and Knowledge*, trans. Walter Cerf and H. S. Harris. Albany: State University of New York Press, 1977.

———. *Vorlesungen über die Philosophie der Religion*, in *Sämtliche Werke*, ed. Hermann Glockner, Vols. 15–16. Stuttgart: Fr. Frommanns Verlag, 1928.

———. *Lectures on the Philosophy of Religion*, trans. E. B. Speirs, B. D. Sanderson, and J. Burdon Sanderson. 3 vols. London: Routledge and Kegan Paul, 1968.

———. *Ästhetic*. 2 vols. Berlin and Weimar: Aufbau-Verlag, 1976.

———. *On the Arts*, trans. Henry Paolucci. New York: Frederick Ungar, 1979.

———. *On Art, Religion and Philosophy*, trans. J. Glenn Gray. New York: Harper Torchbooks, 1970.

HEGEL—SECONDARY WORKS

Butler, Judith P. *Subjects of Desire: Hegelian Reflections in Twentieth-Century France*. New York: Columbia University Press, 1987.

Christensen, Darrel F., ed. *Hegel and the Philosophy of Religion*, The Wofford Symposium. The Hague: Martinus Nijhoff, 1970.

Coletti, Lucio. *Marxism and Hegel*, trans. Lawrence Garner. London: Verso, 1979.

De Man, Paul. "Sign and Symbol in Hegel's Aesthetics," *Critical Inquiry*, Vol. 8, No. 4 (Summer 1982).

De Nys, Martin J. "'Sense-Certainty' and Universality: Hegel's Entrance into the Phenomenology," *International Philosophical Quarterly*, Vol. 18, No. 4 (Dec. 1978).

Deleuze, Gilles. *Nietzsche et la philosophie*. Presses Universitaires de France, 1962.

———. *Nietzsche and Philosophy*, trans. Hugh Tomlinson. New York: Columbia University Press, 1983.

Derrida, Jacques. *Marges de la philosophie*. Paris: Les Editions de Minuit, 1972.

———. *Margins of Philosophy*, trans. Alan Bass. Chicago: University of Chicago Press, 1982.

———. "From Restricted to General Economy: A Hegelianism without Reserves," *Semiotext(e)*, Vol. II, No. 2, 1976.

Desmond, William, ed. *Hegel and His Critics: Philosophy in the Aftermath of Hegel*. Albany: State University of New York Press, 1989.

Fackenheim, Emil. *The Religious Dimension in Hegel's Thought*. Chicago: University of Chicago Press, 1967.

Feuerbach, Ludwig. *Principles of the Philosophy of the Future*, trans. M. H. Vogel. Indianapolis: Bobbs-Merril, 1966.

Findlay, J. N. *Hegel: A Re-examination*. London: George Allen & Unwin, 1958.

Forster, Michael N. *Hegel and Skepticism*. Cambridge, Mass.: Harvard University Press, 1989.

Gadamer, Hans-Georg. *Hegel's Dialectic*, trans. P. Christopher Smith. New Haven, Conn.: Yale University Press, 1976.

Geraets, Theodore. "The End of the History of Religions 'Grasped in Thought,'" *Hegel-Studien*, Vol. 4 (1989).

Harris, H. S. *Hegel's Development: Toward the Sunlight 1770–1801*. Oxford: Clarendon Press, 1972.

------. *Hegel's Development: Night Thoughts (Jena 1801–1806).* Oxford: The Clarendon Press, 1983.

Hartmann, Klaus. "Hegel: A Non-Ontological View," in Alasdair MacIntyre, ed. *Hegel: A Collection of Critical Easays.* Notre Dame, Ind.: University of Notre Dame Press, 1976.

Hegel-Studien, ed. Friedhelm Nicolin and Otto Pöggeler. Bonn: H. Bouvier Verlag, Vols. 1 (1961)- .

Heidegger, Martin. *Hegels Phänomenologie des Geistes.* Frankfurt am Main: Vittorio Klostermann, 1980.

------. "Hegels Begriff der Erfahrung," in *Holzwege.* Frankfurt am Main: Vittorio Klostermann, 1950.

Henrich, Dieter, and Rolf-Peter Hortsmann, eds. *Hegels Logik der Philosophie: Religion und Philosophie in der Theorie des absoluten Geistes.* Stuttgart: Ernst Klett Verlag, 1984.

Hook, Sidney. *From Hegel to Marx.* New York: Humanities Press, 1958.

Hyppolite, Jean. *Genesis and Structure of Hegel's Phenomenology of Spirit,* trans. Samuel Cherniak and John Heckman. Evanston, Ill.: Northwestern University Press, 1974.

------. *Studies on Marx and Hegel,* trans. John O'Neill. New York: Basic Books, 1969.

The Independent Journal of Philosophy, Vol. III, 1979: Hegel Today.

Jaeschke, Walter. *Reason in Religion: The Foundations of Hegel's Philosophy of Religion,* trans. J. Michael Stewart and Peter C. Hodgson. Berkeley: University of California Press, 1990.

Kainz, Howard P. *Hegel's Phenomenology*, Parts I and II. Athens: Ohio University Press, 1976 and 1983.

Kaufmann, Walter. *Hegel: A Reinterpretation.* Notre Dame, Ind.: University of Notre Dame Press, 1978.

------. *Hegel: Texts and Commentary.* Garden City, N.Y.: Doubleday Anchor, 1966.

Kiminsky, Jack. *Hegel on Art.* Albany: State University of New York Press, 1970.

Kojève, Alexandre. *Introduction to the Reading of Hegel,* trans. James H. Nichols, Jr., ed. Allan Bloom. New York: Basic Books, 1969.

------. *Introduction à la lecture de Hegel,* ed. Raymond Queneau. Paris: Edition Gallimard, 1947.

Kroner, Richard. *Von Kant bis Hegel.* 2 vols. Tübingen: Verlag von J. C. B. Mohr, 1921.

Lauer, Quentin, S.J. *A Reading of Hegel's Phenomenology of Spirit.* New York: Fordham University Press, 1976.

Lichtheim, George. *From Marx to Hegel.* New York: Herder and Herder, 1971.

Löwith, Karl. "Mediation and Immediacy in Hegel, Marx and Feuerbach," trans. K. R. Dove, in Warren E. Steinkraus, ed. *New Studies in Hegel's Philosophy.* New York: Holt, Rinehart, and Winston, 1971.

------. "Hegel und die Sprache," *Neue Rundschau*, No. 76, 1965.

Loewenberg, J. *Hegel's Phenomenology: Dialogues on the Life of the Mind.* La Salle, Ill.: Open Court, 1965.

──── . "The Comedy of Immediacy in Hegel's *Phenomenology*," *Mind*, Vol. XLIV (1936).

Loewenberg, J., ed. *Hegel Selections*. New York: Charles Scribner's Sons, 1957.

Lukács, Georg. *The Young Hegel*, trans. Rodney Livingstone. Cambridge: MIT Press, 1976.

MacIntyre, Alasdair, ed. *Hegel: A Collection of Critical Essays*. Notre Dame, Ind.: University of Notre Dame Press, 1976.

Marcuse, Herbert. *Hegel's Ontology and the Theory of Historicity*, trans. Seyla Benhabib. Cambridge, Mass.: MIT Press, 1987.

──── . *Reason and Revolution*. Boston: Beacon Press, 1960.

Marx, Karl. *Selected Writings*, ed. David McLellan. Oxford: Oxford University Press, 1977.

Marx, Werner. *Hegel's Phenomenology of Spirit*, trans. Peter Heath. New York: Harper & Row, 1975.

McCumber, John. *The Company of Words: Hegel, Language, and Systematic Philosophy*. Evanston, Ill.: Northwestern University Press, 1993.

McTaggart, J. M. E. *Studies in Hegelian Cosmology*. 2d ed. Cambridge: Cambridge University Press, 1918.

Miklowitz, Paul. "The Ontological Status of Style in Hegel's *Phenomenology*," *Idealistic Studies*, Vol. XIII, No. 1 (Jan. 1983).

O'Regan, Cyril. *The Heterodox Hegel*. Albany: State University of New York Press, 1994.

Pelczynski, Z. A., ed. *Hegel's Political Philosophy: Problems and Perspectives*. Cambridge: Cambridge University Press, 1971.

Pinkard, Terry. *Hegel's Phenomenology: The Sociality of Reason*. Cambridge: Cambridge University Press, 1996.

Pippin, Robert B. *Hegel's Idealism: The Satisfactions of Self-Consciousness*. Cambridge: Cambridge University Press, 1989.

Ricoeur, Paul. "The Status of *Vorstellung* in Hegel's Philosophy of Religion," in *Meaning, Truth, and God*, ed. Leroy S. Rouner. Notre Dame and London: University of Notre Dame Press, 1982.

──── . *Freud and Philosophy*, trans. Denis Savage. New Haven, Conn.: Yale University Press, 1970.

Riley, Patrick. "Introduction to the Reading of Kojéve," in *Political Theory*, Vol. 9, No. 1 (1981).

Rockmore, Tom. *Hegel's Circular Epistemology*. Bloomington: Indiana University Press, 1986.

Rosen, Stanley. *G. W. F. Hegel*. New Haven, Conn.: Yale University Press, 1924.

Roth, Michael S. "A Problem of Recognition: Alexandre Kojève and the End of History," *History and Theory*, VOl. XXIV, No. 3 (1985).

Soll, Ivan. *An Introduction to Hegel's Metaphysics*. Chicago: University of Chicago Press, 1969.

Solomon, Robert C. *In the Spirit of Hegel*. Oxford: Oxford University Press, 1983.

Stace, W. T. *The Philosophy of Hegel: A Systematic Exposition.* New York: Dover, 1955.

Steinkraus, Warren E., ed. *New Studies in Hegel's Philosophy.* New York: Holt, Rinehart, and Winston, 1971.

Taylor, Charles. "The Opening Arguments of the *Phenomenology*," in Alasdair MacIntyre, ed. *Hegel: A Collection of Critical Essays.* Notre Dame, Ind.: University of Notre Dame Press, 1976.

————. *Hegel.* Cambridge: Cambridge University Press, 1975.

NIETZSCHE—PRIMARY WORKS

Nietzsche, Friedrich. *Sämtliche Werke*, Kritische Studienausgabe, 15 vols., ed. Giorgio Colli and Mazzino Montinari. Berlin: Walter de Gruyter, 1980.

————. *Sämtliche Briefe*, Kritische Studienausgabe, 8 vols., ed. Giorgio Colli and Mazzino Montinari. Berlin: Walter de Gruyter, 1986.

————. *Philosophy and Truth*, Selections from Nietzsche's Notebooks of the Early 1870s, trans. and ed. Daniel Breazeale. New Jersey: Humanities Press, 1979.

————. *Untimely Meditations*, trans. R. J. Hollingdale. Cambridge: Cambridge University Press, 1983.

————. *Human, All Too Human*, trans. R. J. Hollingdale. Cambridge: Cambridge University Press, 1986.

————. *Daybreak*, trans. R. J. Hollingdale. Cambridge: Cambridge University Press, 1981.

————. *The Birth of Tragedy*, trans. Francis Golffing. New York: Doubleday Anchor, 1956.

————. *The Birth of Tragedy*, trans. Walter Kaufmann. New York: Random House Vintage Books, 1969.

————. *The Gay Science*, trans. Walter Kaufmann. New York: Random House Vintage Books, 1974.

————. *Thus Spoke Zarathustra*, in *The Portable Nietzsche*, trans. Walter Kaufmann. New York: Viking Press, 1954.

————. *On the Genealogy of Morals*, trans. Walter Kaufmann. New York: Random House Vintage Books, 1969.

————. *Beyond Good and Evil*, trans. Walter Kaufmann. New York: Random House Vintage Books, 1966.

————. *Ecce Homo*, trans. Walter Kaufmann. New York: Random House Vintage Books, 1969.

————. *The Case of Wagner*, trans. Walter Kaufmann. New York: Random House Vintage Books, 1969.

————. *Twilight of the Idols*, in *The Portable Nietzsche*, trans. Walter Kaufmann. New York: Viking Press, 1968.

————. *The Antichrist*, in *The Portable Nietzsche*, trans. Walter Kaufmann. New York: Viking Press, 1968.

————. *Nietzsche Contra Wagner*, in *The Portable Nietzsche*, trans. Walter Kaufmann. New York: Viking Press, 1968.

————. *The Will to Power*, trans. Walter Kaufmann and R. J. Hollingdale, ed. Walter Kaufmann. New York: Random House Vintage Books, 1968.

————. *Selected Letters of Firedrich Nietzsche*, ed. and trans. Christopher Middleton. Chicago: University of Chicago Press, 1969.

NIETZSCHE—SECONDARY WORKS

Alderman, Harold. *Nietzsche's Gift*. Athens: Ohio University Press, 1977.

Allison, David B., ed. *The New Nietzsche: Contemporary Styles of Interpretation*. New York: Delta Books, 1977.

Andreas-Salomé, Lou. *Nietzsche in Seinen Werken*. Dresden: Carl Reissner Verlag, 1927.

Ansell-Pearson, Keith, ed. *Nietzsche and Modern German Thought*. London and New York: Routledge, 1991.

————. "Nietzsche and the Problem of the Will in Modernity," in *Nietzsche and Modern German Thought*, ed. Keith Ansell-Pearson. London and New York: Routledge, 1991.

Aschheim, Steven E. *The Nietzsche Legacy in Germany 1890–1990*. Berkeley: University of California Press, 1992.

Babich, Babette. *Nietzsche's Philosophy of Science: Reflecting Science on the Ground of Art and Life*. Albany: State University of New York Press, 1994.

Bataille, Georges. *On Nietzsche*, trans. Bruce Boone. New York: Paragon House, 1992.

Bauschinger, Sigrid, Susan L. Cocalis, and Sara Lennox, eds. *Nietzsche Heute: Die Rezeption Seines Werks nach 1968*. Bern and Stuttgart: Franke Verlag, 1988.

Berkowitz, Peter. *Nietzsche: The Ethics of an Immoralist*. Cambridge, Mass.: Harvard University Press, 1995.

Binion, Rudolph. *Frau Lou, Nietzsche's Wayward Disciple*. Princeton, N.J.: Princeton University Press, 1968.

Blanchot, Maurice. "The Limits of Experience: Nihilism," in David B. Allison, ed. *The New Nietzsche*, New York: Delta Books, 1977.

————. *Sur Nietzsche*. Paris: Éditions Gallimard, 1945.

Bloom, Harold, ed. *Modern Critical Views: Friedrich Nietzsche*. New York: Chelsea House, 1987.

Boundary 2, Spring/Fall 1981: "Why Nietzsche Now? A *Boundary 2* Symposium." Binghamton: State University of New York Press, 1981.

Brinton, Crane. *Nietzsche*. New York: Harper Torchbooks, 1965.

Bulhof, Ilse N. "Nietzsche: The Divination Paradigm of Knowledge in Western Culture," in *History of European Ideas*, Vol. II, 1989.

Caygill, Howard. "Affirmation and Eternal Return in the Free-Spirit Trilogy," in *Nietzsche and Modern German Thought*, ed. Keith Ansell-Pearson. London and New York: Routledge, 1991.

Clark, Maudemarie. *Nietzsche on Truth and Philosophy*. Cambridge: Cambridge University Press, 1990.

Danto, Arthur. *Nietzsche as Philosopher*. New York: Columbia University Press, 1980.

Davey, Nicholas. "Hermeneutics and Nietzsche's Early Thought," in *Nietzsche and Modern German Thought*, ed. Keith Ansell-Pearson. London and New York: Routledge, 1991.

Derrida, Jacques. *Spurs—Nietzsche's Styles/Éperons—Les Styles de Nietzsche*, trans. Barbara Harlow. Chicago: University of Chicago Press, 1978.

Donnellan, Brendan. *Nietzsche and the French Moralists*. Bonn: Bouvier Verlag Herbert Grundman, 1982.

Eliade, Mircea. *The Myth of Eternal Return*. Princeton, N.J.: Princeton University Press, 1971.

Foucault, Michel. "Nietzsche, Genealogy, History," in Donald F. Bouchard, ed. *Language, Counter-Memory, Practice*, trans. Donald F. Bouchard and Sherry Simon. Ithaca, N.Y.: Cornell University Press, 1977.

Frenzel, Ivo. *Friedrich Nietzsche: An Illustrated Biography*. New York: Pegasus Books, 1967.

Fuss, Peter, and Henry Shapiro, eds. *Nietzsche: A Self-Portrait from His Letters*. Cambridge, Mass.: Harvard University Press, 1971.

Gillespie, Michael Allen, and Tracy B. Strong, eds. *Nietzsche's New Seas: Explorations in Philosophy, Aesthetics, and Politics*. Chicago: University of Chicago Press, 1988.

Gilman, Sander L. *Nietzschean Parody: An Introduction to Reading Nietzsche*. Bonn: Bouvier Verlag Herbert Grundmann, 1976.

Gilman, Sander L., ed. *Conversations with Nietzsche: A Life in the Words of His Contemporaries*. Oxford: Oxford University Press, 1987.

Goicoechea, David, ed. *The Great Year of Zarathustra (1881–1981)*. Lanham, Md.: University Press of America, 1983.

Harrison, Thomas, ed. *Nietzsche in Italy*. Saratoga, Calif.: ANMA LIBRI, 1988.

Hayman, Ronald. *Nietzsche: A Critical Life*. Middlesex, U.K.: Penguin Books, 1980.

Heidegger, Martin. *Nietzsche*. 2 vols. Pfullingen: Günther Neske Verlag, 1961.

———. *Nietzsche*, ed. David Farrell Krell. Vol. I, *The Will to Power as Art*, trans. David Farrell Krell; Vol. II, *The Eternal Recurrence of the Same*, trans. David Farrell Krell; Vol. III, *The Will to Power as Knowledge and as Metaphysics*, trans. Joan Stambaugh, David Farrell Krell, and Frank A. Capuzzi; Vol. IV, *Nihilism*, trans. Frank A. Capuzzi. San Francisco: Harper & Row, 1979, 1984, 1987, 1982.

Heller, Erich. *The Importance of Nietzsche*. Chicago: University of Chicago Press, 1988.

Higgins, Kathleen Marie. "Zarathustra Is a Comic Book," *Philosophy and Literature*, Vol. 16, No. 1 (April 1992).

———. *Nietzsche's Zarathustra*. Philadelphia: Temple University Press, 1987.

Hollingdale, R. J. *Nietzsche*. London: Routledge and Kegan Paul, 1973.

Howey, Richard Lowell. "Some Reflections on Irony in Nietzsche," *Nietzsche-Studien*, Vol. 4 (1975).

———. *Heidegger and Jaspers on Nietzsche*. The Hague: Martinus Nijhoff, 1973.

Janz, Curt Paul. *Friedrich Nietzsche Biographie*. Munich: Carl Hanser, 1978.

Jaspers, Karl. *Nietzsche: An Introduction to the Understanding of His Philosophical Activity*, trans. Charles F. Wallraff and Frederick J. Schmitz. South Bend, Ind.: Regnery/Gateway, 1979.

Kaufmann, Walter. *Nietzsche: Philosopher, Psychologist, Antichrist.* 4th ed. Princeton, N.J.: Princeton University Press, 1968.

Klossowski, Pierre. "Nietzsche's Experience of the Eternal Return," in David B. Allison, ed. *The New Nietzsche.* New York: Delta Books, 1977.

Lampert, Lawrence. *Nietzsche's Teaching: An Interpretation of Thus Spoke Zarathustra.* New Haven, Conn.: Yale University Press, 1986.

Luke, F. D. "Nietzsche and the Imagery of Height," in Pasley, Malcolm, ed. *Nietzsche: Imagery and Thought.* Berkeley: University of California Press, 1978.

Magnus, Bernd. *Nietzsche's Existential Imperative.* Bloomington: Indiana University Press, 1978.

Magnus, Bernd, Stanley Stewart, and Jean-Pierre Mileur, *Nietzsche's Case: Philosophy as/and Literature.* New York: Routledge, 1993.

McFadden, George. "Nietzschean Values in Comic Writing," *Boundary 2* (Spring/Fall 1981).

Middleton, Christopher, ed. and trans. *Selected Letters of Friedrich Nietzsche.* Chicago and London: University of Chicago Press, 1969.

Miklowitz, Paul. "Unreading Nietzsche: Nazi Piracy, Pyrrhic Irony, and the Postmodern Turn," *New Nietzsche Studies,* Vol. 1:1/2 (Fall/Winter 1996).

———. "New Recordings of Nietzsche Music," *Nietzsche-Studien,* Vol. 24 (1995).

———. "Same As It Ever Was: Plagiarism, Forgery, and the Meaning of Eternal Return," *Journal of Nietzsche Studies,* Vol. 6 (Autumn 1993).

———. "Also Sang Zarathustra: Reflections on Friedrich Nietzsche and Music," *Piano Quarterly,* Vol. 40, No. 158 (Summer 1992).

Nehamas, Alexander. "Different Readings: A Reply to Magnus, Solomon, and Conway," in *International Studies in Philosophy,* Vol. 21, No. 2 (1989).

———. "How One Becomes What One Is," in Harold Bloom, ed., *Modern Critical Views: Friedrich Nietzsche.* New York: Chelsea House, 1987.

———. *Nietzsche: Life as Literature.* Cambridge, Mass.: Harvard University Press, 1986.

———. "The Eternal Return," *Philosophical Review,* Vol. LXXXIX, No. 3 (July 1980).

Neumann, Harry. "Socrates and History: A Nietzschean Interpretation of Philosophy," *Nietzsche-Studien,* Vol. 6 (1977).

Nietzsche-Studien, ed. Mazzino Montinari, Wolfgang Müller-Lauter and Heinz Wenzel. Berlin: Walter de Gruyter, Vol. 1 (1972)– .

O'Flaherty, James C., Timothy F. Sellner, and Robert M. Helm, eds. *Studies in Nietzsche and the Judeo-Christian Tradition.* Chapel Hill: University of North Carolina Press, 1985.

Pasley, Malcolm, ed. *Nietzsche: Imagery and Thought.* Berkeley: University of California Press, 1978.

Peters, H. F. *Zarathustra's Sister.* New York: Crown Publishers, 1977.

Pippin, Robert B. "Nietzsche, Heidegger, and the Metaphysics of Modernity," in Keith Ansell-Pearson, ed., *Nietzsche and Modern German Thought.* London and New York: Routledge, 1991.

――. "Irony and Affirmation in Nietzsche's *Thus Spoke Zarathustra*," in Michael Allan Gillespie and Tracy B. Strong, eds., *Nietzsche's New Seas.* Chicago: University of Chicago Press, 1988.

――. "Nietzsche and the Origin of the Idea of Modernism," *Inquiry*, Vol. 26 (1983).

Roberts, R. H. "Nietzsche and the Cultural Resonance of the 'Death of God,'" *History of European Ideas*, Vol. II, 1989.

Rorty, Richard. "The Contingency of Selfhood," in Harold Bloom, ed., *Modern Critical Views: Friedrich Nietzsche.* New York: Chelsea House, 1987.

Schutte, Ofelia. *Beyond Nihilism: Nietzsche without Masks.* Chicago: University of Chicago Press, 1984.

Semiotext(e), Vol. III, No. 1 (1978): "Nietzsche's Return."

Shaw, George Bernard. "Nietzsche in English," in Robert C. Solomon, ed. *Nietzsche: A Collection of Critical Essays.* Notre Dame, Ind.: University of Notre Dame Press, 1980.

Simmel, Georg. *Schopenhauer and Nietzsche*, trans. Helmut Loiskandl, Deena Weinstein, and Michael Weinstein. Urbana and Chicago: University of Illinois Press, 1991.

Sloterdijk, Peter. *Thinker on Stage: Nietzsche's Materialism*, trans. Jamie Owen Daniel, foreword by Jochen Schulte-Sasse. Minneapolis: University of Minnesota Press, 1989.

Small, Robin. "Incommensurability and Recurrence: From Oresme to Simmel," *Journal of the History of Ideas*, Vol. 52, No. 1 (January–March 1991).

Solomon, Robert C., ed. *Nietzsche: A Collection of Critical Essays.* Notre Dame, Ind.: University of Notre Dame Press, 1980.

Solomon, Robert C., and Kathleen M. Higgins, eds., *Reading Nietzsche.* New York and Oxford: Oxford University Press, 1988.

Stack, George J. "Kant, Lange, and Nietzsche: Critique of Knowledge," in Kieth Ansell-Pearson, ed., *Nietzsche and Modern German Thought.* London and New York: Routledge, 1991.

――. *Lange and Nietzsche.* Berlin and New York: Walter de Gruyter, 1983.

Stambaugh, Joan. *Nietzsche's Thought of Eternal Return.* Baltimore: Johns Hopkins University Press, 1972.

Staten, Henry. *Nietzsche's Voice.* Ithaca, N.Y.: Cornell University Press, 1990.

Sterling, M. C. "Recent Discussions of Eternal Recurrence: Some Critical Comments," *Nietzsche-Studien*, Vol. 6 (1977).

Stern, J. P. *A Study of Nietzsche.* Cambridge: Cambridge University Press, 1979.

Strong, Tracy B. *Friedrich Nietzsche and the Politics of Transfiguration.* Expanded ed. Berkeley: University of California Press, 1988.

Thiele, Leslie Paul. *Friedrich Nietzsche and the Politics of the Soul: A Study of Heroic Individualism.* Princeton, N.J.: Princeton University Press, 1990.

Vaihinger, Hans. *Nietzsche als Philosoph.* Berlin: Reuther und Richard Verlag, 1902.

Zimmermann, Robert L. "On Nietzsche," *Philosophy and Phenomenological Research*, Vol. XXIX (Dec. 1968).

HEGEL AND NIETZSCHE

Beerling, R. F. "Hegel und Nietzsche," *Hegel-Studien*, Vol. 1 (1961).

Breazeale, Daniel. "The Hegel-Nietzsche Problem," *Nietzsche-Studien*, Vol. 4 (1975).

Brose, Karl. *Kritische Geschichte: Studien zur Geschichtsphilosophie Nietzsches und Hegels*. Frankfurt am Main: Peter Lang Verlag, 1928.

Bulhof, Nina. *Apollos Wiederkehr: Eine Untersuchung der Rolle des Kreises in Nietzsches Denken über Geschichte und Zeit*. The Hague: Martinus Nijhoff, 1969.

Fukuyama, Francis. *The End of History and the Last Man*. New York: Free Press, 1992.

———. "The End of History?," *The National Interest* (Summer 1989).

Gilman, Sander L. "Hegel, Schopenhauer and Nietzsche See the Black," *Hegel-Studien*, Vol. 16 (1981).

Granier, Jean. *Le Probléme de la vérité dans la philosophie de Nietzsche*. Paris: Editions du Seuil, 1966.

Green, Murray. "Hegel's 'Unhappy Consciousness' and Nietzsche's 'Slave Morality,'" in Darrel E. Christensen, ed. *Hegel and the Philosophy of Religion*. The Hague: Martinus Nijhoff, 1970.

Halder, Alois. "Hegel und Nietzsche—Gott als die absolute Wahrheit und die Erfahrung des Nihilismus," in B. Casper, ed. *Der Menschen Frage nach Gott*. Donauwörth, 1976.

Houlgate, Stephen. *Hegel, Nietzsche, and the Criticism of Metaphysics*. Cambridge: Cambridge University Press, 1986.

Krell, David Farrell. "The Mole: Philosophic Burrowing in Kant, Hegel and Nietzsche," *Boundary 2* (Spring–Fall 1981).

———. "Heidegger, Nietzsche, Hegel: An Essay in Descensional Reflection," *Hegel-Studien*, Vol. 5 (1962).

Kremer-Marietti, A. "Hegel et Nietzsche," *La Revue des lettres modernes*, Vols. 76/77 (1962/63).

Löwith, Karl. *From Hegel to Nietzsche: The Revolution in Nineteenth-Century Thought*, trans. David E. Green. New York: Holt, Rinehart, and Winston, 1964.

———. *Meaning in History*. Chicago: University of Chicago Press, 1949.

Morel, George. *Nietzsche: Introduction à une première lecture*. Paris: Editions du Seuil, 1971.

Pautrat, Bernard. *Versions du soleil: figure et systeme de Nietzsche*. Paris: Editions du Seuil, 1971.

Röttges, Heinz. *Nietzsche und die Dialektik des Aufklärung*. Berlin: Walter de Gruyter, 1972.

Schmidt, Alfred. "Zur Frage der Dialektik in Nietzsches Erkenntnistheorie," in Max Horkheimer, ed. *Zeugnisse: Theodor W. Adorno zum sechzigsten Geburtstag*. Frankfurt am Main: Europäische Verlaganstalt, 1963.

Stegmaier, Werner. "Leib und Leben: Zum Hegel-Nietzsche-Problem," *Hegel-Studien*, Vol. 20 (1985).

GENERAL

Abrams, M. H. *Natural Supernaturalism.* New York: W. W. Norton, 1971.

Altizer, Thomas J. J. *History as Apocalypse.* Albany: State University of New York Press, 1985.

Arendt, Hannah. *Between Past and Future.* New York: Viking Press, 1961.

Augustine, Saint. *The City of God,* trans. Marcus Dods, D.D. New York: Modern Library, 1950.

Bachelard, Gaston. *The Poetics of Reverie: Childhood, Language and the Cosmos,* trans. Daniel Russell. Boston: Beacon Press, 1971.

Baynes, Kenneth, James Bohman, and Thomas McCarthy, eds. *After Philosophy: End or Transformation?* Cambridge, Mass.: MIT Press, 1991.

Barfield, Owen. *Poetic Diction: A Study of Meaning.* Middletown, Conn.: Wesleyan University Press, 1976.

———. *Saving the Appearances: A Study in Idolatry.* New York: Harcourt, Brace, Jovanovich, no date.

Barthes, Roland. *Mythologies.* Paris: Editions du Seuil, 1957.

———. *Le Degré Zéro de L'Ecriture.* Paris: Editions du Seuil, 1953.

Baudrillard, Jean. *Forget Foucault.* New York: Semiotext(e) Foreign Agents Series, 1987.

Behler, Ernst. *Confrontations: Derrida/Heidegger/ Nietzsche,* trans. Steven Taubeneck. Stanford: Stanford University Press, 1991.

Beilharz, Peter, Gillian Robinson, and John Rundell, eds. *Between Totalitarianism and Postmodernity: A Thesis Eleven Reader.* Cambridge, Mass.: MIT Press, 1992.

Benjamin, Walter. *Gesammelte Schriften,* ed. Rolf Tidemann and Hermann Schweppenhäuser. Frankfurt am Main: Suhrkamp Verlag, 1977.

Berman, Marshall. *All That Is Solid Melts Into Air: The Experience of Modernity.* New York: Penguin Books, 1988.

Bernstein, Richard J. *The New Constellation: The Ethical-Political Horizons of Modernity/Postmodernity.* Cambridge, Mass.: MIT Press, 1992.

———. *Beyond Objectivism and Relativism: Science, Hermeneutics, and Praxis.* Philadelphia: University of Pennsylvania Press, 1983.

Blanchot, Maurice. *The Gaze of Orpheus,* trans. Lydia Davis. Barrytown, N.Y.: Station Hill Press, 1981.

Bloom, Harold. *The Anxiety of Influence: A Theory of Poetry.* Oxford: Oxford University Press, 1973.

Blumenberg, Hans. *Die Legitimität der Neuzeit.* Frankfurt am Main: Suhrkamp, 1966.

———. *The Legitimacy of the Modern Age,* trans. Robert M. Wallace. Cambridge, Mass.: MIT Press, 1983.

———. *Arbeit am Mythos.* Frankfurt am Main: Suhrkamp, 1979.

———. "On the Lineage of the Idea of Progress," *Social Research* (Spring 1974).

Borges, Jorge Luis. *Borges: A Reader: A Selection from the Writings of Jorge Luis Borges,* ed. Emir Rodriguez Monegal and Alasdair Reid. New York: E. P. Dutton, 1981.

Boyce, Mary. *Zoroastrians: Their Religious Beliefs and Practices.* London: Routledge and Kegan Paul, 1979.

Bradbury, Malcolm, and James McFarlane, eds. *Modernism, 1890–1930.* Middlesex, U.K.: Penguin Books, 1974.

Brown, Harold O. J. *Heresies.* Garden City, N.Y.: Doubleday, 1984.

Brown, Norman O. *Love's Body.* New York: Random House Vintage Books, 1966.

———. *Life against Death.* New York: Random House Vintage Books, 1959.

Bürger, Peter. *The Decline of Modernism,* trans. Nicholas Walker. University Park: Pennsylvania State University Press, 1992.

———. "The Significance of the Avant-Garde for Contemporary Aesthetics: A Reply to Jürgen Habermas," *New German Critique,* No. 22 (Winter 1981).

Carr, Karen L. *The Banalization of Nihilism: Twentieth-Century Responses to Meaninglessness.* Albany: State University of New York Press, 1992.

Castoriadis, Cornelius. "The 'end of philosophy'?," *Salmagundi,* No. 82–83 (Spring-Summer 1989).

Cohen, Avner, and Marcelo Dascal, eds., *The Institution of Philosophy: A Discipline in Crisis?* La Salle, Ill.: Open Court, 1990.

Cohn, Norman. *Cosmos, Chaos and the World to Come: The Ancient Roots of Apocalyptic Faith.* New Haven, Conn.: Yale University Press, 1993.

———. *The Pursuit of the Mellennium.* New York: Oxford University Press, 1970.

De Man, Paul. *Allegories of Reading.* New Haven, Conn.: Yale University Press, 1979.

Deleuze, Gilles. *Difference and Repetition,* trans. Paul Patton. New York: Columbia University Press, 1994.

Deleuze, Gilles, and Felix Guattari. *L'Anti Oedipe.* Paris: Les Editions de Minuit. 1972.

Derrida, Jacques. *Raising the Tone of Philosophy,* ed. and trans. Peter Fenves. Baltimore: Johns Hopkins University Press, 1993.

———. *Of Spirit: Heidegger and the Question,* trans. Geoffrey Bennington and Rachel Bowlby. Chicago: University of Chicago Press, 1989.

———. *The Ear of the Other: Otobiography, Transference, Translation,* ed. Christie McDonald, trans. Peggy Kamuf and Avital Ronell. Lincoln: University of Nebraska Press, 1988.

———. *Dissemination,* trans. Barbara Johnson. Chicago: University of Chicago Press, 1981.

———. *Writing and Difference,* trans. Alan Bass. Chicago: University of Chicago Press, 1978.

———. *Glas.* Paris: Éditions Galilée, 1974.

———. *Of Grammatology,* trans. Gayatri Chakravorty Spivak. Baltimore: Johns Hopkins University Press, 1974.

———. *De la grammatologie.* Paris: Les Editions de Minuit, 1967.

Earle, William. *Mystical Reason.* Chicago: Regnery Gateway, 1980.

———. *The Autobiographical Consciousness.* Chicago: Quadrangle Books, 1972.

Eco, Umberto. *Interpretation and Overinterpretation.* With Richard Rorty, Jonathan Culler, and Christine Brooke-Rose. Ed. Stefan Collini. Cambridge: Cambridge University Press, 1992.

Edie, James M., ed. *Phenomenology in America: Studies in the Philosophy of Experience.* Chicago: Qaundrangle Books, 1967.

Findlay, J. N. *Ascent to the Absolute.* New York: Humanities Press, 1970.

Flynn, Thomas R., and Dalia Judovitz, eds., *Dialectic and Narrative.* Albany: State University of New York Press, 1993.

Foster, Hal, ed. *The Anti-Aesthetic: Essays on Postmodern Culture.* Port Townsend, Wash.: Bay Press, 1983.

Foucault, Michel. *The Archaeology of Knowledge,* trans. A. M. Sheridan Smith. New York: Harper Torchbooks, 1972.

———. *Les Mots et les choses.* Paris: Editions Gallimard, 1966.

Freud, Sigmund. *Character and Culture.* New York: Collier Books, 1963.

———. *General Psychological Theory.* New York: Collier Books, 1963.

———. *Three Essays on the Theory of Sexuality,* trans. James Strachey. New York: Basic Books, 1962.

———. *Beyond the Pleasure Principle,* trans. James Strachey. New York: W. W. Norton, 1961.

———. *Civilization and Its Discontents,* trans. James Strachey. New York: W. W. Norton, 1961.

———. *The Interpretation of Dreams,* trans. James Strachey. New York: Science Editions, 1961.

———. *Totem and Taboo,* trans. James Strachey. New York: W. W. Norton, 1950.

Gadamer, Hans-Georg. *Truth and Method.* New York: Seabury Press, 1975.

Gasché, Rodolphe. *The Tain of the Mirror: Derrida and the Philosophy of Reflection.* Cambridge, Mass.: Harvard University Press, 1986.

Geuss, Raymond. *The Idea of A Critical Theory.* Cambridge: Cambridge University Press, 1981.

Gioachino da Fiore. *Il Libro Delle Figure,* ed. Leone Tondelli, Marjorie Reeves, and Beatrice Hirsch-Reich. 2 vols. Torino: Società Editrice Internazionale, 1953.

Goldmann, Lucien. *Lukács and Heidegger,* trans. William Q. Boelhower. London: Routledge and Kegan Paul, 1977.

Grossman, Allen R. *Poetic Knowledge in the Early Yeats.* Charlottesville: University of Virginia Press, 1969.

Guinness, H. Grattan, D.D. *History Unveiling Prophecy, or Time as an Interpreter.* New York and Edinburgh: Fleming H. Revell, 1905.

Habermas, Jürgen. *The Philosophical Discourse of Modernity,* trans. Frederick Lawrence. Cambridge, Mass.: MIT Press, 1987.

———. *Der Philosophische Diskurs der Moderne: Zwölf Vorlesungen.* Frankfurt am Main: Suhrkamp Verlag, 1985.

———. "Modernity—An Incomplete Project," in Hal Foster, ed., *The Anti-Aesthetic: Essays on Postmodern Culture.* Port Townsend, Wash.: Bay Press, 1983.

———. "Modernity and Postmodernity," *New German Critique,* No. 22 (Winter 1981).

——. *Theory and Practice*, trans. John Viertel. Boston: Beacon Press, 1973.

——. *Knowledge and Human Interests*, trans. Jeremy J. Shapiro. Boston: Beacon Press, 1971.

Harari, Josué V., ed. *Textual Strategies*. Ithaca, N.Y.: Cornell University Press, 1979.

Harvey, David. *The Condition of Postmodernity*. Oxford: Basil Blackwell, 1980.

Hassan, Ihab. *The Postmodern Turn: Essays in Postmodern Theory and Culture*. Ohio State University Press, 1987.

Heidegger, Martin. *Sein un Zeit*. Tübingen: Max Niemeyer Verlag, 1979.

——. *The Question Concerning Technology*, trans. William Lovitt. New York: Harper Torchbooks, 1977.

——. *On the Way to Language*, trans. Peter D. Hertz. New York: Harper & Row, 1971.

——. *Poetry, Language, Thought*, trans. Albert Hofstadter. New York: Harper Colophon Books, 1971.

——. *Being and Time*, trans. John Macquarrie and Edward Robinson. New York: Harper & Row, 1962.

——. *Kant and the Problem of Metaphysics*, trans. James S. Churchill. Bloomington: Indiana University Press, 1962.

——. *Unterwegs zur Sprache*. Pfullingen: Günther Neske Verlag, 1959.

——. *Holzwege*. Frankfurt am Main: Vittorio Klostermann, 1950.

Heine, Heinrich. *Religion and Philosophy in Germany*, trans. John Snodgrass. Boston: Beacon Press, 1959.

Heller, Erich. *The Disinherited Mind*. New York: Harcourt, Brace, Jovanovich, 1975.

——. *The Artist's Journey into the Interior*. New York: Random House, 1965.

Herwitz, Daniel. *Making Theory/Constructing Art: On the Authority of the Avant-Garde*. Chicago: University of Chicago Press, 1993.

Hoesterey, Ingeborg, ed. *Zeitgeist in Babel: The Post-Modernist Controversy*. Bloomington: Indiana University Press, 1991.

Horkheimer, Max, and Theodor W. Adorno. *Dialectic of Enlightenment*, trans. John Cumming. New York: Continuum Press, 1982.

Horkheimer, Max, ed. *Zeugnisse: Theodor W. Adorno zum sechzigsten Geburtstag*. Frankfurt am Main: Europäische Verlagsanstalt, 1963.

Husserl, Edmund. *Ideas*, trans. W. R. Boyce Gibson. New York: Humanities Press, 1976.

——. *Cartesian Meditations*, trans. Dorion Cairns. The Hague: Martinus Nijhoff, 1973.

——. *Die Krisis der europäischen Wissenschaft und die transzendentale Phänomenologie*, ed. Walter Biemel. The Hague: Martinus Nijhoff, 1954.

——. *Formale und transzendentale Logik*. Halle: Niemeyer, 1929.

——. *Logische Untersuchungen*, 2d rev. ed. 2 vols. Halle: Niemeyer, 1913.

Huyssen, Andreas. "The Search for Tradition: Avant-Garde and Postmodernism in the 1970s," *New German Critique*, No. 22 (Winter 1981).

Jameson, Fredric. *Postmodernism; or, The Cultural Logic of Late Capitalism*. Durham, N.C.: Duke University Press, 1991.

Jonas, Hans. *The Gnostic Religion*. Boston: Beacon Press, 1963.

Jung, Carl G. *Synchronicity*, trans. R. F. C. Hull. Princeton, N.J.: Princeton University Press, 1973.

Kermode, Frank. *The Sense of an Ending: Studies in the Theory of Fiction*. New York: Oxford University Press, 1981.

Kierkegaard, Soren. *Repetition*, trans. Howard V. Hong and Edna H. Hong. Princeton, N.J.: Princeton University Press, 1983.

―――. *Concluding Unscientific Postscript*, trans. David F. Swenson and Walter Lowrie. Princeton, N.J.: Princeton University Press, 1941.

Kolb, David. *The Critique of Pure Modernity: Hegel, Heidegger and After*. Chicago: University of Chicago Press, 1986.

Lange, Friedrich Albert. *The History of Materialism and Criticism of Its Present Importance*, trans. Ernest Chester Thomas. 3d ed. (3 vols. in one), intro. by Bertrand Russell, F.R.S. New York: Humanities Press, 1950.

―――. *Geschichte des Materialismus und Kritik seiner Bedeutung in der Gegenwart*. Iserlohn: Verlag von J. Baedeker, 1873.

Lerner, Robert E. *The Powers of Prophecy*. Berkeley: University of California Press, 1983.

―――. *The Heresy of the Free Spirit*. Berkeley: University of California Press, 1972.

Lobkowitz, Nicholas. *Theory and Practice*. Notre Dame, Ind.: University of Notre Dame Press, 1967.

Lukács, Georg. *The Theory of the Novel*, trans. Rodney Livingstone. Cambridge, Mass.: MIT Press, 1976.

Lyotard, Jean-Francois. *The Postmodern Condition: A Report on Knowledge*, trans. Geoff Bennington and Brian Massumi, intro. Fredric Jameson. Minneapolis: University of Minnesota Press, 1984.

MacIntyre, Alasdair. *After Virtue: A Study in Moral Theory*. Notre Dame, Ind.: University of Notre Dame Press, 1984.

Marcuse, Herbert. *Negations*. Boston: Beacon Press, 1968.

―――. *Eros and Civilization*. New York: Random House Vintage Books, 1962.

Marquard, Odo. *In Defense of the Accidental: Philosophical Studies*, trans. Robert M. Wallace. Oxford: Oxford University Press, 1991.

Marx, Karl. *Grundrisse*, trans. Martin Nicolaus. New York: Random House, 1973.

―――. *Capital*. 2 vols., trans. Samuel Moore and Edward Aveling. New York: International Publishers, 1967.

Maurois, André. *Illusions*. New York: Columbia University Press, 1968.

McGinn, Bernard. *The Calabrian Abbot: Joachim of Fiore in the History of Western Thought*. New York: Macmillan, 1985.

Megill, Allan. *Prophets of Extremity: Nietzsche, Heidegger, Foucault, Derrida*. Berkeley: University of California Press, 1985.

Murray, Michael. *Modern Philosophy of History: Its Origin and Destination*. The Hague: Martinus Nijhoff, 1970.

Nagl, Ludwig. "The Enlightenment—A Stranded Project? Habermas on Nietzsche as a 'Turning Point' to Postmodernity," *History of European Ideas*, Vol. II, 1989.

Origen. *On First Principles*, trans. G. W. Butterworth. Gloucester, Mass.: Peter Smith, 1973.

Poster, Mark. *Critical Theory and Poststructuralism: In Search of a Context.* Ithaca, N.Y.: Cornell University Press, 1989.

Plato. *The Dialogues of Plato*, trans. B. Jowett, M.A. 2 vols. New York: Random House, 1937.

Rajchman, John, and Cornell West, eds., *Post-Analytic Philosophy.* New York: Columbia University Press, 1985.

Reeves, Marjorie. *Joachim of Fiore and the Prophetic Future.* London: SPCK, 1976.

Reeves, Marjorie, and Warwick Gould. *Joachim of Fiore and the Myth of the Eternal Evangel in the Nineteenth Century.* Oxford: Clarendon Press, 1987.

Reeves, Marjorie, and Beatrice Hirsch-Reich. *The Figurae of Joachim of Fiore.* Oxford: Clarendon Press, 1972.

Ricoeur, Paul. "Narrative Time," *Critical Inquiry*, Vol. 7, No. 1 (Autumn 1980).

———. *The Rule of Metaphor*, trans. Robert Czerny. Toronto: University of Toronto Press, 1977.

———. *The Conflict of Interpretations*, ed. Don Ihde. Evanston, Ill.: Northwestern University Press, 1974.

Rorty, Richard. *Contingency, Irony, and Solidarity.* Cambridge: Cambridge University Press, 1989.

———. *Philosophy and the Mirror of the Nature.* Princeton, N.J.: Princeton University Press, 1980.

Rosen, Stanley. *The Limits of Analysis.* New York: Basic Books, 1980.

———. *Nihilism.* New Haven, Conn.: Yale University Press, 1969.

Royce, Josiah. *Lectures on Modern Idealism.* New Haven, Conn.: Yale University Press, 1919.

Sartre, Jean-Paul. *Being and Nothingness*, trans. Hazel E. Barnes. New York: Philosophical Library, 1956.

———. *L'Etre et le néant.* Paris: Editions Gallimard, 1943.

Schiller, Friedrich. *Über die ästhetische Erziehung des Menschen.* Stuttgart: Philipp Reclam Jun., 1973.

———. *On the Aesthetic Education of Man.* Oxford: Oxford University Press, 1967.

Schopenhauer, Arthur. *The World as Will and Representation*, trans. E. F. J. Payne. 2 vols. London: Dover Books, 1969.

———. *Die Welt als Wille und Vorstellung.* 2 vols. Berlin: Hans Heinrich Tillgner-Verlag, 1924.

Seyhan, Azade. *Representation and Its Discontents: The Critical Legacy of German Romanticism.* Berkeley: University of California Press, 1992.

Spengler, Oswald. *The Decline of the West*, trans. Charles Francis Atkinson. New York: Alfred A. Knopf, 1932.

———. *Der Untergang des Abendlandes.* 2 vols. Munich: Oskar Beck, 1923.

Spiegelberg, H. *The Phenomenological Movement.* 2 vols. The Hague: Martinus Nijhoff, 1976.

Vaihinger, Hans. *The Philosophy of 'As-if'*, trans. C. K. Odgen. 2d ed. London: Routledge & Kegen Paul, 1935.

——. *Die Philosophie des Als-Ob.* Leipzig: Meiner Verlag, 1911.

Vattimo, Gianni. *The End of Modernity*, trans. Jon R. Snyder. Baltimore: Johns Hopkins University Press, 1991.

Voeglin, Eric. *From Enlightenment to Revolution*, ed. John H. Hallowell. Durham, N.C.: Duke University Press, 1975.

——. *Science, Politics and Gnosticism.* Washington, D.C.: Regnery Gateway, 1968.

Wallace, Robert M. "Progress, Secularization and Modernity: The Löwith-Blumenberg Debate," *New German Critique*, No. 22 (Winter 1981).

Wasson, R. Gordon, Albert Hoffmann, and Carl A. P. Ruck. *The Road to Eleusis.* New York: Harcourt Brace Jovanovich, 1978.

Wellbery, David E. "Nietzsche—Art—Postmodernism: A Reply to Jürgen Habermas," in Thomas Harrison, ed., *Nietzsche in Italy.* Saratoga, Calif.: ANMA LIBRI, 1988.

White, Hayden. *The Content of the Form.* Baltimore: Johns Hopkins University Press, 1987.

——. "The Value of Narrativity in the Representation of Reality," *Critical Inquiry*, Vol. 7, No. 1 (Autumn 1980).

——. *Metahistory.* Baltimore: Johns Hopkins University Press, 1973.

Yack, Bernard. *The Longing for Total Revolution: Philosophic Sources of Social Discontent from Rousseau to Marx and Nietzsche.* Berkeley: University of California Press, 1992.

Zizek, Slavoj. *Tarrying with the Negative.* Durham, N.C.: Duke University Press, 1993.

——. *Looking Awry: An Introduction to Jacques Lacan through Popular Culture.* Cambridge, Mass.: MIT Press, 1991.

——. *The Sublime Object of Ideology.* London: Verso, 1989.

INDEX

Abrams, M.H.
  on Marx as synthesis of Hegel and
    apocalypse, 165 n. 1
  on the *Phenomenology* as literary
    narrative, 140
absolute Spirit
  implicit in the 'I' of sense-certainty,
    16
  recursive teleology of, 137
"aesthetical conduct" (Nietzsche),
    113–15, 177 n. 23
  not recognized by Hegel, 15
alienation (*Entfremdung*)
  of consciousness from itself in
    religious thinking, 70
  as indistinguishable from
    "externalization"
    (*Entaußerung*), 59
  of knowing and being, 9
  overcome in the absolute, 75–76
  Vorstellung as medium of, 75
Altizer, Thomas J.J., 167 n. 9
ambiguity, productive of meaning,
    156 n. 15
animals, implicitly aware of thought
    as the foundation of being, 23
aphoristic style, 28, 108, 116, 152 n.
    8, 175 n. 10, 189 n. 63
apocalypse, xiii, 5
  "genre of Hegelian" (O'Regan),
    88
  as literary genre, 139–40, 173–74
    n. 2
  Löwith on modern, 91–92
  in Marx (Abrams), 165 n. 1
  repetition of impossible, 93–94
Aquinas, "denarratizing operations"
    in, 98

argumentation, Hegel's repudiation
    of, 74
Aristotle
  on God's comprehensive
    knowledge of creation, 186 n.
    58
  Nichomachaen Ethics, 168 n. 24
  Poetics, 91, 127
Auden, W.H., on erotic paradigms in
    Western literature, 160 n. 27
Augustine
  against circular temporality, 93,
    97–98, 186 n. 58
  against millenarian hopes, 91
  "denarratizing operations" in,
    97–98
  "theory of the phallus," 162–63 n.
    12

Baeumler, Alfred, 181–82 n. 36
Baudrillard, Jean, 145 n. 18
Barth, John, 189 n. 62
Barthes, Roland, 178 n. 23
Baumgarten, Alexander Gottlieb, 146
    n. 40
Beckett, Samuel, 178 n. 23
Begriff, translated as "Notion," 156
    n. 25
Bennholdt-Thomsen, Anke, 184 n. 44
Benz, Ernst, 169–70 n. 37
Bildungsroman, 7, 99, 115, 137,
    153–54 n. 14, 154 n. 2
Blanchot, Maurice, 110
Blessed Isles, 185–86 n. 57
Bloom, Harold, xxi, 170 n. 40 (94),
    185 n. 55
Blumenberg, Hans, 168 n. 19
Boehme, Jacob, 88